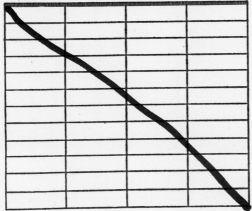

Da Capo Press Reprints in

# AMERICAN CONSTITUTIONAL AND LEGAL HISTORY

GENERAL EDITOR: LEONARD W. LEVY

*Claremont Graduate School*

# JOSEPH McKENNA

## Associate Justice of the
## United States

by
Brother Matthew McDevitt, M. A.

DA CAPO PRESS • NEW YORK • 1974

Library of Congress Cataloging in Publication Data

McDevitt, Matthew, Brother, 1904-
  Joseph McKenna: Associate Justice of the United
States.

  (Da Capo Press reprint in American constitutional and
legal history)
  Thesis—Catholic University, 1945.
  Reprint of the ed. published by Catholic University
of America Press, Washington, D.C.
  Bibliography: p.
  1. McKenna, Joseph, 1843-1926.
KF8745.M25M3  1974      347'.73'2634 [B]  73-21874
ISBN 0-306-70632-6

Copyright 1946 by The Catholic University of America Press

Published by Da Capo Press, Inc.
A Subsidiary of Plenum Publishing Corporation
227 West 17th Street, New York, N.Y. 10011

JOSEPH McKENNA
ASSOCIATE JUSTICE OF THE UNITED STATES

This dissertation was conducted under the direction of Professor Richard J. Purcell as major professor, and was approved by Professor Herbert Wright and Associate Professor Brendan Brown, as readers.

The Catholic University of America

# JOSEPH McKENNA
## ASSOCIATE JUSTICE OF THE UNITED STATES

BY

Brother Matthew McDevitt, M.A.

OF THE BROTHERS OF THE CHRISTIAN SCHOOLS

A DISSERTATION

Submitted to the Faculty of the Graduate School of Arts
and Sciences of the Catholic University of America
in Partial Fulfillment of the Requirements
for the Degree of Doctor of Philosophy

THE CATHOLIC UNIVERSITY OF AMERICA PRESS
WASHINGTON, D. C.
1946

MURRAY & HEISTER—WASHINGTON, D. C.
PRINTED IN THE UNITED STATES OF AMERICA
 9

*To My Mother*

# CONTENTS

# PREFACE

The third Catholic and second California justice on the Supreme Court of the United States was Joseph McKenna, an astute legislator of sharp political prudence, and a worthy and courtly gentleman with an extraordinary ability to concentrate on the business at hand. A competent attorney, rather than a learned, progressive jurist, he was an Irishman who was bound to grow with the new California country and to attain success if given half a chance in the vicissitudes of American political and economic life. This is the way Richard J. Purcell described Justice McKenna in a lengthy treatment in his series of articles on Catholic justices of the Supreme Court.

As is the case of the majority of Supreme Court justices, McKenna has been largely ignored except in a few scattered articles in encyclopedias, legal periodicals and local histories and in three unpublished investigations of a specialized nature. Other than the aforementioned and published study, there are two typed papers. One by George Denman Martin, a student of Professor Felix Frankfurter, was based largely on information furnished by McKenna's daughter, Mrs. Marie McKenna Brown, and disclosed little material not contained in printed biographical sketches. The other investigation by Sister Geraldine Miller was an incompleted master's dissertation, which had benefited from the assistance of the late Attorney Garret W. McEnerney of San Francisco, a close friend and political supporter of McKenna. The present dissertation attempts to give a reasonably full account of McKenna's life and a logical consideration of his theory of the law and his contribution to American judicial philosophy.

The materials for this study are fragmentary and scattered with practically nothing in the histories of California, San Francisco, Benicia and Solano County. Justice McKenna destroyed most of his personal papers and the small portion remaining is in the possession of his daughter, Mrs. Marie McKenna Brown. Letters and papers other than these were found in the collections and archives of persons and institutions with which he was associated. These documents, together with California newspaper accounts and the Supreme Court Reports, constitute the chief sources of this study.

To discover the thought and contributions of Justice McKenna in his legal career, all of his opinions were compiled, analyzed, and classified. Certain of these were selected for discussion in this essay because they illustrated pertinent features in the development of McKenna's thought, application of principle, method of reasoning, procedure of attack, style and formulation of conclusions. Many opinions, because of their brevity or similarity to discussed cases, were omitted. It is thought that the opinions reviewed offer adequate material for evaluation of McKenna's theories of and contribution to the law and orientate him in American life.

The writer takes this occasion to thank his Provincial, Reverend Brother U. Alfred, F.S.C., Ph.D., for the opportunity to pursue graduate studies. He is deeply grateful for the direction, encouragement and assistance of Professor Richard J. Purcell, Ph.D., LL.B., who proposed the topic and guided this essay even when on leave of absence with the War Production Board. Appreciation is likewise due to Associate Professor Brendan Brown, J.U.D., D.Phil., Acting Dean of the School of Law and to the late Professor Herbert Wright, Ph.D., who read the manuscript and made helpful criticism. Valuable information was obtained through the kindness of Justice McKenna's daughters, Mrs. Isabel Duffield and Mrs. Marie McKenna Brown, the staff members of the National Archives, Library of Congress, California State Library and the Bancroft Library of the University of California. The writer also wishes to express deep esteem and gratitude to Chief Justice Charles Evans Hughes, Oscar D. Clarke, librarian, United States Supreme Court, Marian Hughes, of the Library of Congress, Gerald Davis, Chief, Division of Justice Department Archives and Brother Edmund McDevitt, St. Mary's College, California.

GENEALOGY OF JOSEPH McKENNA

John and Mary (Johnson) McKenna     Francis and Marie Bornemann

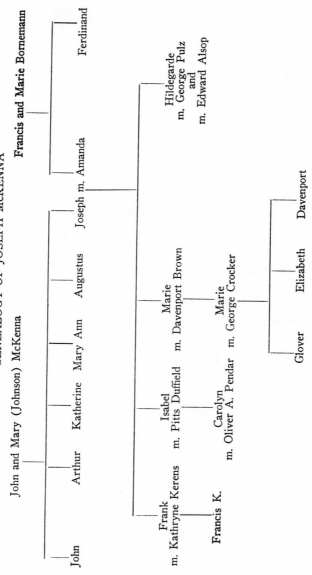

John

Arthur    Katherine   Mary Ann   Augustus    Joseph m. Amanda      Ferdinand

Frank
m. Kathryne Kerens

Isabel
m. Pitts Duffield

Marie
m. Davenport Brown

Hildegarde
m. George Pulz
and
m. Edward Alsop

Francis K.

Carolyn
m. Oliver A. Pendar

Marie
m. George Crocker

Glover    Elizabeth    Davenport

# CHAPTER I

## GROWING WITH CALIFORNIA

The multitude of Irish immigrants who came to the United States in the years before the Famine included the parents of Joseph McKenna. Mary Ann Lucy Johnson McKenna, his mother, born in Manchester, England, April 18, 1817,[1] came to the United States at a comparatively early age. His father, John McKenna, was born in Ireland, attended, according to the family tradition, the University of Dublin for a year,[2] and then emigrated to America in 1842, in the hope of a more prosperous future. Settling in Philadelphia, he met and married Mary Johnson and August 14, 1843,[3] their first child, Joseph, the subject of this paper, was born.[4] On the twenty-seventh of the same month the infant was baptized in St. Philip Neri Catholic Church by Reverend John P. Dunn, the pastor and founder of the parish.

Although the residence of the McKenna family was not in the immediate vicinity of the anti-Catholic and Nativist riots of May, 1844, it may reasonably be presumed that John and Mary Ann McKenna spent several days and nights in apprehension as the unruly mobs surged up and down the streets searching to destroy

---

[1] *The Davenport Brown Scrapbook* consists of an uncatalogued collection of letters, newspaper clippings, personal notes and handbills in possession of Justice McKenna's daughter, Mrs. Davenport Brown, of Boston. Hereafter cited as *Brown Scrapbook*.

[2] This statement is based upon a letter from Mrs. Pitts Duffield, eldest daughter of Justice McKenna, March 2, 1944.

[3] Baptismal Certificate, St. Philip Neri Church, states that Joseph McKenna was born August 14, 1843. This date conflicts with that given in practically all biographical sketches including the rather inaccurate *Biographical Directory of the American Congress* (Washington: 1928), p. 1267, which records August 10, 1843, as the birth date of McKenna.

[4] The probable address of the McKenna family was 21 Mead Alley. Edward C., and John Biddle, *McElroy's Philadelphia Directory for 1843* (Philadelphia: 1843), p. 178.

1

or injure Irishmen in their property or their persons. The center of disorders of the three days of May 6–8, 1844, was in Kensington Township, about two miles directly north of the McKenna bakery,[5] but there was sufficient unrest in all parts of Philadelphia to cause alarm and even terror among the persecuted minority. For an entire week the objects of this fury lived in consternation as they watched the burning of Catholic churches, convents, and homes.[6] As John McKenna plied his trade, he was doubtless able to derive some assurance of security from the steady tramp of the militia which maintained a twenty-four-hour watch and patrol of the streets leading to St. Joseph's and St. Mary's Catholic Churches only a block away. Although the home and the bakery business of the McKennas escaped fire and vandalism, their peace of mind was not restored, for during the following month there was a series of minor street fights and quarrels that kept the populace continually aroused.

Their worst fears were realized on July 6, 1844, when the Southwark riots in southeastern Philadelphia broke forth.[7] The center of these disturbances was St. Philip Neri Catholic Church at Second and Queen Streets. The McKenna home had been moved farther west in the previous months, but their bakery was located only a quarter of a mile from this church. The immediate cause of the outbreak was traced allegedly to a legally authorized collection of guns in its basement. When news of the so-called arsenal was bruited abroad, some of the more choleric members

---

[5] Edward C. and ·John Biddle, *McElroy's Philadelphia Directory for 1845* (Philadelphia: 1845), p. 231. For a detailed description of the rioting and destruction of property, consult *Philadelphia North American and Daily Advertiser*, May 7, 8, 9, 10, 1844 and the *Philadelphia Pennsylvanian*, May 7, 8, 9, 10, 1844; cf., Joseph L. Kirlin, *Catholicity in Philadelphia* (Philadelphia: 1909), pp. 304 ff.

[6] *Philadelphia North American and Daily Advertiser*, May 10, 1844, reports six companies of militia were assigned to protect St. Mary's and St. Joseph's Churches, and sentinels were stationed at the intersection of the streets in the vicinity.

[7] *Philadelphia Pennsylvanian*, July 8, 1844; *Historical Sketches of the Catholic Churches and Institutions of Philadelphia* (Philadelphia: 1895), p. 67, judged it unwise for the Catholics to display guns stored in the basement of the church; cf., J. Thomas Sharf and Westcott Thompson, *History of Philadelphia* (Philadelphia: 1884), II, 1392.

of the Native American Party accepted this as proof that the " papists " were going to inaugurate a reign of terror in retaliation for their defeat in May.[8]  On July 5, an immense throng of Nativists gathered around the church and listened to several inflammatory speeches.  As the mob became more unruly, General Cadwalader in command of the militia ordered the people to disperse.  On their refusal, he commanded his artillery to prepare to fire.

At this juncture, Charles Naylor, a former United States Representative, stepped before one of the fieldpieces and vehemently condemned the action of Cadwalader.  Seized immediately, he was imprisoned in the church.  This only served to make Naylor a martyr and a symbol around which the agitators could rally their forces.[9]  Some hours later the crowd scattered, only to reassemble the following morning increased in numbers and more pugnacious in spirit.  Two cannon were dragged to the rear of the church with a view to making a breach in the walls, when Naylor was freed and the danger was averted momentarily.  All during the day fist fights between the opposing forces kept the tension at high pitch.  A few volleys of gunfire discharged at nightfall became the spark which ignited an all-night battle.  The high point of the fray was a small-scale artillery duel between the militia and the Nativists.  The latter had procured three obsolete but still serviceable cannon from a ship.  These were loaded with pieces of chain, glass, steel, nails, stones and spikes and discharged with deadly effect at the soldiers.  The Nativist artillerymen were well drilled and performed their work with dispatch and efficiency.  Not until daybreak was the militia able to seize the ordnance when the resistance crumbled quickly.[10]

A few blocks to the north of the area of this disturbance, John McKenna doubtless watched the armed mob as it jostled and elbowed its way in front of his shop and listened with apprehension as the battle heightened in tempo during the day.  On Juniper Street, where the McKenna home was now located, Mary Ann McKenna could see the volunteers patrolling the streets and can-

---

[8] Kirlin, *op. cit.*, p. 324.
[9] *Philadelphia North American and Daily Advertiser*, July 8, 1844.
[10] *Philadelphia Pennsylvanian*, July 9, 1844.

non ominously unlimbered at the intersection of the streets in the
neighborhood of St. John the Evangelist's Church and rectory.[11]
Her nervousness may have been allayed if she caught sight of
Bishop Francis Patrick Kendrick as he trudged on his nightly
rounds through the streets of his parish.[12]   Good fortune was
again with the McKennas, for as quiet people they escaped the
danger without injury to person or loss of property.[13]

The animosity engendered by the unrest, disorder, violence and
destruction of these disturbances continued to be the source of
frequent quarrels and minor clashes between the Nativists and
the Irish immigrants.   Thus Joseph McKenna grew up in an environment that was highly charged with race prejudice and religious bigotry.   No doubt he was a spectator, but hardly a
participator, in the frequent gang fights that marred the peace of
the city.   It would be impossible for him to escape the feeling that
there was a local stigma attached to the Catholic religion and the
Irish nationality.   That this impression was indelibly stamped
on his mind may be deduced from the actions of his later life in
matters that touched his faith or his race.   In spite of the virulent
anti-Catholic bias in Philadelphia, the Catholics determined to
open another school in 1851.   Like the little church of the same
name, St. Joseph's College was inconspicuously located in Willing's Alley, ten blocks directly east of Joseph McKenna's home.

Among the thirty or forty youths who came trooping down
Willing's Alley on the morning of September 15, 1851,[14] was the
eight-year-old Joseph McKenna.   The boys assembled in one of
the schoolrooms and then marched to the church where they
assisted at the Holy Sacrifice of the Mass, recited the *Veni
Creator,* and received a short instruction from the president of the
college and pastor of the church, Felix Barbelin, S.J.   After religious services were completed, the lads were reassembled in the

---

[11] *Philadelphia North American and Daily Advertiser,* July 9, 1844.
[12] Kirlin, *loc. cit.*
[13] *Philadelphia North American and Daily Advertiser,* July 8, 9, 10, 1844,
lists the names of the injured.
[14] Letter of Thomas J. Love, S.J., President of St. Joseph's College,
Dec. 7, 1943.

school and segregated into classes.[15] From two until five o'clock that afternoon the classes were in session, and when young McKenna returned to his home that evening he more than likely gave a minute description of what had been said and done by his teachers and classmates.

In common with some other Catholic institutions of that time St. Joseph's was called a college but in reality it was only a primary school. The curriculum was divided into the commercial and the classical departments, and it was in the former that Joseph studied from 1851 to 1855. The staff consisted of two Jesuit scholastics, a coadjutor brother and a layman. The school day began at eight o'clock with the celebration of Mass and continued until five with an intermission of two and a half hours from eleven-thirty until two. Tuesday and Thursday afternoons were holidays, and on Wednesday and Saturday, during the last half hour of the day, religious instruction was given to the pupils on the significance of the liturgy and the purport of the Holy Sacrifice. The courses in the commercial grades were arithmetic, penmanship, history, reading, geography, grammar, public speaking and religion.[16] The tuition of eight dollars a quarter in 1851 was raised to ten dollars in 1852, and, since this was no inconsiderable sum in those days, it may be taken as an indication of the comparatively comfortable circumstances in which John McKenna was able to rear his growing family.

Between 1844 and 1848 four more children, John, Arthur, Catherine and Mary Ann, were born to the McKennas, all of whom were baptized in St. John the Evangelist Catholic Church.[17] To support this progeny was a task which obliged John McKenna to husband his resources and to budget thriftily the profits of his business. That he was not too successful as a tradesman may be

---

[15] Francis X. Talbot, S.J., *St. Joseph's College, Philadelphia, 1851–1926* (Philadelphia: 1927), pp. 37 ff.; *Metropolitan Catholic Directory, 1852* (New York: 1852), p. 82.

[16] For pertinent data on faculty and curriculum, see *Ibid.*, pp. 82 f.; Information on St. Joseph's College in the *Metropolitan Catholic Directory,* 1851, 1852, 1853, 1854, and 1855 is summarized in Talbot, *op. cit.*, pp. 37 ff.

[17] *McElroy's Philadelphia Directory* for each year from 1844–1854 lists the McKenna home address as "Juniper below Walnut Street," which was in St. John the Evangelist's parish.

surmised from the fact that during the course of ten years he changed the location of his place of business on five different occasions.[18]  In addition to keen competition and meager returns for long hours of labor, there was always present the threat that renewed riots might destroy his property and imperil the lives of his family.  Hence, when the first signs of an economic depression began to appear in 1854, it was only reasonable that he should begin to consider removal to the much advertised Pacific Coast where opportunity and religious freedom existed.

Scarcely more than five years had elapsed since the news about the discovery of gold in California had reached the East and sent thousands from the Atlantic seaboard cities trekking westward to seek their fortunes in the Sierra Nevada Mountains.  By 1854 the gold fever had somewhat subsided but the new El Dorado still continued to be the topic of interest that was featured in the newspapers.  It was pictured as a land of rich fertility, unbounded wealth, abundant employment, high wages and opportunity.[19]  Religious intolerance and racial prejudice had little chance to flourish in a population that was over forty per cent alien born.[20]  The substantial colony of thirty thousand Irishmen could help make Catholicism the most numerous religious denomination in the State [21] without fear of arousing Nativist persecution.  Perhaps such reports caused John McKenna to toy with the idea of going to California.  In 1854 such a desire seemed beyond the realm of possibility to one in the financial status of this small baker.  To travel overland would mean untold hardship and possible

[18] *Ibid.,* 1843, p. 140; 1844, p. 201; 1846, p. 229; and 1848, p. 228.

[19] *New York Herald,* Sept. 11, Dec. 11, 1854, Mar. 14, Apr. 6, 1855.

[20] *Statistics of the United States in 1860* (Washington: 1866), pp. 497-500.

[21] John Francis Maguire visited most of the Irish colonies in America and concluded that California was the ideal home for an Irishman. *The Irish in America* (New York: 1873), pp. 264 ff.  Peyton Hurt, "The Rise and Fall of the Know Nothings in California," *California Historical Society Quarterly,* IX (March, 1930), 22, demonstrates the lack of religious antipathy in California.  For the influence of bigotry in national politics, see Paul Foik, C.S.C., "Anti-Catholic Parties in American Politics, 1776-1860," *Records of the American Catholic Historical Society,* XXXVI (March, 1925), 41-69.  For a highly favorable account of the Catholic Church in California, consult *Dublin Review,* LVIII (January, 1866), 1-35.

death; to sail around the Horn was far too risky even for this adventuresome Irishman's family; and to go by way of the Isthmus of Panama was too expensive.[22]

The last-named route was preferable because of regular steamer service to Panama and a railroad across the isthmus which eliminated the inconvenience of mule and canoe travel.[23] It was the only one that offered transportation with a certain degree of security. The single obstacle was the fare of seven hundred dollars for family steerage passage to California and this was beyond the means of the McKennas. Not even the fondest dreams could have fancied the opportunity that soon presented itself. There was a bitter rate war between the steamship lines of William Henry Aspinwall [24] and of the Vanderbilt interests. The fare to California by way of the Isthmus of Panama or of Nicaragua dropped to ten dollars.[25] Since the usual charge to cross the Isthmus was twenty-five dollars, this meant that the companies were paying the passengers to travel on their ships. With little loss of time the McKennas, bag and baggage, were packed up to New York, where they boarded a Panama-bound steamer.

Aboard ship conditions were overcrowded, and all conveniences were scarce, especially in times of bargain rates. Even at best, accommodations for steerage passengers were poor, for the berths were arranged in three tiers around a cabin and each berth was intended to serve three persons, with the inner occupant climbing

---

[22] John H. Kemble, *The Panama Route to the Pacific Coast* (Seattle: 1937), p. 9, asserts that the price of a passage varied but the average was $200 for first class, $175 for second, and $100 for steerage.

[23] *New York Herald,* December 10, 1854, March 14, July 2, 1855.

[24] William Henry Aspinwall, prior to 1848, when he helped to found the Pacific Mail Steamship Company, had been a successful importer and exporter of New York City. To facilitate traffic across the isthmus he constructed the Panama Railroad. It was due to his guidance that his companies were able to survive the competition of the Vanderbilts and eventually monopolize isthmian traffic to California. Richard J. Purcell, " William Henry Aspinwall," *Dictionary of American Biography,* I, 396, henceforth will be cited as *D. A. B.* Concerning the contract, problems, and money involved in the construction of the Panama Railroad, see Hubert H. Bancroft, *History of Central America* (San Francisco: 1890), III, 701 f.

[25] Kemble, *op. cit.,* p. 7.

in and out over his two mates.  However, these discomforts were borne for twenty-one days with the trip across the Isthmus on the newly completed railroad, a highlight of the trip.[26]

The McKennas arrived in San Francisco to find the city, in common with the rest of the nation, still suffering from the effects of the previous year.[27]  The tide of prosperity, which had steadily risen since the discovery of gold, began to subside in 1853 and by the beginning of 1855 had ebbed so far that there was a financial stringency.  To add to the economic woes, a severe drought had caused a suspension of the work in the placer mines.  As a result the miners required credit to purchase their daily necessaries, and the retailer and wholesaler in their turn needed an extension of time.  As long as the banks could support the economic structure, business continued in the accustomed channels without much difficulty.  However, the burden proved to be too great, and, when in February, 1855, Page, Bacon and Company, the leading bank in San Francisco, crashed, it was followed by Wells, Fargo and Company and Adams and Company.[28]  These failures precipitated the collapse of a third of the business houses in the city.  In addition to this business crisis, the moral character of San Francisco had little appeal to a woman of Mary Ann McKenna's nature.  The successive waves of immigration had increased the population too rapidly.  As a consequence, murder,

26 Otis N. Fessenden, *Illustrated History of the Panama Railroad* (New York: 1861), pp. 15 f.

27 John Swett, *Reminiscences of a Half Century* (San Francisco: 1910), p. 117; Hubert Bancroft, *History of California* (San Francisco: 1890), VII, 173; Theodore Hittell, *History of California* (San Francisco: 1897), III, 423 ff.

28 Bancroft depicts the manipulation connected with the removal of the funds of the insolvent banks, *op. cit.*, VII, 173–180; Swett, who was in San Francisco at the time, claimed that the political ramifications involved in the bankruptcy of these firms gave rise to the movement for the vigilantes, *loc. cit.*; James King of William, a former employee of one of the bankrupt firms, established the *San Francisco Bulletin* and publicly attacked the administration of the banks, especially Palmer, Cooke and Co.  It was King's murder that precipitated the establishment of the Vigilante Committee in 1856.  Robert C. Cleland, *History of California, the American Period* (New York: 1922), p. 292; see Richard J. Purcell, "Alvin Adams," *D. A. B.*, I, 36.

robbery, bribery, political corruption and immorality were the order of the day. So venal did the law courts become that, in 1851 and 1856, native-born citizens banded into the vigilante committees to take the law into their own hands.[29] It is quite understandable how the McKennas preferred the little town of Benicia, with a considerable Irish colony whose respectability and economic future seemed assured.[30]

When the McKennas settled in Benicia, in 1855, the town was hardly nine years old. The original grantee, Mariano Guadalupe Vallejo, had conveyed the site of the city to two Americans, Doctor Robert Semple and Thomas O. Larkin.[31] The only stipulations attached to this gift were that a city be founded which should bear one of the names of his wife, Francesca Benicia Felipsa Carrillo Vallejo and that the profits of ferryboats on the Straits of Carquinez be devoted to the establishment of public schools in the town.[32] Thus the settlement was named Francesca; but when Yerba Buena was called San Francisco, Doctor Semple and Larkin changed Francesca to Benicia in order to avoid confusion.[33] Its salubrious climate, deep, capacious and well-sheltered harbor, a position astride the lines of communication to the interior, and a fertile and unsettled back-country aroused the expectations of its promoters for a prosperous future. However, not until the gold rush did these hopes materialize.

Toward the end of 1848, Semple, foreseeing that many forty-niners would come by sea, prepared to draw some of them to Benicia. In 1849 a housing project was launched; but so quickly

---

[29] Bancroft, *op. cit.,* VII, 746–754; Hittell, *op. cit.,* III, 460–648.

[30] Wood, Alley and Co. (publishers), *History of Solano County* (Oakland: 1879), p. 156.

[31] Thomas Oliver Larkin, at one time reputed the richest man in America, was born in Massachusetts, in 1803, and migrated to California in 1832. As American Consul at Monterey, he used his funds and his credit to help separate California from Mexico. When Commodore Jones brought the USS *Southampton* to Benicia in March, 1849, Larkin gave each of the officers a lot in Benicia; Bancroft, *History of California,* VII, 286.

[32] The deed was executed before Lilburn W. Boggs, Alcalde of the District of Sonoma. Held invalid, it was later entered in accordance with the California law of February 20, 1866.

[33] Hittell, *op. cit.,* II, 597; Wood-Alley, *op. cit.,* p. 149.

did the populace increase that these stores and dwellings were only half completed when they were snatched up by the new-comers.[34]   In spite of the high cost of lumber and wages of carpenters at twenty dollars a day [35] with a corresponding increase in the price of a house, the supply was not able to satisfy the demand.   Persons of position and influence had to wait their turn for a house like an ordinary artisan or laborer.[36]

The prospects of Benicia were further brightened with the arrival in March, 1849, of Commander Thomas Catesby Jones to seek a site for a naval base on the Pacific Coast.   Although he refused to make any commitments, he did admit that the anchorage at Benicia was highly satisfactory and predicted that the city would become the future emporium of the West.   A visit productive of more tangible results was made by General Percifer F. Smith, of the United States Army.   He was authorized to select a site for an army depot that would supply the entire coastal area. On April 6, 1849, General Smith began an intensive study of the topography of Benicia, and he finally announced that he was completely satisfied and that Benicia would be the location for the new army base because of the excellent climate, water supply, strategic position, and both land and water facilities.[37]

Construction work was soon started on warehouses, supply depots, barracks, and arsenals.   In 1850, the Pacific Mail Steamship Company, the largest operator of steamers running into San Francisco, made Benicia its northern terminus.   It erected an elaborate machine shop, boiler factory, coal yard, warehouse and refitting plant where its ships could be overhauled, painted, provisioned and re-coaled after their run up from Panama.   For over fourteen years after the McKennas took up their residence in

---

[34] Thomas Gregory, *History of Solano and Napa Counties* (Los Angeles: 1912), p. 68.

[35] Wood-Alley, *op. cit.,* p. 155.

[36] When Colonel Silas Casey, the first commander of the United States arsenal at Benicia, arrived in the spring of 1849, he housed his family for five months in the abandoned French bark *Julie,* until a house was built on the reservation.

[37] General Percifer Smith was military governor of California from February to April, 1849.   As military governor he selected Benicia as the site of the United States arsenal.   Hittell, *op. cit.,* II, 723.

Benicia, there was a steady monthly payroll of approximately sixty thousand dollars for the workers in the shipyards.[38] Besides this lucrative source of income Benicia was the shipping center for the farm products produced in the rapidly developing hinterland.[39] It was hardly possible to spend any time in the town without being told that the State capital had been moved from there in 1854 as the result of a corrupt bargain between the political machine of David Broderick and the politicians of Sacramento.[40]

For masculine tastes the chief center of amusement and relaxation was Tom Maguire's saloon, reputedly the finest in the State, with two bars and an elaborate orchestra.[41] The sporting element, however, became eloquent when they discoursed about the virtues and abilities of John C. Heenan, the famous " Benicia Boy " who was considered the greatest American heavyweight prize fighter.[42]

---

[38] *San Francisco Alta California,* June 27, 1850, November 30, 1852.

[39] *Agriculture of the United States in 1860* (Washington: 1864), pp. 10–12.

[40] Hittell, *op. cit.,* IV, 149; Bancroft, *History of California,* VI, 659–662, 664–666, 681–686, 691–730. David Colbert Broderick was born in Washington, D. C., February 4, 1820, of Irish parents. He was initiated into machine politics in Tammany Hall, failed to be elected to Congress, arrived in California penniless in 1849, and rose rapidly in the ranks of the Democratic Party to the position of boss. He was thwarted in an attempt to replace his arch Democratic rival, William Gwin, in the United States Senate in 1854. However, he was elected to that body in January 1857 and was slain in a duel with a former henchman, Judge David S. Terry, in 1859. Richard J. Purcell, " Senator David C. Broderick," *Studies,* XXVIII (Dublin) (September, 1939), 415–430; cf., Hugh Quigley, *Irish Race in California and on the Pacific Coast* (San Francisco: 1878), pp. 295–302; Oscar Shuck, *Representative and Leading Men of the Pacific* (San Francisco: 1870), pp. 385–393.

[41] Maguire later sold his saloon in Benicia and became an impresario in the Tivoli Opera House in San Francisco. " Blind Chris " Buckley, a native of Ireland, came to the United States in the seventies and in 1880 opened a saloon in Benicia, where he entered politics as a Republican. In 1882 he moved to San Francisco, where he established a saloon on Bush Street in the midst of the business district. Identifying himself with the Democrats and the San Francisco firemen, he became a leader in the Democratic Party. When his party obtained political control of San Francisco, he took over the actual administration and filled all appointive offices with his henchmen who were nicknamed " Buckley's Lambs."

[42] John Carmel Heenan was born in West Troy, New York, went to

Soon after his arrival in Benicia, John McKenna opened a bakery and began to invest in real estate.[43] That he was successful from the start may be concluded from the fact that he could afford to send Joseph to the public school [44] and that Catherine and Mary Ann attended Miss Atkins' Young Ladies Academy, although the Dominican Sisters conducted St. Catherine's Female Academy nearby.[45] In this respect the McKenna children were more fortunate than some seventy per cent of the adolescents in the State whose parents would not or could not send them to school.[46] Many Catholic parents believed that they were inviting destruction of their children's faith by sending them to public schools.[47]

---

California in 1852, and after prospecting in the mines, settled down to a twelve hour daily stint as a laborer in the Pacific Mail Steamship shops in Benicia. After establishing a reputation as a master pugilist, he returned to New York and won and lost several championship fights that attracted national and international attention. Richard J. Purcell, " Fists Across the Sea," *Columbia* (April, 1926) ; " John Carmel Heenan," D.A.B., VIII, 499.

[43] Interview with Mrs. Davenport Brown, January 2, 1944.

[44] The following offer no foundation for the belief that McKenna studied for the priesthood : *Biographical Directory of the American Congress,* p. 1267 ; St. Joseph's College, Records, St. Dominic's Church, Registers, San Francisco Archdiocesan Archives. Letters of Thomas J. Love, S.J., December 7, 1943 ; of Albert Muller, O.P., of St. Dominic's Church, Benicia, December 8, 1943 ; of Gerald Geary, Archivist of the Archdiocese of San Francisco, April 29, 1944 ; of James T. O'Dowd, Superintendent of Schools, Archdiocese of San Francisco, April 5, 1944. Mrs. Pitts Duffield insists that her father never studied for the priesthood.

[45] The Young Ladies' Academy was founded under Protestant auspices in 1852 and became the property of Miss Atkins (later wife of Judge John Lynch, Surveyor General of Louisiana) in 1854. Wood-Alley, *op. cit.,* pp. 172–175 ; cf., Rosalind A. Keep, *Fourscore Years—A History of Mills College* (Oakland: 1921) ; *Metropolitan Catholic Directory* (1855), p. 209.

[46] *Annual Report of the Superintendent of Public Instruction of the State of California, 1855* (Sacramento: 1855), p. 4 ; John Swett, *History of the Public School System of California* (San Francisco: 1876), p. 217, lists statistics of school attendance from 1855 to 1862 and attributes the decrease in numbers to the abandonment of the practice of granting financial subsidies to Catholic schools.

[47] William Gleeson, *History of the Catholic Church in California* (San Francisco: 1872), pp. 273–275 ; Swett, *op. cit.,* p. 24.

In the Benicia Public School Joseph continued most of the courses which he had started in St. Joseph's College. The curriculum consisted in the study of geography, arithmetic, grammar, reading, spelling and " such other subjects as the trustees shall see fit to introduce." [48] The ability of the teachers and the discipline maintained in Solano County Schools were considered to be above the average. In this little school, young McKenna was drilled in habits of punctuality [49] and methodical action that later characterized his life, while his mother instilled those attitudes of mind that he so frequently mentioned when he recalled his boyhood. Even the military bearing which marked his carriage could be attributed to his mother, who, he asserted humorously, " put a stick down my back to keep me straight." [50]

During his free time, Joseph often went duck hunting in the expansive marsh lands with a boyhood chum, Lansing Mizner,[51] or fished off the banks of Carquinez Straits. On Sunday mornings he assisted at Mass in St. Dominic's Church where he was instructed in his religion by Father Francis Sadoc Vilarassa, who came to California in 1850, with Bishop Joseph S. Alemany, of San Francisco. In 1853, Father Vilarassa established a Dominican

---

[48] *Annual Report of the Superintendent of Public Instruction of the State of California,* 1854, pp. 3 f.; 1857, p. 6; 1858, pp. 11–12, 27, 28, 31.

[49] Writer's interview with Robert F. Cogswell, law clerk to Justice McKenna (1921–1925), November 18, 1943.

[50] George Denman Martin, "A Study of the Life of Joseph McKenna," p. 2. Manuscript copy in possession of Mrs. Davenport Brown. The story was told to Martin by Ashton F. Embry, secretary to Justice McKenna.

[51] Lansing B. Mizner, a lifelong friend and law partner of Joseph McKenna. His father was one of the first settlers in Benicia, engaged in several commercial ventures with Dr. Robert Semple and operated a stage line from Benicia to Sacramento, prior to the establishment of boat service on the Sacramento River. The Mizner family was among the wealthiest in Benicia and were said to have substantially aided the McKennas in times of stress. Mizner became an ardent supporter of McKenna in his campaigns and was appointed United States Minister to the Central American States. Involved in a diplomatic tangle, he was recalled and McKenna is supposed to have made such an effective speech in his defense that McKinley remarked, "I want that man—McKenna—for my friend." Interview with Mrs. Pitts Duffield.

priory and church in Benicia.[52]   Another priest of young McKenna's acquaintance was James T. Aerden, a native of Belgium, who settled in Benicia after laboring in Oregon among the Indians for seven years.   For many years he took a leading part in the activities of the town and was loved for his devotion and zeal.[53]

Besides the novelty attendant on setting up a home, becoming acclimated, and adjusting their pattern of life to a frontier environment, the McKenna family was increased by the birth of George Augustus Aloysius in June, 1856.   A few days later, June 28, 1856, the infant was baptized by Father Vilarassa in St. Dominic's Church.   At the ceremony Joseph and his sister, Catherine, became the godparents of their baby brother.[54]   The birth of little George Augustus was the last noteworthy event of happiness for the family in the next six years, which were marked by three deaths.   The first was that of John McKenna, on April 22, 1858.[55] He was buried with the rites of the Catholic Church from St. Dominic's Church, and his remains interred in the little cemetery atop the hill that overlooked Carquinez Straits.[56]   Hardly had the widow and the children adjusted themselves when, October 31, 1859, baby George Augustus died.   Again the little family trudged

---

[52] Zephyrin Engelhart, O.F.M., *The Missions and Missionaries of California* (San Francisco: 1915), IV, 682; Sister M. Aloysius, "Dominicans in California," *Dominicana*, I (December, 1900), p. 48; Gleeson, *op. cit.,* II, 185 f.; *Metropolitan Catholic Directory* (1855), p. 208.

[53] Sister M. Aloysius, *op. cit.,* p. 50.

[54] *Records of Baptisms,* Book One, St. Dominic's Church, Benicia, p. 22, no. 88. For Francis Vilarassa and the growth of the Catholic Church in California, see Sister Gertrude Mary Gray, S.H.N., "The Life of the Most Reverend Joseph Sadoc Alemany, O.P." (Unpublished master's essay, Dept. of History, Catholic University, 1942), pp. 16, 22, 26, 30, 31, 42.

[55] Tombstone on lot 925, Old Catholic Cemetery, Benicia; *Record of Burials,* St. Dominic's Church, Benicia.

[56] In the same cemetery is buried Dona Concepcion de Arguello, the heroine of a famous California blighted romance with the Russian Chamberlain, Nikolai Petrovich Rezanof. After the death of her suitor, Miss de Arguello entered the Dominican Convent in Monterey and received the habit from Bishop Alemany, April 11, 1851. Engelhart, *op. cit.,* IV, 688. She accompanied the Dominicans to Benicia when St. Catherine's Female Academy was founded in 1854, and died there in 1857, at the age of 67. Bancroft, *History of California,* II, 64–78.

its weary way up the hill to the white picketed burial grounds where the child's remains were placed alongside those of his father. Another severe shock for the mother came in 1862, when her namesake, Mary Ann, succumbed.[57]

For this woman with a brood to rear in a frontier settlement, life did not seem to hold bright prospects. Nevertheless, she was able to clothe and feed her offspring without exacting hardship because of some income from real estate investments made by her late husband.[58] As a supplementary source of income, Joseph organized a route in the town and sold bread.[59] In spite of her numerous duties, Mrs. McKenna found time to prepare Joseph for the Benicia Collegiate Institute by 1862. This was the same year in which he received the Sacrament of Confirmation at the hands of Bishop Eugene O'Connell.[60] By attendance at day and evening classes, Joseph was able to complete the college course in two years, that is, in 1864. He then enrolled in a law course which had just been inaugurated.[61] Within a year he thought that

---

[57] Tombstone on lot 925, Old Catholic Cemetery, Benicia, reads: " Mary Ann McKenna, Died March 26, 1862, Age 15 years, 10 months."

[58] This statement is based upon a letter from Mrs. Pitts Duffield to the writer, March 2, 1944.

[59] The exact occupation of Joseph McKenna is not agreed upon. A contemporary, Judge Crooks of Benicia, asserts that McKenna's parents were poor and that "little Joe" sold bread on the streets of Benicia at twelve loaves for a dollar. He reports that when President Hayes toured the country, he stopped at Benicia with McKenna to shoot ducks and, in order not to leave any wrong impressions, McKenna jumped off the train before the President and told an old friend, Jerry O'Donnell, to say nothing about his bread selling activities: "Keep it shady, Jerry, keep it shady." Reverend Mr. Clark, pastor of the Anglican Church, Benicia, claims that "Joe" sold water from door to door; *The Vallejo News,* January 19, 1897, has him running a bakery with his mother. Mrs. Pitts Duffield insists that her father's family derived a substantial income from the wise real estate investments of her grandfather.

[60] *Record of Confirmations,* Book One, p. 6, St. Dominic's Church, Benicia.

[61] Wood-Alley, *op. cit.,* p. 166; Marguerite Hunt, *History of Solano County* (Chicago: 1926), p. 166; Reverend Randolph Crump Miller, Archivist of the Protestant Episcopalian Diocese of San Francisco, writes in a letter, January 12, 1944, that no school was established by his denomination until 1867. This corresponds with statements in the above cited works that St. Augustine's College was founded in 1867 under Episcopalian auspices.

he was sufficiently grounded to take the examination for the bar.

In California any person was eligible to practice before the courts if he were white, male, twenty-one years of age and " of good moral character and who possess the necessary qualifications of learning and ability." Applicants were examined by a judge of the State Supreme Court, and if they proved to have the necessary qualifications, they were admitted to the bar.[62] On April 4, 1865, McKenna with four of his classmates, George A. Lamont, John Hunt, Jr., Thomas J. Hart and Thomas Lamont, appeared before Judge Alonzo Sawyer of the Supreme Court who questioned the aspirants as to their legal knowledge and signed the order which admitted them to the practice of the law.[63] He admonished the new practitioners to relinquish the idea that their education was completed. " It was," he was careful to emphasize, " just begun." The future offered rich rewards for those who were determined to give their strength and time unstintingly to the tasks that lay at hand. With this paternal advice ringing in his ears and a license clasped in his hands, Joseph McKenna struck forth into the world.

Shortly after their admission to the bar, Joseph McKenna and George A. Lamont [64] opened a law office in Fairfield, the seat of Solano County. Like most attorneys in frontier settlements, McKenna became interested in politics. In the summer of 1865,

---

Therefore McKenna could not have graduated from St. Augustine's College in 1865. It is more likely that he was graduated from the Benicia Collegiate Institute which was sold in Dec. 1867 to the Pacific Coast Mission of the Episcopalian Church and became the nucleus of St. Augustine's College. The first law school was not organized in California until 1878. Oscar Shuck, *History of Bench and Bar in California* (San Francisco: 1901), p. 456.

[62] Theodore Hittell, *The General Laws of the State of California from 1850 to 1864* (San Francisco: 1865), I, 71.

[63] *Brown Scrapbook, San Francisco Chronicle,* n.d.

[64] George A. Lamont was born in Ohio in 1844 and moved with his parents to Vallejo, California (1854) where he was enrolled as a student in the Benicia Collegiate Institute. Admitted to the bar in 1865, he was elected District Attorney for Solano County, 1869–1871. In 1876 he married Hattie E. Yount, daughter of John E. Yount, a wealthy landowner of central California.

as the nominee of the Republican Party, he was elected to the office of district attorney of the county.[65]

Thus was McKenna initiated into the body politic of a community that had hardly completed the fifteenth year of its life, yet had experienced most of the effects of public corruption, dishonesty and inefficiency. These unwholesome conditions were variously attributed to primitive surroundings, machine politics, sudden wealth, indifference and inexperience in the procedures of responsible government. The control of the government fell into the hands of one or two individuals whose bitter rivalry for supremacy overshadowed and tainted every detail of legislative, judicial and executive action. The struggle for power culminated in the bitter feud between David Broderick [66] and William M. Gwin,[67] resulting in the murder of Broderick, disruption of the Democratic Party and the entrance of the first Republican administration in 1861 under the leadership of Governor Leland Stanford. In the meantime the State Legislation had embarked on a career of graft and venality [68] and so well entrenched were the forces of evil that, when an independent reform group was

---

[65] Wood-Alley, *op. cit.,* p. 126; Frank A. Leach, a close friend and supporter of McKenna, has a graphic account of electioneering in California during the sixties. *Recollections of a Newspaper Man* (San Francisco: 1917), pp. 14 ff.; Theodore Hittell, *History of California,* II, 702, 809. For excerpts from memoirs and contemporary accounts, see Hubert Bancroft, *History of California,* VI, 275; Winfield Davis, *History of Political Conventions in California, 1849–1892* (Sacramento: 1893), p. 4.

[66] David Colbert Broderick had become leader of the Democratic faction which sought to oust William Gwin.

[67] William McKendree Gwin (1805–1885) was born in Tennessee, the son of an itinerant Baptist preacher. After graduating from the medical school of Transylvania University, he practiced a short time in Mississippi before moving to California in 1849 with the early gold seekers. For his services to California, he was elected to the United States Senate. At the outbreak of the War between the States he was imprisoned by the Federal Government for pro-slavery activities but was released within a few months. He failed to interest the Emperor of France, Napoleon III, in a plan to establish a colony of Confederate sympathizers in Mexico. For some time after the War, he lived in California and then moved to New York where he died in 1885.

[68] Edith Dobie, *Political Career of Stephen Mallory White* (Stanford University: 1927), p. 21.

elected, they too fell into the habit of prostituting political trust for financial consideration.[69]

During the War between the States, little sympathy was manifested in California for the Union cause. The absence of national political and economic ties and the presence of a large foreign element contributed to this spirit of isolation and aloofness. On the other hand, the supporters of the South, neither apathetic nor inactive, strove to separate California from the Union.[70] They planned to establish California as a Republic in order to financially and morally weaken the North. The schemes of the rebels were thwarted only when a minority of the Democrats combined with the Republicans to place most of the State offices in the hands of the loyalists.

The faithful support of the United States troops, stationed in California, was assured when President Lincoln replaced Brigadier General Albert Sidney Johnston by Brigadier General Edwin V. Sumner, as commander of the Pacific Division of the United States Army.[71] It was, however, the activities of enthusiastic and earnest pro-Union men that firmly linked California to the North. In San Francisco a campaign was launched to arouse sentiment for the Federal cause. Thomas Starr King [72] toured the State and enlisted thousands in the loyalist program, prodded the Legislature to pledge adherence to the Lincoln Administration, raised a million dollars for the Sanitary Commission and induced fifteen thousand

---

[69] Cleland, *op. cit.*, pp. 405 f.

[70] John J. Earle, "Sentiment of the People of California with Respect to the Civil War," *Annual Report of the American Historical Association, 1907*, I (1908), 125; Bancroft, *History of California*, VII, 275 ff., gives a balanced narrative of the secession movement; Joseph Ellison, *California and the Nation, 1846–1869* (Berkeley: 1927), orientates California in the national picture.

[71] The dispatch of General Sumner to California was an integral part of the Lincolnian strategy to keep the doubtful border States in the Union.

[72] Thomas Starr King (1824–1864) was born in New York and at the age of fifteen was the support of his widowed mother and five sisters and brothers. After fourteen years as pastor of the Universalist Church at Charlestown, Massachusetts, he accepted the call of the Unitarian Church in San Francisco, where he labored for the cause of the Union from 1860 until his death in 1864.

men to enroll in the Federal Army.[73]  Despite their best efforts, the Unionists were  unable to completely suppress pro-slavery activities.  Albert Sydney Johnston was permitted to depart for the South where he served with distinction, while William Gwin of the Gwin-Broderick controversy joined the diplomatic corps and represented Jefferson Davis in France.  In certain sections of California the secessionist sentiment was so strong that there was no hesitation in publicly advocating the principles of disunion.[74] During the entire four-year conflict the Southern supporters kept the Union sympathizers on edge by intrigue and conspiracy.

Aside from the question of secession and the change from Democratic to Republican control, little material change was noted in the politics of California from 1860 to 1865.  The low ebb of public morality was similar to that of the preceding decade. Professional politicans accepted public trust for private gain and official laxity did not disturb public complacency.[75]  During the life and death struggle of the nation, Republicans controlled most of the State and national offices and it was this condition that prompted McKenna to abandon the political party of his father, and cast his lot with the Republicans.

On October 18, 1865, the voters of Solano County elected McKenna their district attorney.[76]  His service being satisfactory he was reelected in 1867.[77]  During his incumbency most of the

---

[73] Hittell, *History of California,* IV, 289.  Meetings were held in San Juan, Marysville, Vallejo, Eureka, Los Angeles and other towns.  Ellison, *op. cit.,* pp. 189–207.  One journal, *The Visalia Equal Rights Expositor,* October 18, 1862, characterizes Lincoln as " a narrow minded bigot, an unprincipled demagogue, a drivelling, idiotic imbecile creature," cited by Earle, *op. cit.,* p. 132.

[74] *Official Records of the Union and Confederate Armies* (Washington: 1880–1901), Series I, Part I, 496, 556, 629, 759, 879; Part II, 107, 130, 453, 521, 930, 938; for the oaths taken by the members of the organizations, see Part I, 556 and Part II, 938.

[75] Cleland, *op. cit.,* p. 406, quotes the *San Francisco Bulletin* as extending congratulations to the people of the State for electing a legislature which, though ignorant and incapable, was influenced by political prejudice and personal ambition rather than by mercenary motives; cf., Hittell, *History of California,* IV, 335–337.

[76] Wood-Alley, *op. cit.,* p. 143,

[77] *Loc. cit.*

cases reflected the rough life of the frontier.  One of the first, the
*People v. Frank O'Grady*,[78] arose from a murder committed when
an abolitionist berated a group of rebels for celebrating the assassi-
nation of Lincoln.  After two trials, O'Grady was acquitted.  In
the *People v. William Westphal* [79] the accused was charged with
the murder of his wife's half brother.  Despite testimony that
Westphal had struck the deceased immediately before death, the
jury returned a verdict of acquittal and McKenna again failed to
win a widely publicized trial.  Although he obtained a death
sentence against the defendants in the *People v. James Campbell
and Annie Robinson*,[80] the Supreme Court of California overruled
the verdict on the ground that the jury had failed to specify the
degree of murder in their findings.[81]  But McKenna was not to be
denied for he finally obtained some solace when the highest
tribunal of the State refused to heed the appeal of one convicted
of assault with a deadly weapon, on the basis that the court's
jurisdiction did not extend to crimes less than a felony.[82]

In 1879, after the completion of his second term as District
Attorney, McKenna retired to private practice, but not before he
shrewdly arranged that his partner, George A. Lamont, should be
his successor in office.[83]  In the same year McKenna felt sufficiently secure to seek and win the hand of Amanda Frances
Bornemann, of San Francisco.[84]  The future Mrs. McKenna was
born on the edge of the German Black Forest and came as a girl
with her parents to San Francisco.  She attended Notre Dame

---

[78] Wood-Alley, *op. cit.,* p. 144.

[79] *Ibid.,* p. 143.

[80] *Reports of Cases Determined in the Supreme Court of the State of
California, October, 1870–January, 1871* (Sacramento: 1872), XL, 129.
Henceforth cited as *California Reports.*

[81] *Ibid.,* p. 144.

[82] *Ibid.,* XXXV, 389.

[83] Mrs. M. Donohue, of Benicia, recalls that George Lamont was far
superior to McKenna in ability, but the latter was more ambitious and active
in political life.

[84] *San Francisco Bulletin,* June 10, 1869, remarks, " The marriage vows
were taken in the presence of Reverend Father L. A. Auger at the home of
the bride's parents."  Louis Auger was pastor of the Catholic Church in
Suisun, California.  *Metropolitan Catholic Directory, 1869,* p. 99.

Academy in San Jose and after graduation became prominent in the work of Catholic charities.[85] Her marriage resulted in four surviving children, three girls and a boy.[86] During forty-five years of wedded life, this woman, frequently referred to as " strikingly handsome," was the constant confidante of her husband.[87] So affectionate was their companionship that when McKenna died in 1926, it was generally concluded that his wife's death two years previously was a contributing factor in his failing health and last illness.

As District Attorney and in private practice, McKenna achieved a good reputation.[88] Although his residence was in Suisun, the greater part of his business was in Fairfield, which was reputed to have a " very strong bar." [89] In his tilts with the legal lights of San Francisco and Oakland, McKenna because of his quick thinking and effective speaking was always able to " hold his own." A friendly observer asserted that " in mental sense he is as nimble as a cat and in cross-examination, repartee and argument " never at a loss for the apt word.[90]

One jurist before whom McKenna frequently pleaded, noticed:

> McKenna always had a procedure marked out but was
> capable of varying it when occasion demanded. If he

[85] McKenna courted Elizabeth Hanlon without success but he in turn was pursued without avail by Miss Barry of Benicia. In the midst of the courtships, McKenna created quite a stir by going to San Francisco and marrying Amanda Bornemann. Statement made by Mrs. Donohue of Benicia.

[86] The children were Isabel, later Mrs. Pitts Duffield, of New York, Frank, Marie, who married Davenport Brown of Boston, and Hildegarde, who became the wife of George Pulz and, later, of Edward Alsop of New York. Statement made by Mrs. Pitts Duffield.

[87] Statement made by Mrs. Davenport Brown; cf., *New York Times,* January 6, 1925; *The Woodland Democrat,* February 18, 1892, maintains that McKenna "always sought her advice and approval" and had great respect for her judgment.

[88] Leach, *op. cit.,* p. 203.

[89] McKenna was liaison man for several law firms in the nearby cities. The task consisted primarily in keeping these attorneys informed as to the time that their cases would be called up in the Solano County courts. *Brown Scrapbook,* clipping from the *San Francisco Wasp,* n.d.

[90] *Brown Scrapbook,* newspaper clipping, n.n. ; n.d.

was forced to abandon one line of attack through a ruling
of the court, he unhesitantly launched out on a new approach without any loss of force or effectiveness. "He
is never at a loss and never gets rattled." [91]

McKenna was noted for his ability as an advocate, whether before
judge or jury, and his versatility in legal skirmishes became
proverbial.[92]  His friends emphatically denied that McKenna was
an "obscure crossroads lawyer" [93] simply because his practice was
confined to one county.  Rather they included him among those
prominent western attorneys who had served their novitiate in
rural courtrooms.[94]

In 1874 McKenna received considerable attention when he
represented Fairfield in its endeavor to remain the county seat.
An election in the previous year decided that distinction should be
Vallejo's and February 8, 1874, designated as the date for the
change.  However, McKenna enjoined the removal by a temporary
restraining order.  When the court refused to issue a permanent
injunction, McKenna sponsored a bill in the State Legislature
which would isolate Vallejo from the rest of the county.[95]  After
the bill had passed both Houses the Vallejoites appealed to the
Governor.  That official consented to use his veto only if Fairfield
were re-established as the county seat.  The Vallejo contingent
agreed.  A bill was expeditiously framed, rushed through the
Assembly and the Senate, signed by the Governor and transmitted
in sufficient time to forestall the transfer.[96]  The legal competence

---

[91] *Brown Scrapbook,* newspaper clipping, n.n.; n.d.

[92] *Oakland Enquirer,* January 21, 1898.

[93] Gustavus Myers, *History of the Supreme Court of the United States*
(Chicago: 1918), p. 640.

[94] Martin, *op. cit.,* p. 8.

[95] Marguerite Hunt, *History of Solano County* (Chicago: 1926), I, 57 ff.;
during the controversy, Frank Leach was a lobbyist for the Vallejo interests.
Leach, *op. cit.,* pp. 182–185.  Leach was born in New York in 1847 and was
brought to California via the Panama route in 1852.  In 1867 he established
the *Vallejo Chronicle* which became an enthusiastic supporter of McKenna.
For his work on the *Chronicle* and on the *Oakland Enquirer,* he was rewarded by President McKinley with the position of Director of the San
Francisco Mint, in which capacity he served from 1897 to 1907 when he
became Director of Mints at Washington, D. C.

[96] Leach, *op. cit.,* p. 184.

displayed by McKenna established his name prominently in the public mind and facilitated his election to the State Assembly in 1875.

While McKenna was preparing for further political experience, significant events were transpiring in California. The demoralization of public life which plagued the national government with Credit Mobilier, Indian Frauds, the Whiskey Ring, corruption of judges, trafficking in appointments and bribery of Congressmen, gave birth in California to similar crimes against the body politic. The State Legislature was the most debased of all departments in the matter of political morality. The legislators, reputedly of " mediocre ability and second-rate morals," [97] were entrusted with a free hand in matters of taxes, appropriations, franchises and special legislation.[98] The Legislature so misused these prerogatives that it became a symbol of waste and corruption.[99] The bid for votes was so brisk that the Central Pacific Railroad had to employ " everybody who could pull a pound." [100] A seat in the United States Senate was sold to the highest bidder [101] and even the influential Leland Stanford was reputed to have spent $250,000 for that honor.[102] It made little difference which party was in

[97] Dobie, *op. cit.,* p. 21.

[98] *Federal and State Constitutions,* Francis N. Thorpe, ed. (Washington, D. C.: 1909), I, 403, 410.

[99] Cleland, *op. cit.,* p. 405.

[100] Stuart Daggett, *Chapters on the History of the Southern Pacific* (New York: 1922), p. 204.

[101] Dobie, *op. cit.,* p. 426.

[102] Leland Stanford, with whom McKenna formed a close and profitable friendship, was born in New York, March 4, 1824, and moved to California after a temporary sojourn in Wisconsin. In the West, he spent the first three years, 1852–1855, as a keeper of a general store in a mining camp called Michigan Bluff. He then moved to Sacramento, where he established a large mercantile business and came in contact with three other merchants in whose company he was destined to build a fortune which made his name well known in western railroad history. From the time he arrived in California until his death in 1893, Stanford maintained an interest in politics. As Republican leader, Governor, United States Senator and lobbyist for the Southern Pacific interests, Stanford was recognized as a potent factor in the political life of his community. In Washington, Stanford and McKenna became associates and there is reason to believe that Stanford

power, the special interests and the large corporations had little trouble in buying and manipulating votes for the support of their favored legislation.[103]

Reputedly a most lavish dispenser of bribes was the Central Pacific Railroad. The Act of 1862 [104] under which it was incorporated and the supplementary law of 1864 [105] fixed the maximum rates, but they were ignored and the traffic was charged all that it could bear. Although continual demands besought the State Legislature to initiate a rate-tariff, the railroad was sufficiently powerful to thwart such movements. Furthermore, the carriers contended that statistics demonstrated that their profits were not exorbitant.[106]

In the face of these recognizable grievances it was only natural for the public to seek a sacrificial victim and the lot fell upon the Chinese. The unfortunate Oriental, symbolizing the fears and racial prejudices of the discontented, was the composite of all that was inferior, alien, and strange and therefore could easily be imagined as evil, dangerous and ominous. The first Chinese presumably came to California in 1848 and by 1850 eight hundred had followed them. They were welcomed and the Governor described them as one of "the most worthy classes of our citizens." [107]

By 1876 the Chinese influx had changed the feeling of hos-

---

persuaded President Harrison to nominate McKenna for the United States Circuit Court.

[103] U. S. Congress, Senate, *Report of the United States Pacific Railway Commission,* Executive Document 51, U. S. Senate, 50th Congress, 1st Session (Washington: 1887), V, 3284, reports the testimony of railroad officials who contended that legislators had to be constantly watched lest they pass legislation detrimental to the carrier. When asked to estimate the sums that the railroad spent in order to influence legislators, the railroad representatives refused to answer on advice of counsel. *Ibid.,* pp. 3287, 3721. Hereafter cited as *Report of Pacific Railway Commission.*

[104] *12 U. S. Statutes,* 489.
[105] *13 U. S. Statutes,* 356.
[106] Hittell, *History of California,* IV, 496; Daggett, *op. cit.,* pp. 242, 245, quotes "Report of the California Commissioner of Transportation"; for testimony of Stephen T. Gage, assistant to Leland Stanford and lobbyist at Sacramento, consult *Report of Pacific Railway Commission,* V, 2534, 2536.
[107] Bancroft, *History of California,* VII, 12.

pitality to suspicion and opposition. The Chinaman had been disliked almost from the time that his industry and thrift brought him into competition with the white man. The 116,000 Chinese were represented as a peril to the economic, social and political welfare of the community.[108] The imagined evils which threatened the State caught hold of the public imagination and by 1876 the hysteria had developed to a universal demand that " the Chinese must go." [109] Demagogues found it comparatively easy to exaggerate the shortcomings of the coolie and attribute to him the plight of the unemployed, particularly since the railroad, the target of most rabble rousers, had imported the Oriental in shipload lots.[110] Thus antagonism for the railroad and prejudice against the yellow man were combined to make exclusion of the Chinese a leading political issue.[111]

In 1875, the year of McKenna's initial campaign, the political parties molded their platforms into proposed solutions for these problems. There were four groups in the field, i.e., Republican, Democratic, People's Independent and Temperance Reform.[112] The last two, offshoots of the Republican Party, indicated the discontent among the conservative and respectable members of that organization. The split in Republican ranks was influenced by the repudiation of the Grant Administration and the formation of the Liberal Republican Party by Carl Schurz, Charles Francis Adams, Horace Greeley, Senator Lyman Trumbull and Governor B. Gratz Brown of Missouri. The State Convention of the

---

[108] Winfield Davis, *History of Political Conventions in California, 1849–1892* (Sacramento: 1893), p. 507.

[109] The phrase " The Chinese must go " was supposed to have been coined by a political campaigner and became the rallying cry for Dennis Kearney and his followers as well as for many of the mediocre office seekers in the State. Cleland, *op. cit.,* p. 51.

[110] It was admitted that the Central Pacific began to import Chinese labor in 1864 and the number rose to eleven thousand in 1866 and 1867 and then fell in 1869 to five thousand. The Chinese were paid $35 a month and were required to furnish their own board whereas the white labor obtained $35 a month and free board. *Report of Pacific Railway Commission,* V, 3139–3141.

[111] Davis, *op. cit.,* pp. 334, 352, 357, 360.

[112] *Ibid.,* pp. 335–356.

Republicans, conscious of the truth of the charges of nepotism, corruption, inefficiency and misrule levelled against them, carefully disclaimed dependence on corporate power and decried, without denying, the manipulation of their party by the monied interests.[113]

In general the platforms censured the abuse of monopolists, and proposed to free the public schools from sectarian influence.[114] In addition each party offered one or more interesting propositions. The People's Independent naively requested that each candidate be carefully scrutinized and that the vote be cast for the one who would be faithful to the people and to the principles of good government.[115] The Temperance group sought the abolition of the corner saloon by a monthly tax of thirty dollars.[116] The Democrats naturally condemned the maladministration of the Republicans, demanded Chinese exclusion, censured discriminatory taxes against saloons and championed the cause of the workingman.[117] The Republicans, in glorifying President Grant, contended that the attacks on him had their source in the same ungenerous spirit that had prompted vilification of Washington, Jackson and Lincoln. One-half of the platform was devoted to a discussion of the origin, privileges and abuses of the Central Pacific Railroad and in a somewhat startling conclusion the party advocated regulation of the railroad.[118]

In August, 1875, Joseph McKenna and his friend, Lansing B. Mizner, were nominated by the Solano County Republican Convention for the Assembly.[119] In his campaign McKenna's speeches were hewn close to the party line and based on those parts of the platform most appealing to his audiences, namely, irrigation and transportation. On the former the candidate insisted that all resources of the State should be employed for the benefit of agriculture [120] and the means most conducive to that end was a

[113] *San Francisco Bulletin,* June 11, 1875.
[114] *Ibid.,* June 22, 30, 1875.
[115] *Ibid.,* June 22, 1875.
[116] Davis, *op. cit.,* p. 354.
[117] *San Francisco Bulletin,* June 11, 1875.
[118] Davis, *op. cit.,* p. 333.
[119] *Weekly Solano Republican,* August 27, 1875.
[120] Davis, *op. cit.,* p. 334.

series of subsidized irrigation projects.[121] Farm produce could
be moved profitably by cheap transportation and it was the
obligation of the commonwealth to procure that by regulating the
railroads.[122] McKenna was convinced that only the fiat of the
State could control carriers " who often disregard the welfare and
convenience of the public which they were created to serve." [123]

In populated areas the candidate dwelt on the advantages of the
public school which he visualized as " an institution of the state,
established as a preventive of crime and poverty which attend
ignorance." [124]    It might be observed here that the assurances
which McKenna gave were scrupulously observed when he became
a member of the State Assembly.    Always cautious in making
promises, once he had committed himself, he did his utmost to
have those pledges as " nearly realized by appropriate performance
as belongs to the duty of a representative." [125]

On election day, September 1, 1875, McKenna received the
highest total of four competitors.[126]  His vote of 1,586 was 53
more than Democrat Stephen W. Swan who in turn led Lansing
B. Mizner, 1,533 to 1,532.    So close was the Swan-Mizner race
that the final result was not announced until a week after
election.[127]  On September 8, 1875, Joel Harvey, county clerk,
certified McKenna as legally elected and administered the oath
of office to the new assemblyman.[128]  In state-wide returns the
Democrats enjoyed a landslide.    Not only would they control
sixty-four of the eighty seats in the Assembly and a majority in
the Senate, but they had also made a clean sweep of offices.[129]

The Twenty-First Biennial Session of the California State
Assembly opened on Monday, December 6, 1875.    During the four

---

[121] *San Francisco Bulletin,* June 11, 1875.

[122] *Brown Scrapbook,* newspaper clipping, n.n. ; n.d.

[123] *Ibid.,* newspaper clipping, n.n. ; n.d.

[124] *Daily Alta California,* August 11, 1876.

[125] The remark was made by McKenna before the Republican Convention
which had tendered him the nomination for the Third Congressional District.

[126] *Solano County Republican,* September 16, 1875.

[127] *San Francisco Bulletin,* September 9, 12, 13, 15, 1875.

[128] The document is found in the Archives of Solano County, *List of
Assemblymen,* County Court House, Fairfield, California.

[129] Davis, *op. cit.,* p. 355.

months of its existence it labored under many difficulties, the most important of which was an obligation to legislate on a multiplicity of state, county, town and municipal matters within a maximum of 120 days.[130] The result was a welter of unconsidered legislation in which hundreds of unread bills were passed.[131] In this confusion there were few legislators who were sufficiently shrewd to draw commendation on the performance of their prosaic tasks. Yet McKenna was able to find time and opportunity to distinguish himself.[132] The secret of his success was partially explained by a colleague, Morris M. Estee, who noted that McKenna did not seek to legislate on every permissible subject, but simply introduced a few measures of importance and " watched them carefully in committee." [133]

After the preliminaries at the initial session, the Assembly elected officers. McKenna was nominated for Speaker by John B. Reddick, one of the twelve Republican Assemblymen. The Democrats chose for their candidate, Gideon J. Carpenter of Hangtown, later dignified with the more respectable name of Placerville. The vote was according to strict party line and Mc-Kenna was overwhelmingly defeated by 61 to 12.[134] It is interest-

---

[130] Thorpe, *op. cit.,* I, 408.

[131] Cleland, *op. cit.,* p. 407; Martin, *op. cit.,* p. 13.

[132] *Solano County Republican,* January 20, 1876; *Brown Scrapbook* contains an undated clipping from the *San Francisco Examiner* in which McKenna was congratulated for the address on the Education Bill. It was predicted that he would some day occupy a prominent position in the councils of the Republican Party, therefore "it is but natural that he should come to the advocacy of such measures as have received the impress of dogmatic definition of the councils of the Radical organization. His speech was an able exposition of Radical ideas on this subject. He stood right up for his cause . . . but his cause is wrong."

[133] Morris M. Estee had a long, but not particularly impressive political career. He was elected to the State Assembly from Sacramento in 1863 and from San Francisco in 1873 when he was selected to be the Speaker of the Assembly. In 1879 he participated in the formation of a constitution for the State. In 1876 and 1888 he was one of the Republican presidential electors.

[134] *Journal of the Assembly, 21st Session of the Legislature of the State of California, 1875–1876* (Sacramento: 1876), I, 2. The Journal was written in longhand and signed each day by G. J. Carpenter, Speaker of the

ing to note that McKenna offered a proposal to abolish the office of chaplain, but when it was defeated, he cast his vote for the Republican nominee.[135] A similar attempt failed in the Senate, and one observer believed that these irreligious motions were the outgrowth of a political philosophy that credited ordinary men with as much power as the clergy in drawing down the blessing of God.[136]

When committees were formed, McKenna was on the roster of those concerned with Elections, Judiciary and Federal Relations.[137] As a member of the last named he wrote a minority report in favor of a proposed amendment to the United States Constitution which would prohibit subsidizing sectarian schools. McKenna championed the measure because diversion of common school funds was " opposed to the admitted interests of all." [138] Thus it was evident that Assemblyman McKenna either ignored or was ignorant of the widespread Catholic opposition to such a proposal. When President Grant first broached the subject in Des Moines, September 29, 1875 [139] and later incorporated it in his annual message to Congress,[140] the Catholic press roundly criticized a presidential blessing that was given to an educational system that created a " generation of infidels." [141]

---

Assembly, and Robert Ferral, chief clerk. File No. 1237, Archives of the Secretary of State, Sacramento, California. Hereafter cited as *Assembly Journal.*

[135] *Ibid.,* p. 19.

[136] Hittell, *History of California,* IV, 570.

[137] *Assembly Journal,* I, 50, 69.

[138] On this occasion McKenna wrote: " I dissent from the report of the majority of your committee and recommend the passage of the resolution set out in the said report. The appropriation of public moneys raised by taxation for Educational purposes to the support of sectarian schools is repugnant to that which is conceded to be a proper National and State policy. No State therefore should be allowed the power of doing that which is opposed to the admitted interests of all. Respectfully, McKenna." *Ibid.,* I, 1071.

[139] " The President's Speech at Des Moines," *The Catholic World,* XXII (January, 1876), 433.

[140] *A Compilation of the Messages and Papers of the Presidents, 1789–1899,* James D. Richardson, ed. (Washington: 1896–1899), VII, 334.

[141] W. M. Marshall, " Secular Education in England and the United

*Joseph McKenna*

On February 12, 1876, McKenna again clashed with his fellow Catholics when he fought the repeal of the compulsory school law. Some of his co-religionists averred that these institutions were controlled and conducted by Protestants and " debauched the faith of Catholic children." [142] They argued that the right of parents to educate their offspring was violated and that the so-called " common " schools were actually un-American, atheistic, oppressive and destructive of the true aims of education.[143] Assemblyman John R. McConnell of Los Angeles cited statistics to prove that the compulsory school law was ineffective and that for the thousand infractions not one conviction had been recorded. Mandatory education, in the eyes of a Democrat, was compatible with despotic and tyrannical government and odious to an enlightened people.[144]

In answering the challenge McKenna levelled his attack at two basic points in his opponent's argument. The legislation was neither undemocratic nor un-American because it distinguished between " well-regulated freedom and unlicensed liberty." The right of the parent to educate the child was admitted, but some curb must be placed on its exercise. The law compelling the parent to educate his child was as logical as that which obliged him to feed and clothe it. The act did not " imperatively say where, when or how; but somewhere, sometime or somehow the child must be given an opportunity to develop its intellectual capacities . . . if the parent has given the child existence then he should . . . render that existence a profit and a pleasure, not a burden and a pain." [145]

McKenna's address was greeted by Republican journals as a severe blow to the forces of reaction and bigotry.[146] His debate with John McConnell was termed the most pointed, terse and

---

States," *The American Catholic Quarterly Review,* I (January-October 1876), 299, 308.

[142] John G. Shea, " Catholic Free Schools in the United States," *ibid.,* IX (January-October, 1884), 715–718.

[143] James Conway, " Rights and Duties of Family and State in Regard to Education," *ibid.,* pp. 114 f.

[144] *San Francisco Bulletin,* February 14, 1876.

[145] *Brown Scrapbook,* newspaper clipping, n.n.; n.d.

[146] *Weekly Solano Republican,* February 24, 1876.

spirited encounter of the session [147] yet never in the heat of controversy did he lose for a moment his self-control or spirit of fair play.[148] Although younger and less brilliant than his opponent, his arguments were more effective because his methods of thought and content of ideas were more concentrated and finished.[149] Despite his efforts the Assembly voted to repeal the law 43 to 26,[150] but it was effectively pigeon-holed in the Senate.[151]

The popularity of Assemblyman McKenna was materially enhanced when he became identified with two bills aimed at placing the railroads under strict surveillance. Attempts had been made since 1866 to initiate a rate schedule but the legislators thought such legislation superfluous since the railroads could deliver freight and passengers in one quarter of the time and at one-fourth the expense of other vehicles.[152] The laissez-faire supporters asserted that the railroad was a national project and that State interference would be an infringement on the exclusive power of Congress over interstate commerce.

In his comments on the Archer Freight and Fare Bill [153] McKenna dwelt on the universal desire for control of the railroad and the competency of the Legislature to create a supervisory body. In McKenna's judgment the railroad was so powerful that unless the government enforced an equitable tariff " the people

---

[147] A summary of the school controversy may be found in William Gleeson, *History of the Catholic Church in California* (San Francisco: 1872), II, 275; after withdrawing financial aid to sectarian schools, the legislature enacted a measure which made it obligatory for children to attend school. *Statutes of California Passed by the 20th Session, 1873–1874* (Sacramento: 1874), p. 751. The Catholics of California were opposed to the compulsory school bill and are alleged to have been behind the movement to repeal it. It was against this attempt that McKenna contended. *Weekly Solano Republican,* February 24, 1876.

[148] *Brown Scrapbook,* newspaper clipping, n.n.; n.d.

[149] *Assembly Journal,* p. 332.

[150] *Senate Journal,* p. 85.

[151] Bancroft, *History of California,* VII, 625.

[152] *San Francisco Bulletin,* February 28, 1876, contains the provisions of the bill.

[153] *Brown Scrapbook,* newspaper clipping, n.n.; n.d.

are helpless." [154] Aside from the usual laudatory notices in the Republican press, the remarks of McKenna were applauded by the anti-railroad publications. One of the latter remarked, " The contents of the addresses of Lawrence Archer [155] and Joseph McKenna would form a fairly complete treatise on the popular side of the railroad question." [156] The Archer Bill was approved by the Assembly 66 to 8,[157] but was defeated in the Senate.[158] Disappointed in his first attempt, McKenna resumed the fight for the O'Connor Transportation Bill. In this issue he was successful and for the first time railroads in California were constrained to publish and maintain a scale of reasonable rates.[159]

In addition to advocating popular measures, McKenna was sufficiently prudent to keep his political fences well mended. He sponsored a bill which authorized the Board of-Supervisors of Solano County to re-establish and re-locate the public roads and entrusted to those officials a fund from which the faithful adherents could be rewarded.[160] Another measure enacted under the egis of McKenna provided for a new Great Register of Voters for Solano County. A fee of twenty cents was granted to the County Clerk for each name recorded and in this way approximately seven hundred dollars were meted out to loyal supporters.

---

[154] *San Francisco Bulletin,* February 17, 1876, summarizes the contents of Judge Archer's speech.

[155] *San Francisco Call,* March 1, 1876.

[156] *Assembly Journal,* p. 381.

[157] The O'Connor Transportation Bill was substituted by the Senate Committee for all other proposals of railroad legislation. *San Francisco Bulletin,* March 15, 1876.

[158] Bancroft, *History of California,* VII, 627.

[159] *Assembly Journal,* pp. 288, 386, 450; *Statutes of California Passed at the 21st Session of the Legislature, 1875–1876,* p. 224, cites the obligation which the bill placed on the railroad and canal companies which utilized the public lands to relocate their roads or canals " at their own expense so that the public highway may cross the same without danger or delay."

[160] *Ibid.,* pp. 181 f.

# CHAPTER II

## CAMPAIGNING FOR CONGRESS

When the California State Assembly adjourned on April 3, 1876, McKenna had established a reputation as a leader among the Republicans. His supporters began to agitate for his selection as the candidate of the party in the Third Congressional District. When McKenna was questioned about this movement, he blandly replied in words that have a characteristic and familiar political ring: " If my friends will tender me the nomination, I will be constrained to receive it." [1]

On August 8, 1876, when the Republican Convention met in San Francisco, potential nominees had dwindled from seven to two, Joseph McKenna and State Senator W. De Haven of Humboldt County. Lansing Mizner, a boyhood friend, nominated McKenna and James McM. Shafter seconded the nomination. Both loquaciously lauded the proposed candidate's fitness. [2] The preliminary balloting was scarcely completed when De Haven withdrew and made McKenna's choice unanimous. After the official count Mizner and Shafter escorted the candidate to the platform where he delivered an address of acceptance and appreciation. McKenna warned his auditors that in view of the traditionally strong Democratic element in the district, success could be attained " only after severe labor and difficult canvass," yet he refused to countenance any wild or impossible promises even though they might be considered as " campaign talk," as Mr. Wendell Willkie might put it. " Promises," he cautioned, " are easily made; but are too often considered as pie crust." [3]

---

[1] *Weekly Solano Republican,* July 27, 1876.

[2] *Daily Alta California,* August 9, 10, 1876; *San Francisco Bulletin,* August 8, 9, 1876 and the *Chico Enterprise,* September 8, 1876, contain a detailed account of the speeches delivered at the nominating convention.

[3] *Daily Alta California,* August 11, 1876; clippings from newspapers with

33

McKenna's nomination was received by the Republican press with satisfaction and approval and even some of the Democratic journals admitted that a " wise choice " had been made.  The independent publications hailed him as the best choice to oppose " Luttrell, the railroad, and the Democratic horde."  Some analysts attributed the nomination to the fact that in the State Assembly he had proved to be the friend of the people and foe of corporations,[4] while others cynically observed that McKenna was nominated because nobody else wanted the thankless task of fighting a losing battle.  A pro-railroad journal noted rather testily that the Third District had not of late been favorable to the Republicans but it was a suitable place " in which a virtual unknown (McKenna) possessed of some energy, capacity to talk and . . . lofty aspirations might be made to realize his own limitations." [5]

In the campaign between John King Luttrell,[6] the Democratic nominee, and Joseph McKenna, national policies and problems rather than local issues were discussed.  By the Democratic victory in the national elections in 1874 and the wholesale exposure of graft and corruption within the Republican ranks, the Republicans realized their only hope of success lay in a thorough housecleaning.  Consequently, Rutherford B. Hayes, thrice governor of

---

out names in the possession of Mrs. Davenport Brown, of Boston, daughter of Justice McKenna.  Henceforth referred to as *Brown Scrapbook*.

[4] *Weekly Butte Record*, September 16, 1876; *Chico Enterprise*, September 8, 1876; reactions to the nomination are found in clippings in *Brown Scrapbook* from *Petaluma Argus, Sacramento Bee, Vallejo Chronicle, Russian River Flag, Contra Costa Gazette, Yolo Mail, Trinity Journal, Yreka Journal*.  Although without date the contents of the articles refer to the place, persons and circumstances of the nominating convention of 1876.

[5] *Sacramento Daily Union*, August 12, 1876; statement made by Mrs. M. Donohue, of Benicia, in a personal interview with the writer.

[6] John King Lutrell was born in Knoxville, Tennessee, June 27, 1831.  He moved with his parents to Alabama and thence to Missouri.  In 1852 the family continued westward to California, where John became a farmer, but soon turned to law and passed the bar in 1856.  Two years later he moved to Fort Jones, Siskiyou County, and from that district was elected to the California State Assembly in 1871.  From 1873 to 1879 he represented the Third District in Congress.  In 1893 he was appointed United States Agent for Alaska, where he died in the same year.  *Biographical Directory of the American Congress, 1774–1927* (Washington: 1928), p. 1245.

Ohio, was made their presidential candidate. Although not completely satisfactory to the reform element, he was acceptable to the less scrupulous and more practical leaders of the rank and file. The platform recalled the Republicans' role in saving the Union, advocated assistance to the farmer and war veteran, favored payment of the public debt in gold, promised reform of the civil service, championed high tariff and supported an amendment to the Constitution forbidding diversion of public school funds.

The Democrats nominated Samuel J. Tilden, prosecutor of the Tweed Ring and progressive governor of New York. Reforms were promised in the tariff, currency and civil service; retrenchment in state and national expenditure; exclusion of the Chinese; and the corruption and graft of Grant's administration condemned.

Some of the difficulties that Luttrell and McKenna experienced in carrying on their campaign in 1876 were due to the vastness of their district, which included twenty-one counties with a total area of 46,000 square miles, a territory larger than the combined States of Maine, New Hampshire and Vermont.[7] The topography of the country may be likened to a large plain traversed from north to south by three parallel chains of mountains. On the east were the Sierra Nevadas, in the middle the Napa chain and on the extreme west, along the ocean, the Coast Range. The two valleys formed by the mountains were the Sacramento and Napa. Most of the large towns being in either of the valleys, it was natural that the candidates would concentrate their efforts in these regions. Since the railroads served only the valley regions, the campaigners did most of their travelling by stage coach, horseback and snow sled. Transportation was expensive, slow, uncomfortable and often dangerous.[8] On these less frequented highways

---

[7] *San Francisco Bulletin,* September 2, 12, 15, 16, 18, 22, 25, 1876.

[8] *Yreka Union,* April 1, 1876; *Yreka Journal,* August 23, 1876; *San Francisco Bulletin,* January 9, September 12, 1876, contains schedules of the rates, distances and times; Artemus Ward related that the stage coach on which he was a passenger travelled along a road "which looked down on either side of an appalling ravine . . . as night came on and it became very dark and began to snow and notwithstanding the brakes were kept hard down, the coach slewed wildly, often fairly touching the brink of the black precipice." *Yreka Journal,* April 19, May 10, November 15, 1876.

delay was occasioned by mud, snow, washed out bridges, land-slides, runaway horses, forest fires, detours and infrequent service, thus making the rate of speed tantalizingly slow.

The Republican campaign in the Third District in 1876 was considered to have been the most thorough and astutely organized in the history of that region.[9] During September and October, twenty stump speakers were on the circuit[10] and in more than one hundred and fifty meetings they contacted the electorate of practically every city, town, hamlet, village cross-roads and camp. A lush campaign fund was generously utilized in the organization and employment of booster units, drill teams, brass bands and glee clubs.[11] Practically every rally was featured by the appearance of local entertainers and with a lavish display of fireworks, Roman candles, Japanese lanterns, torch lights, posters, placards, bunting and flags.[12]

Among the subjects most frequently discussed by the speakers were the records of the parties, the reform movement, tariff, paper money and civil service. In respect to the first named, McKenna emphatically asserted that parties should be " judged by their past performances rather than by their present professions." He recalled that the Democrats were under the control of the South and warned that if their candidates were elected there would be an unparalleled raid on the treasury of the United States.[13]  Once

---

[9] *San Francisco Bulletin,* October 28, 1876.

[10] *San Francisco Bulletin,* September 2, 12, 15, 16, 18, 22, 25, October 2, 1876; *Lassen Advocate,* September 29, 1876; *Mountain Messenger,* September 16, 1876; *Sacramento Daily Record-Union,* August 12, 1876.

[11] *San Francisco Bulletin,* September 20, 1876; *Butte Record,* September 23, 1876; *Santa Rosa Daily Democrat,* October 17, 1876; *St. Helena Star,* October 20, 1876; *Vallejo Evening Chronicle,* October 20, 1876.

[12] *Santa Rosa Daily Democrat,* October 17, 1876; *Healdsburg Enterprise,* October 18, 1876; *San Rafael Herald,* October 19, 1876; *St. Helena Star,* October 2, 1876; *Marysville Daily Appeal,* October 22, 1876; *San Francisco Bulletin,* October 17, 19, 25, 1876, describe the meetings held at Santa Rosa, Healdsburg and Oroville; *Butte Record,* September 23, 1876; *Mountain Messenger,* September 16, 1876; *Weekly Colusa Sun,* October 28, 1876, publicly challenges a leading Republican of Placerville to a debate on the merits of McKenna and Luttrell for a $100 side bet.

[13] *Chico Enterprise,* September 22, 1876; *Marysville Daily Appeal,* October

in power, the rebels would press their suit of over two billion dollars for property which had been confiscated during the late war.   Northern Democrats should be chary in voting the Democratic ticket, for, even if successful, " their compensation would be only an occasional bone from the southern dictators." [14]   At the beginning of the canvass, McKenna indulged in waving the " bloody shirt," but he soon desisted when he aroused bitter feelings in this strongly pro-southern region.[15]

Intimately connected with the records of the parties was the reform movement.   Although this was a source of embarrassment for most Republicans, McKenna boldly attempted to refute the charges of corruption and even endeavored to prove that the Republican administration of finances was more economical than that of the Democrats.[16]   To the charge of venality among high-ranking office holders, the Republican candidate's stock retort was that he was " amazed " that so few dishonest men could be found despite the frequent and minute investigations engineered by the Democratic-controlled House of Representatives.[17]   So unyielding was McKenna in the championship of the Grant regime that an opposition newspaper ironically admitted Grant to be the most upright,

22, 1876; *Colusa Independent,* October 28, 1876; *San Francisco Bulletin,* November 1, 1876.

[14] *San Francisco Bulletin,* September 25, October 10, November 2, 1876.

[15] *Healdsburg Enterprise,* October 18, 1876; *Marysville Daily Appeal,* October 22, 1876; *Weekly Colusa Sun,* October 28, 1876; *Colusa Independent,* October 22, 1876, reports evidence of strong pro-southern feeling was manifested at the presentation of the flag to the Democratic Club of Woodland. One spectator was so incensed that he called the flag "a damned filthy, dirty rag"; *San Francisco Bulletin,* October 28, November 2, 3, 1876, remarks that after a mob had failed to break up the rally held for McKenna, it tore down the flag in front of the hall and " dragged it in the mud "; *Wheatland Free Press,* November 4, 1876, carries an account of this incident.

[16] *Weekly Colusa Sun,* October 18, 1876; *San Francisco Bulletin,* November 4, 1876; *Mountain Messenger,* September 20, 1876; *Santa Rosa Daily Democrat,* October 17, 1876, condemns the alleged economy policy advocated by McKenna.

[17] *Marysville Daily Appeal,* October 22, 1876; *Butte Record,* September 23, 1876.

honest and intelligent executive in the history of the United States.[18]

To claim that the Democratic Party was one of reform and purity was ridiculed by McKenna as " an excessive and careful protestation which always comes from a deceitful purpose." He admitted the benefits of reform, as he unconvincingly protested that, " There may be wisdom in bearing the ills we have than to fly to others we know not of." [19]  In the matter of reform, John Luttrell's position was stronger than McKenna's because he could easily prove the need for it in the National Government and could boast of being the first " to sound the tocsin " for purity in politics on the Pacific Coast.  On this basis it was predicted that " Honest John " Luttrell would be swept into office by an overwhelming majority.[20]

Luttrell flayed the Radical Republicans as devotees of the spoils system and asserted that the few feeble attempts made for the promotion of civil service reform had been throttled by President Grant at the dictates of his professional aides.  McKenna sought to divert attention by stressing the program of Federal employment supported by Hayes.  He insisted that it was under Republican auspices that the foundation had been established for the equitable selection of governmental employees, but confessed quite confusedly that the initial progress had been overcome " by a bad traditional practice." [21]

On the public school question, Luttrell proposed to free the system of all sectarian influence, while McKenna, as the " Champion of Public Education," insisted that it was contrary to State and National constitutional policy to divert public school funds from their proper purpose by using them in sectarian institu-

[18] *Weekly Colusa Sun,* October 28, 1876.

[19] *Chico Enterprise,* September 22, 1876.

[20] *Tehama Tocsin,* September 24, 1876; *Chico Enterprise,* September 22, 1876; *Mountain Messenger,* September 20, 1876; *Marysville Daily Appeal,* October 22, 1876; *Weekly Colusa Sun,* October 28, 1876; *San Francisco Bulletin,* October 28, 1876.

[21] *Chico Enterprise,* September 22, 1876; for a brief account of this reform, see Richard J. Purcell, " Civil Service Versus the Spoils System in the Federal Government," *Catholic Educational Review,* XXX (November, 1932), 549–560.

tions.[22]  Consequently he favored an amendment to the United States Constitution which would prohibit State subsidies for private institutions.  When Luttrell twitted McKenna before an audience in Wheatland because he had made a hobby out of public education, the local press carried an article the following day to the effect that as long as McKenna held to that course " he would not make many enemies." [23]

Although the candidates themselves refrained from indulging in personal invective, their supporters felt no scruple.  From the latter part of August until the day after election a constant barrage of vituperation and insinuation issued from the Republican and Democratic press.[24]  The opening charge was hurled on August 28, when the *Solano County Republican* denounced Luttrell as a " bloviating " trickster whose remarks were " as full of misrepresentations and falsehoods as an egg is full of meat." [25]  Two days later the challenge was answered when McKenna was branded as the fanatical supporter of the most corrupt political machine in history and lampooned as a beardless youth, " who if elected would have no influence in Congress." [26]  The Democrats considered it sheer nonsense for men to be represented by a mere boy who recited " a prepared speech precisely like a young man of eighteen summers." [27]  Repeatedly McKenna was criticized

---

[22] *Daily Alta California,* August 10, 11, 1876; *Brown Scrapbook,* newspaper clipping, n.n.; n.d.

[23] *Wheatland Free Press,* November 4, 1876.

[24] *San Francisco Bulletin,* November 9, 1876, quotes the *Marysville Appeal* that the campaign had been a " long, wearisome irritation and personal warfare."

[25] *Weekly Solano Republican,* August 26, 1876, notes that Luttrell " held forth yesterday afternoon to a little knot of curious spectators about as numerous as usually collects around a corn-doctor or other nostrum vendor but the crowd was not nearly as numerous as Colonel Reuss could gather around a sale of jackasses or merchandise." *Napa Register,* September 5, 1876, wagers that Luttrell, " the leather-lunged, could easily be heard at a distance of one mile from the platform."

[26] *Weekly Butte Record,* September 16, 1876; *Mendocino Democrat,* October 14, 1876; *Santa Rosa Daily Democrat,* October 17, 1876.

[27] *Mendocino Democrat,* October 14, 1876, suggests that Mizner, who admittedly made a good speech " for a bad cause," be substituted for the youthful McKenna.

for committing his speeches to memory, with evincing no originality in thought or action and in immersing himself in the " same old Republican rut." Pictured as a machine-picked candidate, he was derided for his attempt to persuade men to put their fate in the hands of the clique " that runs Mare Island." [28]

For his attempt to recall the war record of the Democratic Party McKenna was castigated for waving the bloody shirt and professing " a doctrine . . . that because a man fought for his country, he has the right to steal everything in her larders." [29]   Opponents sarcastically referred to McKenna as a " peaceful warrior " who, in the words of a disgusted Union soldier " never fought a single battle, or even perhaps dreamed of doing so, becoming warlike in a time of peace." [30]   The unfavorable reaction to his lack of a war record led McKenna to omit further reference to the war records of the parties.   He was reported to have skipped " the bloody shirt part of the program " and presented his case without wounding the feelings of his opponents.[31]

While the Democratic lampooners were aiming their shafts at McKenna, his rival was receiving due share of attention from the Republican columnists.   Luttrell was denounced as a political trickster, sail-trimmer, demagogue, shyster, fencewalker, opportunist, liar and tool of the Central Pacific Railroad.[32]   Surprisingly

---

[28] *Santa Rosa Daily Democrat,* October 17, 1876; *Butte Record,* September 16, 23, 1876.

[29] *Butte Record,* September 23, 1876, contends that McKenna confessed he did not expect to be elected, but that he was making the canvass " to get a record for future occasions."

[30] *Healdsburg Enterprise,* October 18, 1876.   There is some justification for the course which McKenna followed, for he was the principal support of his mother, brothers and sisters.

[31] McKenna must have been particularly careful to avoid any reference to the War between the States when speaking in any of the Sacramento Valley towns.   The area was popularly referred to as the " South Carolina of the West."   *Colusa Independent,* October 28, 1876.

[32] *San Francisco Bulletin,* October 10, 1876; *Colusa Independent,* November 4, 1876; *Lake Democrat,* November 4, 1876.   The charge that Luttrell was a " tool of the railroad " has found some substantiation in letters published in a suit of the widow of David Colton against the Central Pacific Railroad. Some of these letters are published in U. S. Congress, Senate, *Report of the United States Pacific Railway Commission,* U. S. Senate, Executive Docu-

few references were made to the religion of either contestant, although near the end of the campaign one newspaper informed its readers that although the Democrats called McKenna a Roman Catholic, it had it on good authority that " Mr. McKenna's parents are good old Methodists, and he has a warm regard for that denomination." [33]

As the election day, November 7, 1876, approached, it was observed that the race in the Third District would be close. Observers freely conceded that the most bitterly contested fight had been waged in the McKenna-Luttrell struggle, in which McKenna had made a " very plucky and determined onslaught upon Luttrell." For some days after the balloting the Republican press conceded the presidential victory to the Democrats, but there was some doubt as to the victor in the Third District. So close was the count that not until eight days had elapsed did the Republican publications grudgingly admit that Luttrell had been elected by a small majority of less than a thousand out of a total of thirty-eight thousand votes.[34]

McKenna attributed his defeat to the fact that he was a Roman Catholic, but such was not the opinion of the Republican press nor of impartial commentators. Rather it was asserted that McKenna had alienated Catholic voters by sponsoring public school measures in the State Assembly.[35] The principal cause for the failure of McKenna was assigned by both Democrats and Republicans to the

---

ment 51, 50th Congress, 1st Session (Washington, 1887), pp. 1875–1878, 3721, 3722. Henceforth cited as *Report of Pacific Railway Commission;* cf. Stuart Daggett, *Chapters on the History of the Southern Pacific* (New York, 1922), p. 201.

[33] *Chico Enterprise,* November 3, 1876; *The Weekly Colusa Sun,* November 11, 1876, rebukes the *Chico Enterprise* for circulating a report that McKenna would consider it a slander to be called a Catholic and if he did " he would not be the gentleman we have taken him for." *Vallejo Chronicle,* October 26, 1876, describes a joint debate between McKenna and Luttrell at St. Helena.

[34] *Daily Alta California,* November 10, 1876; *San Francisco Bulletin,* November 15, 1876.

[35] Statement made by Mr. J. Tormey, of Vallejo, in a personal interview with the writer. Mr. Tormey recalled that most of the Democrats were Catholics and that they considered McKenna as a " black Republican " on the " wrong side of the fence."

solid and well-organized Democratic support, which Luttrell received. McKenna's defeat was just one more in the long line of Republican setbacks in this District. For McKenna the defeat only served to whet his appetite and in the following election of 1879 he campaigned again.

Soon after the adoption of a new State constitution,[36] May 7, 1879, the Republican, Democratic, New Constitutional and Workingmen's Parties prepared for the September election. The new Constitutional Party was interested solely in electing a slate that would ensure effective operation of the new constitution while the other three were concerned in national as well as State issues. The Workingmen's Party held its convention in San Francisco, on June 3, 1879, and formulated a platform of some forty planks demanding equal wages for both sexes, an eight-hour day, compulsory education, free textbooks, direct election of all national officers, Chinese exclusion and the elimination of contract convict labor. After condemning the Congress for an indifferent attitude toward the vital issues of the day, it concluded with the plea that people be given " not stones but bread." [37]

One bulletin issued by the Workingmen's Convention contrasted the open and democratic system by which it selected candidates and " the disgraceful jobbery now going on in Sacramento where all the old party hacks . . . are assembled to nominate each other, and perpetuate the rule of rings and public plunderers." [38] This reference was made to the Republican State Convention held June 18, 1879. The two contestants for nomination in the Third District were Jerome C. Banks of Red Bluff and Joseph McKenna. The latter was the favorite because of his recognized " gallant fight " in the last election.[39] Mr. Banks was conceded some chance because his managers were cannily exploiting an upstate move-

---

[36] Winfield Davis, *History of the Political Conventions in California, 1849–1892* (Sacramento: 1893), p. 388; Hubert H. Bancroft, *History of California* (San Francisco: 1890), VII, 370-406, contains a fairly complete account of the personnel, debates and provisions of the constitutional convention.

[37] *San Francisco Bulletin,* June 18, 1879.

[38] *Loc. cit.*

[39] *Butte County Register,* July 11, 1879.

ment to give the nomination to some one other than a representative of Solano County.[40] Strong opposition to McKenna failed to materialize, and he was easily nominated on the first ballot by 72 to 37.[41]

After the slate of nominees had been completed the Republicans adopted a platform that denounced Democratic interference in elections, pledged support to the new constitution, favored progressive education, promised reconciliation of differences between farmer and miner and demanded the establishment of reasonable railroad rates.[42]

The Democrats met in the same city on July 1, 1879, and nominated Campbell P. Berry [43] after John Luttrell refused to run again. They, like the Republicans, urged establishment of fair railroad fares, settlement of differences between mining and agriculture and honest enforcement of the new constitution. They branded free use of the veto by President Hayes as an illegal participation in legislation, bade the Republicans " take their hands off the ballot box " and proposed, like the Workingmen, strict exclusion of the Chinese.[44]

---

[40] *San Francisco Bulletin,* June 18, 1879.

[41] *Sacramento Daily Record-Union,* June 20, 1879, reports that Mr. Dudley of Sonoma nominated Joseph McKenna and in complimentary speeches Mr. Jewett, of Yuba, and Mr. Folke, of Siskiyou endorsed the nomination. Jerome Banks, of Tehema, was nominated by Mr. Garter and on the roll call McKenna was made the nominee of the Republican Party; *Daily Alta California,* June 28, 1879, records that the choice was made unanimous after the first ballot; for the reaction of the news that McKenna was nominated, see *Arcata Leader,* August 9, 1879, *Ukiah City Press,* August 15, 1879 and *Brown Scrapbook* which has a clipping from the *Weekly Antioch Ledger,* n.d. Democrats maintained that McKenna was the choice of the Central Pacific Railroad. *Yreka Union,* August 16, 1879.

[42] *San Francisco Bulletin,* June 18, 1879; *Chico Enterprise,* August 1, 1879.

[43] Campbell P. Berry was born in Jackson County, Alabama, November, 1838. He moved with his parents to Arkansas in 1841, then to California in 1857. He settled near Yuba City in the Sacramento Valley. After graduation from the Pacific Methodist College, he entered farming and retail merchandising. Elected to the State Assembly in 1869, 1871, 1873, 1875 and 1877, he decided to run for Congress and was elected as Representative in 1879. From 1894 to 1898 he was United States subtreasurer in San Francisco and died in Wheatland, California, in 1901.

[44] *San Francisco Bulletin,* July 2, 1879.

The speeches of McKenna and Berry were woven around the planks in the platforms except where local issues might demand a different stand. In the mountain areas Berry had antagonized numerous Democrats by supporting a curb on hydraulic mining. Not only had he advocated the measure with enthusiasm but even recommended that hydraulic mining be listed as a felony.[45] Berry had adopted this position only after he had been convinced that it was necessary in order to protect rich farm lands from destruction. Although McKenna was well received in the mining communities, he adroitly avoided any definite statement that would give umbrage to either proponents or opponents of hydraulic mining. Notwithstanding his dubious position, the miners thought that he would make a more favorable representative than their avowed antagonist.[46]

In the Sacramento Valley towns, McKenna and Berry gave particular attention to the obligation of enforcing the new State constitution.[47] In this respect McKenna held the advantage because he had supported the ratification of the Constitution while Berry had remained noncommittal until after adoption and then became its ardent defender. Republican publicists made capital of this favorable circumstance, urging all supporters of the new government to vote for a " dyed-in-the-wool " defender of the constitution rather than one of its fair-weather friends.[48]

---

[45] *Mountain Messenger,* July 19, August 9, 1879 and the *Weekly Solano Republican,* August 30, 1879, condemn Berry for favoring the Ostrom Bill because a " few acres of land along the river bottoms has been injured." *The Yreka Union,* August 9, 1879 and the *Lassen Advocate* justify Berry's support of the Ostrom measure.

[46] *Mountain Messenger,* July 19, 1879; *Oroville Weekly Mercury,* August 29, 1879.

[47] *Ukiah City Press,* August 8, 1879; *Arcata Leader,* August 2, 1879; *Scott Valley News,* July 30, 1879; *San Francisco Bulletin,* July 9, 1879, gives a list of the speaking engagements.

[48] *Chico Enterprise,* August 1, 1879, and the *Arcata Leader,* August 2, 1879, proclaim McKenna as a champion of the new State constitution. The *Sentinel,* August 2, 1879, questions the veracity of McKenna's statements in support of the new constitution because it was unable to understand McKenna and Perkins running on the same ticket, the former a professed constitutionalist and the latter bitterly opposed to it. However, it concluded,

McKenna devoted some time in each of his addresses in justifying the vetoes of President Hayes and in censuring the efforts of the Democratic House to ram bills through the Congress without proper justification.[49]  Berry retorted that the prolific use of the veto by the Executive was an unjustified interference with orderly processes of government and repudiated the wishes of the people. Both candidates agreed on Chinese exclusion, but McKenna contended that the Congress alone had the power to enact the prohibition, whereas Berry insisted that the State and National governments cooperate.  The latter emphasized that the only attempts made to solve the difficulty had been initiated by his colleagues and that the Republicans had not only imported coolies by the shipload, but had negotiated the Burlingame Treaty to keep them here.[50]

Repercussions of the Congressional debates on the Federal Elections Law were felt when McKenna accused the Democrats of being opposed to honest and fair methods of balloting.  To this charge, Berry retorted that McKenna was making a futile attempt to distract attention from an unconstitutional infringement of State power by a barrage of misrepresentation and calumny.  The aim of the Democratic Party in repealing the election law was to preserve the balance for which the founding fathers had established so many safeguards.[51]

The contest of 1879 was less important from the national standpoint than that of 1876, yet the political fanfare and theatrical paraphernalia were no less in evidence.  As in the prior election, the local political machines resorted to the common means calculated to arouse attention, enthusiasm and support among their followers and non-partisan groups.  Banners, placards, fireworks, parades, rallies, pep talks, discussions, badges and posters were employed.[52]

---

" The Republican Party is willing to send McKenna where he can do the most good toward nullifying its provisions and ' Barkus is willin' ' to go."

[49] *Yreka Union,* August 9, 1879.

[50] *Sonoma Democrat,* August 23, 1879; *Marysville Daily Appeal,* September 2, 1879.

[51] *Weekly Butte Record,* August 16, 1879.

[52] *Oroville Mercury,* August 29, 1879; *Mountain Messenger,* July 26, 1879;

Skulduggery was introduced when three members of the Workingmen's Party issued a forged proclamation, repudiating Berry as the official candidate of the party.[53]  The hoax was quickly detected, the culprits expelled [54] and McKenna pilloried for being implicated in the plot.[55]  The Democrats ridiculed the Republican ward-heelers for their stupidity and awkwardness.  It was obvious that any reasonable man would not want an obscure nonentity in Congress, such as "tapeworm . . . McKenna, with all the Republican corruption reeking from his political skirts." [56]

The Republican press glossed over these accusations and proclaimed McKenna a staunch party man who favored "the constructive and worthwhile reforms of the Workingmen's Party." [57] It portrayed Berry as a political chameleon who had assured his neighbors that he favored the Workingmen's Party, yet repudiated that organization when offered the support of the Democrats.  It was only by clever and artful manipulation that Berry later circumvented the prescriptions of the oath of the Workingmen's Party and became the choice of that group as well as of the Democrats.  One caustic critic claimed that the Workingmen had allowed Berry "to spit in their face" and yet kept him on their ticket.[58]  McKenna in turn was castigated for his close as-

---

*Weekly People's Cause,* August 2, 1879, reports, "The quiet stillness on yester evening was suddenly broken by the loud ringing sound of anvil firing . . . announcing the arrival of the Republican speakers Joe McKenna and George T. Bromley"; *Chico Enterprise,* August 1, 1879; *Weekly Butte Record,* August 2, 1879; *Scott Valley News,* August 7, 1879; *Ukiah City Press,* August 8, 1879; *The Sentinel,* August 9, 1879; *Yreka Union,* August 9, 1879; *Vallejo Chronicle,* August 30, 1879.

[53] *Yolo Democrat,* August 21, 1879; *Mountain Messenger,* July 19, 1879, expresses delight upon receiving the news that George T. Elliott has been substituted for Berry because, "that will cook Mr. (Debris) Berry's goose very effectually." Cf., *Benicia New Era,* August 23, 1879.

[54] *Yolo Democrat,* August 21, 1879.

[55] *Loc. cit.*

[56] *Weekly Butte Record,* August 16, 1879; *Yolo Democrat,* August 21, 1879

[57] *Vallejo Chronicle,* August 30, 1879, records that McKenna was in favor of the Workingmen's Party, but wanted to put their proposals into effect through the machinery of the Republican Party.

[58] *Benicia New Era,* August 23, 1879; the oath which was required of all candidates sponsored by the Workingmen's Party was "I . . . . . . . . do sol-

sociation with the Mare Island " ring," which was labelled as a minor Tammany Hall, with its tapeworm ticket, organized and disciplined ranks and well-filled campaign chest.[59]

The issue upon which the followers of Berry became most censorious was the railroad.[60] McKenna sought to avoid discussion of this topic by naively professing that the law which created the railroad commission eliminated the railroad from politics and therefore no discussion was necessary.[61] Berry described this position as " ridiculous," because " if you took the railroad out of politics in this state there would not be enough of the Republican Party to organize a debating club." He asserted McKenna was the stooge of Leland Stanford, president of the Southern Pacific Railroad, and as long as such association continued " all the eloquence of a Demosthenes would be powerless to impart dignity " to his aspirations.[62] One upstate journal told its readers : " Vote for Berry, damn it, vote for every anti-railroad man you can find on either ticket." [63]

As the campaign entered its final stages, it was the consensus

---

emnly pledge my sacred honor that I will, if elected as ........ of the city and county of San Francisco, accept as salary for services as such the sum of ........, and turn in to the Treasury of the city the sum of ........, being the difference of amount between the salary allowed for such services . . ." The oath for county and state officers was similar. *Scott Valley News,* July 30, 1879.

[59] *Yreka Union,* August 9, 1879; *Weekly Butte Record,* August 2, 1879; *Yolo Democrat,* August 28, 1879, refers to the Republican nominee as " Tapeworm " McKenna. It avers that the Mare Island Navy Yard clique would run the district, if McKenna were elected.

[60] *The Sentinel,* July 29, 1879; *Weekly Butte Record,* August 2, 1879, notes with sarcasm that McKenna was of the opinion that the Democratic gubernatorial candidate would not be elected because, " he had no political training, had never bathed in the filthy pool of politics, never danced to the music of the railroad fife and could not possibly be trusted to pilot the ship of state."

[61] *Weekly Butte Record,* August 16, 1879; *Solano Republican,* October 28, 1879.

[62] *Weekly Butte Record,* September 6, 1879.

[63] *Yreka Union,* August 9, 1879; *Weekly Butte Record,* August 16, 1879; *Solano Republican,* October 28, 1879; *Scott Valley News,* August 9, 1879, accuses the Republican candidate of being the choice of the Central Pacific Railroad for governor.

of opinion that the results would be very close,[64] but impartial critics conceded that McKenna had a slight edge. His advantage lay in the fact that since the Workingmen's Party vote would be the decisive factor in the poll, three-fourths of it, being Catholic, would go to McKenna.[65] It was alleged that the adherents of this faith " would obey the injunction of their Archbishop [66] and repudiate Berry." [67]

So evenly matched were McKenna and Berry that, for seventeen days after the election, neither ventured to issue a definite statement of the result. When the first tabulations were reported, it appeared that McKenna would win easily, his votes increasing so quickly that one of the Berry newspapers admitted it had given up hope for victory.[68] At the end of a fortnight all the votes had been counted except those in the two most northern counties, Trinity and Humboldt. When the former gave McKenna a majority of seventy, a Republican victory seemed secured, but hopes were blasted when Humboldt's ballots gave Berry a total of 20,019 and McKenna 19,830 or a majority of 189 out of a total of 39,849.[69] Truly Joseph McKenna could appreciate the

[64] *Weekly Butte Record,* September 20, 1879.

[65] *Dixon Tribune,* September 13, 1879; letter from Gerald Geary, Archivist of the Archdiocese of San Francisco, April 1, 1944, states that the records of the archdiocese are not available prior to 1890.

[66] Joseph Sadoc Alemany, O.P., first Archbishop of San Francisco, was born in Vich, Spain, in 1814. He served as a missionary in the Ohio Valley from 1840 to 1850, when he was appointed Bishop of Monterey, California. In 1853 he was raised to the Archiepiscopal See of San Francisco which he administered for thirty-one years. During the last four years of his life, he lived in retirement in Spain, where he died in 1888.

[67] *Dixon Tribune,* September 13, 1879.

[68] *Colusa Sun,* September 6, 1879, mournfully reports that, although Colusa County had given Berry something like a thousand majority, yet it was almost certain that McKenna was elected. The editor of the *Solano Republican* had been defeated as the Workingmen's candidate for state senator and in his melancholy contended that, " the sharpest, shrewdest rascal succeeds in business . . . and in politics." *Solano Republican,* September 4, 1879; *Dixon Tribune,* September 5, 1879; *Chico Enterprise,* September 12, 1879; *The Weekly Butte Record,* September 20, 1879, attributes the defeat of McKenna to the " swindles of the McKenna faction."

[69] *People's Cause,* September 20, 1879, carries the following: " Hurrah for McKenna! We are out of the woods now and are allowed to halloo

statement of Henry Clay that defeat is most bitter when victory
was thought most secure.

In spite of his defeat McKenna continued to exercise an influence in the councils of the Republican Party so that in 1884,
when his county was relocated in a Democratic gerrymander, he
was in a favorable position to bid for the congressional nomination for the new Third District. This newly created district consisted of the six counties of Alameda, Contra Costa, Marin,
Solano, Sacramento and Yolo, located on or near the eastern and
northern shores of San Francisco Bay.[70] Because the Republican
nomination was considered tantamount to election, there was keen
rivalry for that distinction.

As a departure from the customary rules, the nominating convention was to be held at Benicia on July 14, 1884, nine days prior
to the State convention. This innovation was hailed by the more
conservative and respectable elements as a " blow at the politicians
and wire-workers with their traditional intrigues and coali-
tions." [71]

At the opening of the convention at Benicia there were five
candidates, Carroll Cook, of Oakland, W. W. Camron, of Oakland, Henry Edgerton, of Sacramento, Judge George Tyler, of
Alameda, and Joseph McKenna.[72] For some weeks the newspapers had been agitating for their favorites, and it was one of
these pre-campaign articles that broached the obligation of the
Republican Party to nominate McKenna, through a sense of gratitude, because he had carried the standard in two forlorn and des-
perate struggles.[73] While showering praise upon McKenna, the
editors paused to throw verbal brickbats at two of his opponents.
Henry Edgerton did possess ability, integrity and brilliant powers,
yet " when his services are most needed he is liable to be indis-

as loud as we please. Three cheers for McKenna . . . hip, hip, hurrah!";
*Daily Alta California*, September 17, 1879, gives the first inkling of defeat;
*San Francisco Bulletin*, September 18, 1879.

[70] *Congressional Directory*, 49th Congress, 1st Session, p. 10.

[71] *Contra Costa Gazette*, May 17, 1884; *Berkeley Advocate*, July 19, 1884.

[72] *Oakland Daily Evening Tribune*, July 15, 1884; *Contra Costa Gazette*,
July 26, 1884.

[73] *Berkeley Advocate*, July 12, 1884, implies that Carroll Cook had an
advantage over McKenna because of the former's university training.

posed " and Carroll Cook was " connubiating " too freely with
notorious tricksters and corruptionists to satisfy the discriminating tastes of the Republican Party.[74]

Evidently McKenna's " campaign to campaign " was gaining
momentum too quickly, for some of his rivals essayed to impede
its progress by circulating a rumor that a Catholic nominee would
bring dishonor and defeat to the party. The friends of McKenna
quickly quashed the attack by styling such stories as un-American,
and contrary to fair play so highly esteemed by Protestant and
Catholic alike. The only ones who insisted on qualifying their
support were a few bigots " whose opinions are of no value." [75]

On the scheduled day the convention came to order in the old
town hall of Benicia and, after preliminary ceremonies, the names
of the contestants for the nomination were placed before the
delegates. Lansing B. Mizner again nominated McKenna.[76] A
friendly columnist portrayed McKenna as " sprucely attired, natty
in bearing, graceful in gesture, terse and dainty in language,
earnest in look, musical in voice, as self-possessed as a veteran
schoolmaster." [77] After the first few ballots it was evident that
no agreement could be reached by the two most powerful contenders, Cook and Camron, and that some arrangement must be
made between either of them and a second-rate contestant if the
deadlock was to be broken.

The feeling between Cook and Camron was described as " fierce
and unrelenting " and as a consequence the friends of McKenna
considered this their opportunity.[78] On the streets and in the
saloons, in fact, wherever the delegates congregated, the name of
McKenna was bandied. It was bruited about that Carroll Cook
had made a bargain with the Vallejo Navy Yard clique. In return for giving his followers the State offices, he was willing to

[74] *Contra Costa Gazette,* May 24, 1884.

[75] *Solano Republican,* July 11, 1884.

[76] *Oakland Daily Times,* July 15, 1884; letter from Mrs. Pitts Duffield,
daughter of Justice McKenna to the writer, March 2, 1944.

[77] *Oakland Evening Tribune,* February 12, 1892, records the reactions of
an observer at the convention.

[78] *Oakland Daily Times,* July 16, 1884; *Alameda Encinal,* July 16, 1884,
considers McKenna a " dark horse "; *Berkeley Advocate,* July 19, 1884.

throw his support to McKenna.[79]   This report was given credence
soon after the reassembling of the convention when Cook's followers changed their votes to McKenna and this became the signal
for a stampede to make him the unanimous choice of the convention.[80]

The news of McKenna's nomination was received with approval by the Republicans in and out of the district.[81]   The
majority of the editors expressed the sentiment that, since
McKenna had borne the "brunt and the tears" of battle and
had "gathered only the bitter apples of defeat," it was fitting
that he should be the standard-bearer when there was some chance
of success.   Even the anti-Catholic *San Francisco Argonaut* "entirely approved this nomination." [82]   On the other hand, the Democrats felt that the Republicans had disgraced themselves by
neglecting to nominate either Henry Edgerton or Judge George
W. Tyler.   The former was considered, in many respects, the
outstanding Republican in the State, while Judge Tyler was recognized as a leader in his profession.   The opposition taunted the
Republicans for allowing three second-rate mediocrities, namely
Cook, Camron and McKenna, to steer an inferior character into
the nomination.[83]   In their opinions, if the delegates had been un-
instructed, the unholy triumvirate would have had no influence,
in fact, "the mere mention of their names would only excite
laughter."

The Democratic nominee was John R. Glascock, of Oakland,
who had been elected in 1882 as Congressman at large.   The

[79] *Oakland Daily Times,* July 16, 1884; *Marin County Journal,* July 17,
1884, hints that a deal had been arranged.

[80] *Contra Costa Gazette,* July 19, 1884, reports that, when Judge John
Lynch realized that McKenna had won the nomination, he threw his own
and neighbor's hat "heavenwards" and had to spend a half hour searching
for them.

[81] *Oakland Daily Times,* July 1884; *Marin County Journal,* July 17, 1884;
*San Francisco Argonaut,* July 24, 1884; *Contra Costa Gazette,* July 26, 1884,
quotes the *Napa Reporter, Solano Republican, Antioch Ledger* and the
*Benicia New Era* to demonstrate the general approval.

[82] *San Francisco Argonaut,* July 26, 1884.

[83] *Oakland Daily Times,* July 16, 1884; *Oakland Tribune,* February 13,
1884.

campaign was enlivened by the appearance of Joseph W. Wills, candidate of the Prohibitionists, and of A. B. Burns, representing the Anti-monopoly Party, which was composed of the remnants of the Greenback, Labor, National Union and Anti-monopoly groups.[84]

As 1884 was a presidential year, the utterances of the speakers were shaped by the national platforms and the personal ideas of the presidential candidates. Cleveland, Blaine, General Ben Butler of the Anti-monopoly and John P. St. John of the Prohibition Party were the subjects of criticism and praise. Although the vote of the minor parties was disappointingly small,[85] the proposals which they injected into the contest were of interest. The Anti-monopoly advocated woman suffrage, child labor laws, factory and mine inspection, national ownership of railroads and increased issue of greenbacks. To staid politicians such socialistic measures entailed political suicide.[86] The Prohibitionists championed strict regulation of liquor sales, and, with the Anti-monopolists, they demanded a low tariff, woman suffrage and the elimination of unfair railroad practices. Both the Democratic and Republican platforms opposed further immigration of the Orientals, condemned the abuses of the railroads, sponsored extension of civil service reform. Naturally they differed on the tariff.

The candidates of the two major parties entered the race apparently on equal terms. Glascock had demonstrated his ability to obtain generous appropriations for his district and to protect his constituents' interests.[87] McKenna, on the other hand, had the advantage, campaigning in a district known for its rock-ribbed Republicanism and for its pride in the public school system, of which he was heralded as a champion. In his speeches he denounced the free trade policy of the Democrats as being dangerous to the well-being of the nation and to the welfare of American

[84] Davis, *op. cit.,* pp. 454 ff.

[85] Of a total of over thirty thousand votes the Anti-monopolists polled 273 and the Prohibitionists 322. *Ibid.,* p. 474.

[86] *Contra Costa Gazette,* August 2, 1884.

[87] *Alameda Encinal,* July 23, 1884, calls attention to Glascock's influence in the Congress, his association with Cleveland, his record of protecting California products and his anti-Chinese policy.

labor. He recalled that the Republican Party was founded to oppose slave labor and always fought any proposal to bring American workingmen into competition with alien servile labor.[88] John Glascock chided McKenna for taking his cue from Blaine in the matter of protection as he reproached him for a lack of originality.[89] Democrats identified Glascock as a follower of Cleveland in his program of reform, purity in government, low tariff, civil service and abolition of machine politics.[90]

The canvass of 1884 had less of the biting sarcasm and harsh criticism than the campaign of 1879. Both sides promised at the outset to avoid personalities [91] and Glascock was assured that " Mr. McKenna will never resort to slandering him." [92] Notwithstanding their promises, both sides did slip into a mild attack on the position of their adversaries. In describing the antics of McKenna in a joint debate, the Democratic press pictured him as " fearful of standing up for fear that he would get knocked down," comparing the debate to a recent prize-fight. One of the contenders refused to fight, with the result the better man was unable to display his ability and superior skill.[93] The McKenna contingent admitted Glascock's superiority in debate and in oratorial ability, but contended that truth and logic, as contained in the Republican's statements, were far more effective than the legerdemain of his rival. In addition to the insinuation that McKenna was a machine selection, the most frequently repeated canard concerned a delegate to the Benicia convention who voted for McKenna only after the Navy Yard clique had promised to nominate him for a State senatorship.

---

[88] *Contra Costa Gazette,* September 6, 1884.

[89] *Oakland Daily Tribune,* October 15, 1884, describes the joint meeting held between Glascock and McKenna at Walnut Creek. It asserts that McKenna's speech " bore suspicious traces of a well-kept scrapbook."

[90] *Loc. cit.*

[91] *Oakland Sunday Times,* July 20, 1884, cites Glascock's declaration " My opponent, Mr. McKenna, is a thorough gentleman and there will be no dirty work done by either of us." Cf., *Alameda Encinal,* July 23, 26, 1884.

[92] George A. Knight, an acquaintance of both men for fifteen years, told an audience in Oakland that he was certain neither would " stoop to slander . . . or abuse of any kind." *Oakland Daily Times,* July 26, 1884.

[93] *Oakland Times,* July 17, 1884.

Insipid was the anti-Catholic onslaught against McKenna in comparison with its activity elsewhere. Before and after the nominating convention there were slight and sporadic outbreaks of bigotry, but it was not until the last weeks of the contest that anything resembling a sustained assault was inaugurated.[94] The defenders of McKenna termed such onsets as contemptible and cowardly in an age that prided itself on enlightenment and tolerance. John Glascock inadvertently introduced the religious issue when he ridiculed Blaine's attempt to obtain the votes of Catholics, Protestants and infidels by establishing tenuous relations with each group.[95]

Although both sides were confident of success in the initial days of the contest, the trend toward McKenna became more manifest as the election approached and as a consequence few predictions were upset when McKenna received 17,435 and Glascock 13,197.[96] It was a red-letter day in the life of Joseph McKenna. After two unsuccessful attempts he had finally won the coveted honor of representing his district in the national House of Representatives. The victory marked a milestone in his long trek toward political preferment.

---

[94] *Contra Costa Gazette,* July 12, 1884; *Marin County Journal,* October 16, 1884; *San Francisco Argonaut,* August 28, 1884, agrees that "McKenna was an entirely satisfactory candidate." *The San Francisco Argonaut* was the publicity organ of the Nativist Party.

[95] *Oakland Times,* October 15, 1884.

[96] *Oakland Daily Times,* November 5, 1884; *Oakland Daily Evening Tribune,* July 23, 1884; *San Leandro Reporter,* August 1, 1884; *Contra Costa Gazette,* October 4, November 1, 1884.

# CHAPTER III

## CONGRESSMAN

The Democratic Party had regained strength during twenty years following the War between the States and in 1884 elected a presidential candidate. Success was due to defection in Republican ranks, mistakes by the Republican candidate and the character of the Democratic nominee, Grover Cleveland. Though the trend had swept the Democrats into the White House and into control of the House, yet the Senate remained Republican. In the midst of the spoils-hungry majority little could have been expected of a fledgling Republican Congressman, but McKenna had already cut his political eye-teeth and he was to find little difficulty in adjusting his sights from state to national horizons.

In the first days of the Forty-Ninth Congress, McKenna was named a member of the Committee of Claims and as such placed on the statute books ten of his twenty-five petitions for relief. Among the successful claims was his sponsorship of Senator Leland Stanford's bill for the release of a judgment of $11,000 against the estate of Frank Soule, late collector of internal revenue for the first district of California.[1] McKenna's exertions in behalf of Albert Emery, a government research technician, not only failed but brought some discomfiture. After McKenna had demanded that the government pay Emery $200,000, which the latter had spent without authorization, an opponent obliged McKenna to admit that $129,000 of the total could not be traced to any definite expenditures.[2]

It was quite natural that the new Congressman should introduce measures in the interest of his constituents. He proposed tax exemption for alcohol, distilled from beet root sugar, to suspend

---

[1] *Congressional Record,* 49th Congress, 1st Session, pp. 99, 2351, 2354, 2388, 2418, 2648.

[2] *Ibid.,* 2nd sess., pp. 889, 2570, 2573.

duties on sugar making machinery,[3] and expenditure of $1,000,000 for the fortification of Benicia Arsenal.[4]  In the interests of Californians, he introduced a resolution to extend the unconfirmed land grants of the California and Oregon Railroad ;[5] to authorize California to take lands in lieu of sections 16 and 36 when these were designated as mineral lands ;[6] and failed to restore authority to the San Francisco Mint to coin silver dollars.[7]

Imbued with the hostility to the Orientals, then so prevalent among his fellow-Californians, McKenna spoke with little dispassion against a bill to appropriate $147,000 to indemnify the families of Chinese miners murdered in a riot at Rock Springs, Wyoming Territory.  Basing his arguments on the admissions of Cleveland and Secretary of State Bayard, that we were not liable under international law for the claim, McKenna contended that approval of this requisition would entitle every victim of a riot to reparation from the Government.  McKenna claimed that sentiment, not reason, was the foundation for this petition.  However, his arguments carried little weight with an administration bent on maintaining friendly relations with the Chinese government.[8]

Speaking in behalf of large dairy concerns in the Sacramento Valley, the young legislator branded the sale of oleomargarine as a fraud parading under " the artful and iniquitous masquerade " of butter.  He insisted that the government was justified in levying confiscatory taxes on articles, like oleomargarine, sold under

---

[3] *Ibid.*, 1st sess., pp. 370, 718.

[4] *Ibid.*, p. 7983 ; *24 U. S. Statutes*, 243 ; c. 902.

[5] *Cong. Record*, 49th Cong., 1st sess., pp. 370, 5828.

[6] *Ibid.*, p. 1907.

[7] McKenna proposed to increase the budget for the San Francisco Mint from $170,000 to $250,000 on the ground that silver dollars could be coined in the West cheaper than in Philadelphia.  This contention, as well as his charge that Cleveland was an opponent of silver coinage, was proved to be without basis. *Ibid.*, p. 5724.

[8] The riot occurred at the Union Pacific Coal Mines at Rock Springs, Wyoming Territory, when the Chinese refused to join the Welsh and Swede miners in a strike.  In the disorder, twenty-eight Chinamen lost their lives. The administration wished to make compensation for the loss in order to smooth the way for the abrogation of the Burlingame Treaty.  McKenna was willing to make compensation for the property destroyed but not for the lives that were lost. *Ibid.*, p. 4427.

fraudulent and misleading appearances. Likewise for the benefit of his constituents, McKenna opposed repeal of the Silver Purchase Act on the grounds that bimetallism could be served best by " letting the existing law alone . . . because some things are best done when not done." [9]

In favor of California railroads in their rivalry with the English subsidized Canadian Pacific Railroad, McKenna resisted the long-and-short clause in the Interstate Commerce Bill. So anxious was he for the welfare of the California railroads that he stubbornly opposed the bill even though it authorized the commission to readjust rates to suit local conditions.[10]  In commenting on a measure granting to a Federal judgment-creditor ninety days in which to docket such judgment, McKenna warned that a similar arrangement in California had created grave embarrassment.[11]

In his first term McKenna obtained large appropriations for his district.  After he failed to obtain $15,000 for the construction of three dwellings on Mare Island Navy Yard under the Naval Appropriation Bill [12] he had the measure incorporated in the Appropriation Bill of 1886.[13]  In spite of the share that Benicia Arsenal was assigned in a $50,000 repair fund, McKenna's suggestion for an additional $10,000 might have been accepted had not Democrat Samuel Randall objected.  Among the other appropriations McKenna secured were $250,000 for the Mare Island Navy

---

[9] *Ibid.*, p. 3301.

[10] *Ibid.*, 2nd sess., pp. 737, 881.  The fourth section of the Interstate Commerce Law provides that charges for short distances were not to be more than those for longer hauls under similar circumstances. *24 U. S. Statutes,* 380; c. 104.

[11] *Cong. Record,* 49th Cong., 1st sess., p. 3795.

[12] U. S. Congress, House, *Rules of the House of Representatives,* U. S. House of Representatives, Document 665, 76th Congress, 3rd sess. (Washington: 1941), p. 384, cites Rule XXI, section 2 as " No appropriation shall be reported in any general appropriation bill, or be in order as an amendment thereto, for any expenditure not previously authorized by law."

[13] *24 U. S. Statutes,* 591; c. 391; some justification may be urged for McKenna in proposing his amendment at this time because he had evidently understood that the committee in charge of the bill favored the amendment and that no objection would be made to it.

Yard; [14] $50,000 for dredging the Sacramento River; $60,000 for improving Oakland's harbor and $11,000 to survey San Francisco Bay.[15]

McKenna was careful to keep his political fences well mended and his deftly publicized solicitude for his constituents might be considered as pre-campaign spade work.[16] The Republican newspapers featured McKenna's accomplishments in behalf of the farmer, veteran, sugar grower, merchant and laborer. Therefore he entered the campaign of 1886 with reasonable hope for success. In this year, of the eight parties in the field, the Anti-Chinese Association and the Irrigation Association had their own particular aim to promote and can be omitted in a consideration of the political question which agitated California at this time.[17]

The other six, namely, the Republican, Democratic, Prohibitionist, United Labor, Farmers' Conference and American all demanded Chinese exclusion and State-owned irrigation systems. Free coinage of silver and regulation of the railroads were advocated by the Republican, Democratic and Farmers' Conference platforms while the first two united with the Labor Party in encouraging cooperation among workers. With special emphasis the Farmers' Conference sponsored direct election of United States Senators, pure food laws and equal pay for both sexes.[18] The American Party, as its name would imply, stressed the rule of " America for Americans," proposed repeal of naturalization laws and demanded a curb on immigration. The Prohibitionists desiring liquor control laws were condemned by the Democrats for attempting to " saddle the country with moral

[14] *24 U. S. Statutes,* 237; c. 902.

[15] *Ibid.,* pp. 317, 326, 327.

[16] *Benicia New Era,* August 4, 11, 18, 1886; *San Leandro Reporter,* August 14, 1886; *Marysville Democrat,* August 30, 1886; *Solano Republican,* August 27, 1886.

[17] Winfield Davis, *History of Political Conventions in California, 1849–1892* (Sacramento: 1893), p. 484 gives a list of the proposals and the reasons for the exclusion of the Chinese. Many of the causes enunciated in these resolutions are also used by McKenna in speeches against the Chinese.

[18] *Ibid.,* pp. 454–459.

laws." [19]   The Democrats delighted in opposing the program of the American Party by bombastically sympathizing with the Irish in their struggle for liberty.[20]

On August 26, 1886, McKenna was proposed by Lansing Mizner before the Third Congressional District Convention of the Republican Party and unanimously nominated.[21]   Henry C. McPike was nominated by the Democratic and American Parties while the Farmers' Conference drafted W. W. Smith.   McKenna's chief opposition was expected to come from McPike.[22]   The contest was featured by mass meetings, torchlight parades, bonfires, fireworks, brass bands, drill teams and all the fanfare common to political campaigns.[23]

The leading issue between McPike and McKenna was the free coinage of silver.   The latter had voted to retain the Bland-Allison Silver Purchase Act because it would prevent a flood of cheap silver into the United States, yet he opposed the free coinage of silver and it was for this opposition that he was condemned by McPike.[24]   The latter was commended for having " done the Honorable Joe up for his vote on silver coinage and now Mr. McKenna is beating the air with both hands to catch his breath." [25]

Republican newspapers scored McPike for making himself ridiculous by pretending to understand the silver question, they asserted that " Webster, Calhoun and Haines [sic] had lived too soon . . . they should have waited on McPike on Legislation and

---

[19] The Democratic platform did not mention the Prohibitionists by name but declared unequivocally " that it was contrary to the spirit of democracy to lay excessive license tax upon certain classes of business." *Ibid.*, p. 458.

[20] Davis, *op. cit.*, p. 459.

[21] *Solano Republican,* August 27, 1886; *Sacramento Daily Record-Union,* August 26, 30, 1886; *Oakland Morning Times,* August 27, 1886.   The convention was held in Los Angeles under the chairmanship of W. W. Camron, of Oakland.   Expressions of satisfaction with the nomination are found in *Yolo Mail,* October 8, 1886; *Benicia New Era,* September 1, 1886; *Alameda Encinal,* September 1, 1886.

[22] *Solano Republican,* September 17, 1886.

[23] *Contra Costa Gazette,* October 23, 30, 1886; *Solano Republican,* November 5, 1886.

[24] *Ibid.*, September 17, 1886.

[25] *Ibid.*, October 15, 1886.

the Constitution." [26]   McKenna pointed to McPike's inconsistency
when on the one hand he praised Cleveland " who is distinctly in
favor of suspending the coinage of silver " and yet on the other
hand found fault with him (McKenna) because he supported a
law compelling the administration to coin at least two million
silver dollars each month.[27]

Veterans' bonus was another topic which was frequently discussed in the campaign.   Although it did not appear on the
California Republican platform, yet McKenna's liberal pension
plan was one of his strongest talking points.   He promised that he
would labor for a more equitable scheme of veteran compensation
for he declared " if the country expects volunteers in war time
they must take care of their widows and orphans in peace time." [28]

In 1886 an anti-Catholic American Party entered California
politics and proclaimed that it would support any candidate who
was competent, honest, native-born, opposed to auricular con-
fession, papal temporal power, Irish Home-Rule and papal in-
fallibility.[29]   It assailed the Catholic parochial school system as
un-American and unpatriotic.   Without preferring any specific
charges against McKenna, they asserted that if elected he would
be unduly influenced by priests and papists.[30]

Instead of launching a series of diatribes, the Republican press
appealed to the American sense of fair play and by slyly poking

[26] *Marin County Journal,* September 30, 1886.

[27] In his addresses on the silver question and his defense of his position
on that matter, McKenna quotes Cleveland's phrase " Prosperity hesitates
on our threshold on account of the unsettled condition of the silver question,
I recommend the suspension of silver dollars." *Contra Costa Gazette,* October 30, 1886.

[28] *Sacramento Daily Record-Union,* October 6, 1886.

[29] The American Party offered their official support to the Republican
gubernatorial nominee, John F. Swift, but he refused in a letter to Frank
Pixley, editor of the *San Francisco Argonaut,* stating, " Roman Catholics
are as loyal to republican institutions and to the United States as Protestant
Christians or people of any other faith.   And I believe that whether born
in the United States or in foreign lands, if citizens, they ought to enjoy
precisely the right as to holding office, and all other rights of citizenship
under the constitution and laws with myself or any other native born citizen."
*San Francisco Argonaut,* September 18, 1886, cited by Davis, *op. cit.,* p. 531.

[30] *San Francisco Argonaut,* August 28, 1886.

fun at the American Party destroyed its appeal to the non-Catholic electorate. The American Party had no official candidate but when its leader, Frank Pixley, publicly announced his support of Mc-Pike, the Republican journals ironically sympathized with the latter because it was no light misfortune for a candidate to receive the " kiss of death " from Pixley.[31]

The campaign ended on October 30, in a massive meeting in Martinez attended by delegations from the nearby towns of Concord, Walnut Creek, Crocket, Port Costa, Vallejo and Benicia.[32] At the election, three days later, McKenna received 15,801 to McPike's 13,277, and although defeated, the latter cut McKenna's previous majority in half.

In the Fiftieth Congress, the House was Democratic and the Senate Republican, consequently there was a stalemate in the legislative program of President Grover Cleveland. However, McKenna continued to represent his constituency faithfully by obtaining remission of a $3,000 judgment against the estate of Lieutenant Colonel Edward E. Eyre of the First California Cavalry.[33] Further he established the claim of Henry Glass [34] and paved the way for William S. Rosecrans to retire from the United States Army with the rank of brigadier general.[35] He guided through the House Senator Leland Stanford's bill for.the relief of William R. Wheaton and Charles Chamberlain, former register and receiver, respectively, of the United States Land Office in San Francisco.[36] It was with reluctance that he presented a peti-

---

[31] *Solano Republican,* September 24, 1886.

[32] *Contra Costa Gazette,* October 30, 1886.

[33] Lt. Col. Edward E. Eyre had been ordered, in spite of his protest, to act as quartermaster and thirteen years later was told that the voucher which he had given to his successor had not been accounted for and that he was in default of $3000. *Cong. Record,* 50th Cong., 1st sess., p. 898.

[34] *Ibid.,* p. 591.

[35] Opposition to granting this concession to Rosecrans arose from the fact that when he was a member of the House of Representatives he had protested against a similar proposal to reward Ulysses Grant. *Ibid.,* pp. 2216, 2219.

[36] Stanford's bill S. 664 was substituted for McKenna's H. R. 661. *Ibid.,* pp. 9247, 9250.

tion of San Francisco residents for the impeachment of Circuit Court Judge Lorenzo Sawyer.[37]

In his opposition to the low duties proposed by the Mills Tariff Bill, McKenna ingeniously defended the interests of California. As a stalwart protectionist his antagonism became unreasonable when he declared the Mills Bill " carefully, industriously and cruelly " discriminated against California's economy. By placing borax, wool, lumber, salt, fruits, and marble on the free list it dealt a mortal blow to the nascent industrial life of his State. While free bagging would be a boon to wool growers of California, he would not put it on the free list as that industry could be developed in the United States, for he declared: " I am a protectionist everywhere that the principle of protection applies. I believe as Edmund Burke said of liberty: that protection is the clear right of all industries or none." For fig and raisin growers he could get no protection but he succeeded in having prunes and plums stricken from the free list.[38] Nor could he prevent the reduction of duties on salt [39] or obtain withdrawal of an excise tax on spirits used to fortify wine sold in the export trade. Therefore he was one of the 149 who voted against the bill which the Republicans in the Senate managed to kill.[40]

Likewise in the interest of California was McKenna's proposal to give that State five per cent of the sales of public lands within its confines. California had received the sixteenth and thirty-sixth sections of each township but unlike other western states had not received the bonus from public land sales, which McKenna maintained was needed for educational purposes. Well did he observe that failure of a bill to pass in several sessions of Congress was no criterion for its intrinsic worth.[41]

In addition to espousing the cause of his constituents, McKenna

---

[37] The citizens of San Francisco demanded the impeachment of Lorenzo Sawyer and George M. Sabine because they permitted Chinese to land in violation of the laws. *Ibid.*, p. 7271.

[38] *Ibid.*, pp. 5028, 5029, 5690, 6087.

[39] *Ibid.*, p. 5029.

[40] *Ibid.*, Appendix, p. 337.

[41] *Ibid.*, p. 1879, notes that McKenna again substituted Stanford's bill for his own. McKenna argued that because the measure had been defeated in the 47th, 48th, and 49th Congresses, it was no reason to reject it.

was particularly interested in furthering the interests of railroads. When the Democrats proposed to repossess seventy million acres of public lands fraudulently acquired by railroads, McKenna maintained that the government could only sequester five million acres;[42] he voted against a bill that would authorize the printing of ten thousand copies of the unfavorable *Report of the Pacific Railway Commission;*[43] and favored the disestablishment of the Western Union's monopoly over the telegraph lines of subsidized railroads.[44]

Presumably connected with his concern for the interests of the Southern Pacific, which had vast land holdings in California, was McKenna's support of a bill which enabled homesteaders to mortgage a claim prior to its being proven up in order that they might obtain the necessary money for irrigation facilities. He conceded that the law could easily lend itself to abuse by large corporations but he was convinced that the advantages of the proposal would outweigh the evils.[45]

On August 18, 1888, William D. Bynum, a Democrat from Indiana, condemned the Republican Party and in particular its presidential candidate Benjamin Harrison for favoring the unimpeded flow of cheap Chinese labor into the United States.[46] In reply McKenna conceded that Harrison, while in the Senate, had opposed the Chinese Exclusion Bill but it was picayunish to uncover insignificant actions in the career of General Harrison because the people were not concerned with what he was, but " what he is and will be." The attack on Harrison was made for

---

[42] *Ibid.,* p. 5441.

[43] The United States Pacific Railway Commission was appointed under an act of Congress, March 3, 1887, in order to investigate the accounts and methods of the railways which received aid from the United States. It was the evidence collected by this committee that has formed one of the popular sources of information for writers on the activities of the Southern Pacific Railroad. *Ibid.,* p. 1556.

[44] *Ibid.,* p. 1716.

[45] Opponents of the measure denied McKenna's assertion that the homesteaders needed capital to irrigate their land. They implied that the proposal made it possible for large companies to " garble up the small grants." *Ibid.,* pp. 1879 f.

[46] *Ibid.,* pp. 7701–7706.

the purpose of distracting attention from the economic depression that was paralyzing the nation.[47]   Democrats wanted cheap goods, why not cheap labor, if they were consistent? Republicans favored the exclusion of cheap goods and cheap men, and if Harrison did not he would not be their presidential nominee.

That McKenna was favorably disposed toward labor was evident from his vote for an eight-hour day in the office of the public printer and for the plan to confine the sale of convict-made merchandise to the state in which it was produced.[48]

As in the Forty-Ninth Congress McKenna obtained considerable sums of Federal monies for his district.  Mare Island Navy Yard received $100,000; Oakland, $350,000; $150,000 was appropriated for the new Sacramento post office; $40,000 for the improvement of the Sacramento and San Joaquin rivers; $7,500 for dredging Napa Slough; and $4,000 was set aside to improve Mokelume River and Petaluma Creek.[49]

Four parties participated in the campaign of 1888, the Republican, Democratic, American and Prohibition.  All platforms contained a plank against Chinese Immigration and for the free coinage of silver.  The Republicans desired a tariff high enough to protect American industry and labor, while the Democrats were opposed to any tariff that could be employed to exploit the poor.[50]

As in the campaign of 1886, McKenna entered that of 1888 with political fences well mended.  During the previous two years he had sponsored measures beneficial to his constituents which did not go without their reward of fitting publicity.  His attempt to protect California interests, his advocacy of anti-Chinese legislation and his position as sponsor of irrigation projects, friend of labor and crusader for better public schools were frequently mentioned in the daily press.  Toward the end of July, 1888, the ward heelers were preparing for the approaching election.[51]  On July 28, 1888, the Seventh Ward Republican Club of Oakland expressed gratitude for Congressman McKenna's labors in behalf of the

[47] *Ibid.*, pp. 7748 f.

[48] *Ibid.*, p. 1308.  *25 U. S. Statutes,* 57; c. 47.

[49] *Ibid.*, 467; c. 991.  407; c. 860.  175; c. 371.  422; c. 860.  512; c. 1069.

[50] *Contra Costa Gazette,* August 1, 1888.

[51] *Ibid.*, July 28, 1888.

development of Oakland harbor and advocated his renomination.[52] A few days later the Contra Costa Republican Association instructed its delegates to " use all means " to secure McKenna's renomination.

It was rumored that McKenna would have keen competition for the nomination yet as the time for the convention approached, no opponent appeared. McKenna was so confident of the nomination that he did not even leave Washington.[53] His shrewd analysis proved correct for he was unanimously selected as the Republican nominee.[54]

So well entrenched was McKenna that many commentators thought the Democrats would not enter the campaign but when they nominated Benjamin Morgan, it was considered only a " matter of form." [55] It was of interest to note that Mr. Morgan, like the Republican gubernatorial candidate of 1886, refused to accept the proffered nomination of the American Party. His rejection of the dubious honor lent weight to the supposition that support of Nativists in California was a liability rather than an asset.

The campaign of 1888 was featured by the vigorous but ineffective interjection of the religious issue. The publicity organ of the American Party was Frank Pixley's *San Francisco Argonaut* [56] which sought to dissuade all parties from nominating Catholic candidates because the teachings of their church were antagonistic to American institutions. Pixley proclaimed that it was no longer possible for the papists to disguise their attack on the public schools and that Catholic political bosses " set at defiance every rule of propriety and courtesy as they rule like dictators and criminal blackguards over the destinies of the Democratic and Republican machines." [57] It might be reasonably concluded that

[52] *Oakland Enquirer,* August 1, 1888.
[53] *Oakland Morning Times,* August 18, 1888; *Oakland Enquirer,* August 18, 1888, observes that since McKenna was so far away " it would be strange if some Democrat could not be found to come out and run against him."
[54] *Oakland Enquirer,* August 1, 1888.
[55] *Contra Costa Gazette,* September 15, 1888.
[56] *The San Francisco Argonaut,* July 23, 1888.
[57] *Loc. cit.*

since the Nativistic and anti-Catholic elements in the American
Party were equally balanced, there would be as many for as
against McKenna for although he was a Catholic yet he was in all
else acceptable to the staunchest Nativist.

Another facet of Nativism was discrimination against Chinese.
McKenna averred that Chinese Exclusion was no longer a matter
of partisan politics but one in which all Americans were interested.[58]  He took this position to offset the Democrats who had
succeeded in modifying the Burlingame Treaty, thus temporarily
ending the influx of cheap Oriental labor.  McKenna's record on
anti-Chinese measures was unassailable because he had supported
Democratic as well as Republican bills aimed at Chinese exclusion.

In justifying his position on the tariff question, McKenna referred to his remarks in the *Congressional Record* which proved
that he had fought consistently, though not always successfully,
for the interests of his constituents.  McKenna flayed the Mills
Tariff Bill as a travesty of every economical doctrine; formed by a
committee without consideration of the manufacturer's needs it
discriminated against industries and sections and gave preference
to select political groups.  On the other hand the Republican tariff
would protect all American industry and sections which could
flourish only under the " star spangled banner " and not under the
" red bandana " that flew from the truck of John Bull's merchant
ships.[59]  McKenna's reference to the English flag was made as a
result of a rumor that the Cobden Club of England had raised
a huge propaganda fund to spread free trade ideas in the United
States.[60]

McKenna cautioned his audiences that the Democratic tariff
would neither protect American labor nor American industry
whereas the Republican tariff would insure such prosperity that

---

[58] *Oakland Morning Times,* October 25, 1888.

[59] The " red bandana " of the British merchant ships was pictured as the
symbol of free trade, the Mugwumps and Cobden Club.  The Republican
Party was compared to an arch, the inside of which was inscribed with
" Protection for American Labor." *Contra Costa Gazette,* August 1, 1888.

[60] *Ibid.,* August 25, 1888, records that Lord Brassey had given $5000 and
others had contributed less amounts and the " hat is going around." Cf.
*Oakland Morning Times,* October 25, 1888.

it would "make two blades of grass grow where formerly only one blade grew." [61] McKenna's comments were emphasized by Representative Thomas Reed of Maine, who while visiting California spoke in behalf of McKenna and warned that a low tariff would ruin America and enrich England.[62]

Benjamin Morgan, Democratic nominee, attacked McKenna's tariff policy and claimed that McKenna was one of those protectionists who prostituted their office by serving as "political stooges for big business." A tariff which protected the worker was desirable but one which channeled wealth into the pockets of the few was repellent to the American sense of justice and fair play. Morgan showed the disparity between McKenna's position in the State legislature when he favored a low tariff [63] and his policy in Congress when he supported protection.[64]

As in the previous campaigns that of 1888 was featured by fireworks and mass meetings.[65] A typical meeting began with a parade with drill teams, brass bands, civic groups, fraternal lodges, school children and political organizations.[66] McKenna's opposition was weak and it was a foregone conclusion that he would win with little difficulty. So confident were McKenna's followers that they were willing to concede that Benjamin Morgan was a clever attorney and an able orator but he was on "the wrong side of the fence." [67]

The election held November 7, 1888, resulted in a Republican landslide and McKenna's majority of 5,300 out of a total poll of

[61] *Loc. cit.*

[62] *Contra Costa Gazette,* October 31, 1888.

[63] *Oakland Enquirer,* October 19, 1888.

[64] *Loc. cit.*

[65] *Berkeley Advocate,* August 15, 1888, describes the new uniforms of the Republican Club as consisting of "full dress, a white duck hat with red, white and blue ribbons and spring cane with silk flag." One popular ditty ran "Blaine runs the engine, Morton rings the bell, Harrison goes to the White House and Cleveland goes to hell." *The Emporia Kansas Republican,* cited by *Contra Costa Gazette,* October 31, 1888.

[66] *Ibid.,* October 31, 1888, lists the order of the parade at Antioch, "Martinez Brass Band, Martinez Flambeau Club, Young Men's Republican Club, Speaker's carriage, Martinez Glee Club, visiting citizens, Antioch Band, Antioch Republican Club."

[67] *Berkeley Advocate,* August 15, 1888.

34,000 proved that he was satisfactory to his constituents.   That
California did not take kindly to anti-Catholic and Nativistic
harangues of American Party orators was proved by the fact that
that organization polled only 338 votes, not quite one per cent of
the gross number.[68]

In the Fifty-First Congress, McKenna as a member of the
majority party was appointed to the highly coveted Committee of
Ways and Means as well as to a post on the Committee for the
Eleventh Census.[69]   On the former he was thrown into constant
contact with such stalwarts as its chairman, William McKinley,
Sereno Payne, Nelson Dingley, Thomas Bayne, Robert La Follette
as well as with Democrats John Carlisle, William Breckenridge
and Roswell Flower.[70]

President Harrison had remarked that it was not time to weigh
the claims of old soldiers on apothecary's scales, yet only three of
McKenna's seventeen petitions for relief became law.   Commendable, after three failures, was his procuration of relief for the
crew of the British bark *Chance* which had relinquished all
hope of profit in the short Arctic whaling season in order to rescue
ninety-six shipwrecked Americans.[71]   Less worthy was the care
which he devoted to furthering Senator Stanford's bill to aid
Charles Murphy, a California contractor, whose claim had been

---

[68] Davis, *op. cit.,* p. 550.

[69] *Cong. Record,* 51st Cong., 1st sess., pp. 134, 379; in this Congress
William McKinley and Thomas Reed were candidates for the Speakership.
McKinley depended on McKenna's vote, but when he approached McKenna,
the latter told him he had already pledged his vote to Reed.   McKenna
asked, " Now what would you do, Bill, if you were in my place?   I promised
my vote to Reed before I knew that you were to be in the race."   McKinley
replied, " A promise is a promise, Joe."   McKinley lost the election by one
vote.   Isabel McKenna Duffield, *Washington in the 90's* (San Francisco:
1929), p. 23; William A. Robinson, *Thomas B. Reed, Parliamentarian* (New
York: 1930).

[70] The membership of the committee is noteworthy because of the influential positions that its members were later to hold.   Five became United
States Senators, two chairmen of the Ways and Means Committee, four
governors, one ambassador to Russia, one Attorney General and Justice of
the United States Supreme Court and one President of the United States.

[71] *Cong. Record,* 51st Cong., 1st Session, p. 280; *26 U. S. Statutes,* 1226;
c. 270.

rejected by the Court of Claims. After calling up this bill, Mc-
Kenna intimated that he was going to propose a motion for the
previous question which would automatically cut off debate.
However, McKenna's attempt to steam roller the bill through the
House was frustrated by the insistence of William Breckenridge,
Democrat from Kentucky, that the rules of the House be strictly
observed.[72]

During the debate which ensued the Democrats condemned the
Murphy Bill, McKenna, and the Republican Party. It was
asserted that in spite of the fact that there was no fraud, accident,
mistake or legal right to the hearing, in respect to Murphy's cause,
McKenna was imputed to have unearthed a new interpretation of
the term "equity" in order to place Murphy's case under the
"protective covering of that much abused term." Despite the
vigorous opposition of the Democrats, the House passed the bill.[73]

In the interests of his constituency McKenna renewed his efforts
without success to obtain for his State five per cent of the public
land sales; failed to obtain an appropriation for a public building
in Alameda; guided to legislative enactment his cherished plan to
permit exchange of the sixteenth and thirty-sixth sections of
public lands if they contained minerals;[74] and obtained House
approval of a bill that would permit homesteaders to mortgage up
to one-half the value of their claims. In behalf of the residents of
San Francisco Bay area, he proposed without success to establish
six ports in the Territory of Alaska together with appropriate
customs buildings and staff.[75]

As a member of the Committee of the Eleventh Census he
introduced a bill that would make it mandatory for the Superintendent of the Census to compile a descriptive index of all Chinese
in the United States and give each an identification card, which

---

[72] *Cong. Record,* 51st Cong., 1st Session, p. 7161.

[73] *Ibid.,* pp. 7163 f.; it was signed by the President and became law. *26 U. S. Statutes,* 1226; c. 270.

[74] *Cong. Record,* 51st Cong., 1st Session, p. 707; the bill provides that if settlement is established before the survey is made and is later found to be located on the 16th or 36th section, other tracts would be given in exchange for such lands. *26 U. S. Statutes,* 796; c. 384.

[75] *Cong. Record,* 51st Cong., 2nd Session, p. 1375; *26 U. S. Statutes,* 1087; c. 552.

would be their " sole " evidence of right to remain in this country.
If found without this certificate, the offender was " deemed to be
unlawfully in the United States" and upon trial and conviction
returned to China or imprisoned for five years.[76]

In the McKinley Tariff Bill, McKenna incorporated a protective
clause for California wines by levying a prohibitive tax on imported fruit juices compounded with alcohol;[77] likewise in the
interest of California wine producers was the provision that
placed on the free list spirits used in the fortification of wine.
He opposed a bounty clause of two cents a pound for domestic
sugar which was aimed at offsetting the competition of free
imported sugar. This was not strange in an era of no bounties to
increase or decrease crops when ardent proponents of the tariff
regarded such an arrangement as a doubtful precedent.[78]

In seconding William McKinley's bill which would simplify
collection of customs' duties, McKenna took occasion to record
his attitude toward the " common man." Although dubbed an
" aristocrat " and a " snob " by critical observers, McKenna remarked that he favored the McKinley Bill because it guaranteed a
jury trial in cases arising in customs disputes and " I have never
yet seen or heard of a judge whom on all occasions I would trust
as soon as I would trust the verdict of a petit jury." [79]

In the second session, he supported a deficiency appropriation
of which one item gave the Central Pacific Railroad three million
dollars for the transportation of troops and supplies [80] and consequently he was denounced as a tool of the railroads. Democrats
claimed that it was preposterous for the Central Pacific to demand
payment of a debt for $3,000,000 when it owed the government
$70,000,000. In reply, McKenna quoted decisions of the Cali-
fornia and United States Supreme Courts which held that the

[76] *Cong. Record,* 51st Cong., 1st Session, p. 2309.

[77] *Ibid.,* p. 230; *26 U. S. Statutes,* 590; c. 1244, places a duty of sixty
cents a gallon on juices containing up to eighteen percent alcohol and $2.50
a gallon on those containing over eighteen percent.

[78] *Cong. Record,* 51st Cong., 1st Session, pp. 4661, 4991, 4992, 4993; *26
U. S. Statutes,* 583; c. 1244. 584; c. 1244.

[79] *Cong. Record,* 51st Cong., 1st Session, pp. 827, 828, 833.

[80] *Brown Scrapbook,* newspaper clipping, n.n.; n.d.

railroad was entitled to compensation for services rendered and that the railroad's debt to the government due in 1892 did not justify the latter in postponing payment of its debt due in 1890.[81]

On February 4, 1891, McKenna spoke in defense of his friend Lansing Mizner, who had been recalled from his post as American Consul to the Central American States because he had acted without authority in the Barrundia Affair. General Barrundia, a citizen and political refugee of Guatemala, had taken passage on an American steamer in order to go from Mexico to Panama. Enroute the steamer stopped at Guatemala and the authorities of that country demanded the person of Barrundia. Before complying, the captain of the vessel applied to Mizner who advised him to surrender Barrundia because the State Department recognized that "a ship in a foreign port was amenable to the laws thereof."[82] When the authorities attempted to arrest Barrundia, a scuffle ensued, Barrundia was killed and Mizner was recalled by the State Department because his advice to the ship captain was unwise. In his address McKenna demonstrated that the precedents of the State Department and international law justified Mizner's action and that under the circumstances Mizner had acted wisely and prudently.

McKenna did not vote on the passage of the Sherman Anti-Trust Act but did support the Sherman Silver Purchase Act[83] as well as the Fortification Appropriation Bill, termed by its opponents "an outrage upon the taxpayers of the country."[84] He obtained several large appropriations for his district among which were $110,000 to repair the levies of the Sacramento River;[85] $30,000 for improvement of navigability on the Feather River; and smaller sums for dredging the San Joaquin and Napa Rivers, Redwood Creek and Petaluma Slough. Yerba Buena Island, Benicia Arsenal, Oakland harbor, Sacramento and Humboldt Bay were granted sums ranging from $3,000 to $250,000.[86]

---

[81] *Cong. Record,* 51st Cong., 2nd Session, pp. 3396 f.
[82] *Cong. Record,* 51st Cong., 2nd Session, pp. 2119, 2123, 2124.
[83] *Ibid.,* p. 7226.
[84] *Ibid.,* 1st Session, p. 2893.
[85] *Ibid.,* p. 336; *26 U. S. Statutes,* p. 668.
[86] *Ibid.,* 451; c. 907. 434; c. 907. 118; c. 236. 434; c. 907.

Apparently McKenna satisfied his constituents in most ways and he entered the campaign of 1890 with better prospects for success than at any time in his career. The Prohibition, Democratic, American, and Republican Parties again participated in the campaign. The Prohibitionists advocated the Australian secret ballot, direct election of United States Senators, public ownership of railroads, and a Constitutional amendment prohibiting the manufacture, sale, transportation and importation of intoxicating liquor. The Democrats and Republicans both favored trust regulation, Chinese exclusion and soldiers' bonus. The Republicans favored the Sherman Silver Purchase Act and the McKinley Tariff while the Democrats condemned both measures.[87]

The Republican County Conventions conscious of McKenna's efforts in their behalf instructed their delegates to the State Convention to support McKenna's renomination.[88] On August 12, 1890, McKenna was nominated by the Republicans and a few days later John P. Irish,[89] of Oakland, was selected by the Democratic and American Parties while Prohibitionists drafted O. O. Felkner as their candidate.

In the first part of the campaign there were several criticisms of the religion of the candidates but such comments were considered to proceed from the narrow-minded bigots "who are themselves the most obvious examples of the evil which they deprecate."[90] To the people of the Third Congressional District it must have appeared paradoxical for two parties, holding contradictory views toward the Catholic religion, to sponsor John Irish; and for Frank Pixley, leader of the American Party, to declare that a candidate's religious affiliation was immaterial, " so long

---

[87] *Brown Scrapbook,* newspaper clipping, n.n.; n.d.

[88] *Ibid.,* clipping from the *Pacific Wine and Spirit Review,* n.d., makes an appeal for McKenna's re-election on the strength of the work that he did in protecting California wines. Cf., *Contra Costa Gazette,* August 30, September 24, October 11, 1890.

[89] John P. Irish was reputed to have been a member of the legal department of the Southern Pacific Railroad ever since he arrived in California and had served the interests of the large capitalists in their disputes with labor. Furthermore, he could "count on the water, gas and other corporations" for aid in his campaign.

[90] *Oakland Tribune,* September 8, 1890.

as he was loyal to the government, the constitution and the flag." [91]
Totally unexpected was Pixley's declaration that he considered
McKenna a good American and a serviceable man in Congress
and that he preferred McKenna to John P. Irish.

The McKinley tariff, passed only thirty-five days before election,
was the most frequently discussed topic in the campaign.[92]
McKenna stressed the protection which the tariff afforded to
California's farmers and industrialists and insisted that it brought
prosperity to employees and employers alike. John Irish condemned McKenna for being a " dyed-in-the-wool " protectionist
and as such acting as a tool for the large corporations and vested
interests who utilized the tariff to profit the few and exploit the
many.

With little difficulty John Irish became eloquent in denouncing
the autocratic tactics of Republican Speaker " Czar " Reed in the
House of Representatives who suppressed with unexampled indifference the protests of his opponents. McKenna was equally
guilty of the same conduct when he attempted to railroad bills
through the House in defiance of proper procedure. Undeterred,
McKenna, as befitted a faithful party man, not only defended,
but lauded, the technique of Reed. In rather bombastic fashion
he eulogized the Speaker as one of the most noted and impartial
parliamentarians in the world. Although the Democrats might
denounce his procedure, yet " until they rail and denounce the sun
from the heavens they can't change this judgment of men." [93]

In the election which took place November 4, 1890, the Republicans won practically every place on the National and State
tickets. McKenna polled one of the highest number of votes in
his entire career and enjoyed a very satisfactory majority over
his major opponent, John P. Irish.[94]

---

[91] *Loc. cit.*

[92] *Contra Costa Gazette,* September 24, 1890, quotes a letter from Congressman William Morrow, in which McKenna is held responsible for
placing every industry in California, as well as oranges, raisins, prunes, wool,
wheat, wine, hops, quicksilver and borax, under the protective clauses of
the McKinley Tariff.

[93] *Brown Scrapbook,* newspaper clipping, n.n.; n.d.

[94] Davis, *op. cit.,* p. 565.

In the Fifty-Second Congress McKenna found that only eighty-eight Republicans had weathered the Democratic onslaught in the previous election.  He was reappointed to the Ways and Means Committee, to the Committee for Indian Affairs and to that for the Columbian Exposition.[95]  During his three months service in this Congress McKenna presented twelve petitions for relief, none of which was favorably acted on.  He revived the proposal to give California five per cent of the proceeds from the public land sales in the State; proposed a bill to encourage silk culture; strove to expand the Benicia Arsenal and to extend the bonding time of distilled spirits.[96]  All of these motions were given short shrift by the Democratic majority.

As a member of the minority, McKenna now could find cause to be disgruntled about a majority which rode roughshod over the opposition and employed steam roller tactics to enact its will.[97]  Without much urbanity he condemned the " cunning, masquerading . . . pious and patriotic " Democrats who rigidly enforced the rule which prohibited dilatory motions from the floor.  Strangely enough this was the rule that Republican Speaker Reed had employed to enforce the will of the Republican majority in the previous Congress.  In demurring to the dictatorial tactics of the Democrats, McKenna quoted excerpts from speeches of leading members of that party and then with evident glee turned to the Speaker Pro-tempore, who had just ruled a McKenna motion dilatory, and quoted that official as once stating

> no free representative body in the world has ever entrusted a presiding officer with such unrestricted, such unprecedented power as this rule (against dilatory motions) entrusts to the Speaker.[98]

When Representative William Holman proposed the famous " Holman's Rule," which regulated the amendment of appropria-

---

[95] *Cong. Record,* 52nd Cong., 1st Session, pp. 103 f.

[96] *Ibid.,* p. 126.  All of these resolutions appear on the same page and there is no indication in *27 U. S. Statutes* that they passed.

[97] *Cong. Record,* 52nd Cong., 1st Session, pp. 339 f., reports McKenna's proposals and it is evident that he was utilizing the rules in order to obtain the floor and voice his opposition to the resolution.

[98] *Ibid.,* pp. 566, 677, 678, 813, 822.

tion bills, McKenna protested that the language was ambiguous; that it would impede rather than expedite legislation; that it could be employed to repeal almost any law; that it inverted the principles of legislation; and militated against the proper aims of government.[99] Despite McKenna's opposition the Holman Bill became law and was later recognized as one of the most salutary of House rules. Again he protested against a bill which authorized the Committee on Appropriations to investigate the government-subsidized Columbian Exposition. McKenna insisted that the only purpose of the bill was to provide a junketing expedition for some of the members of the Appropriations Committee.[100] In spite of the overwhelming Democratic majority and the short time he spent in the Congress, Representative McKenna was sufficiently influential to secure recognition for the needs of his district.[101]

Having served but three months of his fourth term in Congress McKenna was selected by President Benjamin Harrison to succeed Lorenzo Sawyer as judge of the Ninth Federal Circuit Court of Appeals.

Despite an engaging personality, McKenna's demeanor as a Congressman was distant and austere.[102] He was reputed to be more " aristocratic than the scion of a colonial first family " ; an associate of the influential rather than the " rougher members " of Congress;[103] a patrician who employed his position as a stepping stone to higher places. He made friends with such substantial figures as William McKinley, Theodore Roosevelt, Mark Hanna, William Taft, Uncle Joe Cannon and Myron T. Hendrick. As to his political integrity even in the heat of an election campaign, Chief Justice Taft and his colleagues on the Supreme Court maintained in their testimonial at the end of his career:

> Put to the test in one of your electoral campaigns, you
> declined to yield your convictions on what you deemed

[99] *Ibid.*, p. 813.
[100] *Ibid.*, pp. 864, 936, 945.
[101] *27 U. S. Statutes*, 241; c. 206. 109; c. 158. 353; c. 380. 111; c. 158.
[102] *Oakland Evening Tribune*, February 13, 1892; *Philadelphia Inquirer*, November 22, 1926; *Baltimore Sun*, November 22, 1926.
[103] *Oakland Evening Tribune*, February 13, 1892.

sound monetary principles, and in the face of overwhelming adverse local sentiment, you carried your own congressional district.

McKenna was a faithful party man and consistently supported high tariff, sound money, big business, laissez faire and the railroads. Certainly free silver, inflation, and agrarianism had little effect upon such a stalwart and conservative Republican as Joseph McKenna. He was aptly described as loyal to friends, party, and country, possibly too loyal to corporations.

# CHAPTER IV

## CIRCUIT COURT JUDGE AND ATTORNEY GENERAL

When Judge Lorenzo Sawyer, of the Ninth Circuit Court of Appeals, died, President Benjamin Harrison received the usual plethora of recommendations in behalf of candidates for the position. Fifteen highly esteemed and publicly approved aspirants filed letters of commendation with the Chief Executive.[1] The four strongest contenders were William Morrow, of San Francisco, John D. Works, of San Diego, Judge William Van Fleet, of Sacramento, and Judge John Spencer, of San Jose.

William Morrow withdrew when he was appointed to the United States District Court in San Francisco[2] and John D. Works was eliminated when opposition developed on account of the support he gave to Daniel W. Voorhees when the latter campaigned for United States Senator in Indiana in 1879. The opponents of Works charged that he professed to be a Republican yet had accepted the support of the Greenback Party and the secret aid of the Democrats in return for his pledge to vote for Voorhees if elected to the State Legislature.[3] The field was thus

---

[1] At the time that a successor to Judge Sawyer was to be selected another seat on the Ninth Circuit Court was created by an act of Congress. Hence there were applicants from the Pacific Coast for both posts. It was generally accepted that a resident of California would fill Judge Sawyer's post while one from either Washington or Oregon would be appointed to the new seat. For the latter position there were seven fairly well supported candidates whose credentials are found in the file with those of the aspirants from California. National Archives, Department of Justice, File *Ninth Circuit Court, 1889–1893*. Henceforth cited as *Ninth Circuit Court, 1889–1893*.

[2] *Sacramento Record-Union*, Feb. 12, 1892; *Woodland Democrat*, Feb. 18, 1892.

[3] *Ninth Circuit Court, 1889–1893*, Manes B. McCrellis to President Harrison, Mar. 21, 1891; among the petitioners for John Works were William F. Herrin, attorney for the Southern Pacific Railroad, and Hall McAllister. John Works was an associate justice of the State Supreme Court at this time.

narrowed to Judges Spencer and Van Fleet,[4] who were so " evenly backed " by influential and uncompromising supporters that a deadlock ensued.[5]  However after some days, during which it was reported that the President had definitely decided to appoint Spencer,[6] McKenna's name was sent to the Senate for confirmation.

Newspapers asserted that Harrison was deterred from nominating Spencer because he feared to arouse the hostility of the Van Fleet contingent and in order to avoid giving offense he had selected McKenna because " he had no enemies." [7]  This incident was similar to the contest for the Republican nomination in Benicia in 1884 which McKenna obtained after the two leading candidates nullified each other's strength.  After McKenna had been chosen, it was stated that the President acted only after consulting close political advisers on the expediency of granting preference to a Catholic in face of the opposition and criticism of the American Protective Association.  The Chief Executive consulted the entire California delegation in Congress and then turned to Senator Leland Stanford, who set at rest all the presidential scruples and reassured him that he could make no mistake in naming Joseph McKenna to the Federal bench.[8]

Immediately after the nomination had been received in the Senate, Senator Charles N. Felton, of California, rushed over to the House and congratulated the nominee.  As the news spread

---

[4] *Brown Scrapbook,* when candidates for the Circuit Court began to campaign, McKenna supported Judge Van Fleet and it was only when the latter's hopes for success were shattered that McKenna allowed his name to be proposed for the post.

[5] *Alameda Argus,* Feb. 12, 1892.

[6] *San Francisco Chronicle,* Feb. 12, 1892.

[7] *San Francisco Post,* Feb. 12, 1892.

[8] *Sacramento Record-Union,* Feb. 12, 1892, remarks, that in addition to Senator Stanford, McKenna's staunchest advocates were Senators Felton, Shoup, Squire and Carey.  Among those who wrote letters of recommendation for McKenna were Claus Spreckels, George L. Shoup, Fred Dubois, Willis Sweet, Representative John S. Cutting, Senator John B. Allen, James A. Waymire, Nathan Frank and Abe Ruef.  The last named was later sent to San Quentin Penitentiary on conviction of charges growing out of a San Francisco graft ring.

through the chambers, Democrats as well as Republicans felici-
tated the Californian.  Thomas B. Reed, of Maine, a warm friend
of McKenna, maintained that Harrison's choice was the best that
could be made but regretted the loss of McKenna from the ranks
of Congress.[9]  Barclay Henley, a Democrat from California,
lauded the wisdom displayed by President Harrison and commended McKenna as a man admired and respected because he was
fair, candid and honorable.  It may be reasonably supposed that
Senator Leland Stanford had some intimation that his fellow
Californian was going to be selected because Mrs. Stanford was
the first to break the news to Mrs. McKenna.[10]

The public journals for the most part approved and applauded
the assignment.[11]  One publication, noted for its animosity toward
the railroads, accepted the appointment as an indication of the
waning power of the Southern Pacific Company,[12] while others
referred to it as in line with the President's policy " to put strong
men on the bench." [13]  The selectee, in response to a reporter's
question, frankly conceded that he was happy to be relieved of
the campaign every two years.  Yet he was wary enough to add
that he had fewer disagreeable experiences with his constituents
than most men.[14]

Some of the more critical newspapers claimed that McKenna
was " happy " to don the judicial robes because he faced inevitable
defeat in the next election.  McKenna, they reported, had labored
feverishly and ingeniously to convert his future from political
innocuousness to respectable retirement.  Others suggested that
McKenna had ambitions of becoming a United States Senator and
therefore the " Senators fearing this, put him on a shelf where indeed there is much cheese for life." [15]  In other quarters it was

[9] *San Francisco Examiner,* Feb. 12, 1892.

[10] *Sacramento Record-Union,* Feb. 12, 1892.

[11] *Brown Scrapbook,* contains clippings from *Vallejo Chronicle,* Feb. 12,
1892; *Inyo Index,* Feb. 17, 1892; *San Francisco Daily Report,* Feb. 18, 1892.

[12] *San Francisco Daily Report,* Feb. 16, 1892.

[13] *Brown Scrapbook,* clipping from *San Jose Mercury,* no date.

[14] *Brown Scrapbook,* clipping from *San Francisco Chronicle,* n.d.

[15] *Ninth Circuit Court, 1889–1893,* contains only one letter of opposition
to McKenna's appointment; *Brown Scrapbook* contains a clipping from
unidentified newspaper dated Oakland, California, Feb. 13, 1892, and notes,

rumored that McKenna was preparing to succeed his fellow Californian, Justice Stephen J. Field, on the Supreme Court of the United States. Although McKenna was acknowledged as " not the man to look for dead men's shoes and certainly will not try on those shoes before the man is dead," yet he was recognized as the logical candidate to succeed Field.[16]   On March 28, 1892, McKenna, who admittedly had steered a very skillful course in troubled political waters, resigned his seat in the House of Representatives [17] and after taking the oath of office entrained for San Francisco.[18]

At the time McKenna was appointed to the Circuit Court, it was asserted that the Southern Pacific Railroad was primarily responsible for his elevation to the bench, and that McKenna would be another tool of that corporation.[19]   However, during his term as a judge of the circuit court, McKenna's action on and off the bench demonstrated that he maintained an impartial attitude toward the Southern Pacific.

The most striking example of this policy occurred during the first year of McKenna's judgeship, when he refused to serve as a contingent executor for the estate of his late friend, Senator Leland Stanford, former president of the Southern Pacific Railroad.[20]   Acceptance of such a position would place McKenna in a rather embarrassing position because of the difficulty of presiding at a hearing in which the Stanford estate or the Southern Pacific,

---

" McKenna had a billet that such a model jurist as Superior Judge W. E. Greene, of Oakland, ought to occupy. Although McKenna will not be an imbecile on the bench, yet if any knotty questions arise they will be solved for the jurist by lawyers who practice at the court . . . findings will be prepared, when solicited, by the counsel who is to be proclaimed winner in the case."

[16] *Brown Scrapbook,* n.n.; n.d.

[17] *Congressional Record,* 52nd Congress, 1st Session, p. 2610.

[18] *Ninth Circuit Court, 1889–1893,* contains a copy of the official decree which notes that McKenna was appointed on March 7, 1892 and took the oath of office in Washington, April 5, 1892.

[19] *San Francisco Examiner,* Dec. 4, 1897.

[20] *Ibid.,* July 20, 1893; the close friendship of McKenna and Stanford was described in personal interviews with McKenna's daughters, Mrs. Isabel McKenna Duffield and Mrs. Marie McKenna Brown; cf., Isabel McKenna Duffield, *Washington in the 90's* (San Francisco: 1929), pp. 11 f.

whose stock formed the bulk of the Stanford millions, would be involved. McKenna explained that he rejected the proffered post in order "to avoid the possibility of criticism in the mind of any person and to satisfy my own idea of what was proper."[21]

A few of the decisions selected from different fields of law in which the Southern Pacific Railroad was concerned gave further grounds for believing that McKenna preserved his neutrality in respect to the corporation. For example, on the day that he refused to act as contingent executor of the Stanford estate, he ruled against the railroad in *Southern Pacific Railroad v. Lafferty*.[22] The railroad was liable for the death of a brakeman, killed by a runaway locomotive because it was negligent in taking all reasonable means and precautions to protect its employees in the performance of their duties. McKenna was convinced that the ordinary incidents of railroading were unusually dangerous and therefore extra precautions must be taken to safeguard employees. A runaway locomotive was not one of the risks incident to the deceased's employment, for an employee did not assume any risk which the master's reasonable care could obviate. In a word, the unusual and extraordinary risk of death by runaway locomotives would not have existed had the master taken ordinary precautions.

It appeared that McKenna's reputation for impartiality suffered considerably when he granted a temporary injunction to the Southern Pacific Railroad against the city of Oakland. For some years the citizens of Oakland were dissatisfied with the Southern Pacific ferry service to San Francisco and agitated for improved transportation.[23] Finally an independent operator, with the unofficial support of Oakland municipal authorities, established a fast, comfortable service and immediately drew most of the patronage from the Southern Pacific.[24]

---

[21] *Brown Scrapbook* contains a copy of the resignation of McKenna as executor of the Stanford estate.

[22] 57 F. R. 536 (July 17, 1893).

[23] Oscar Lewis, *The Story of the Big Four* (New York: 1938), has a popular and rather biased account of the position of the Southern Pacific.

[24] In order to increase the patronage of the independent line, the mayor and the council of Oakland planned to pass an ordinance authorizing the independent line to take possession of a ferry slip controlled by the Southern

In the course of the subsequent struggle for the commuter trade, Oakland city officials prepared to seize a ferry slip held by the Southern Pacific. The latter petitioned the Circuit Court for a temporary injunction to enjoin such trespass. Defendants in *Southern Pacific Railroad Company v. City of Oakland et al.,*[25] insisted that their acts were trespass and, as such, susceptible of pecuniary compensation but not enjoinable. McKenna rejected this viewpoint and maintained that the act to seize the ferry slip was enjoinable on the grounds that if permitted it would result in untold damage to the business of the railroad. The contemplated action of the public officials was tantamount to an act of ownership and if executed would amount to appropriation of property.

The violation of the right to property was the principle upon which McKenna based his reasoning. He claimed that next in degree to the right of personal liberty was that of enjoying private property. The requirement that private property should not be taken without the process of law was an affirmance of a doctrine established by the common law for the protection of private property. It was based on natural equity and recognized as a principle of universal law. In a free government almost all other rights would become worthless if the authorities enjoyed an uncontrollable power over the property of every citizen.

Other railroad cases soon followed, one of the most bitterly contested being that concerned with an attempt of the State to establish a schedule of railroad rates for freight and passengers. McKenna had actively participated in the movement to regulate railroad rates and as a member of the State Legislature had sponsored the first law establishing such regulation. McKenna's opposition to the railroad increased his prestige and popularity and was an important factor in his election to Congress. Hence severe criticism naturally followed when he refused to permit a reduction

---

Pacific. Before the latter could obtain a temporary injunction, the city superintendent had removed a portion of the track to prevent the railroad from blocking the street with a line of empty freight cars.

[25] 58 F. R. 50 (Aug. 21, 1893).

of rates in *Southern Pacific Railroad Company v. Board of Railroad Commissioners of California.*[26]

In sustaining his position, McKenna wrote his lengthiest opinion as a Circuit Judge. He based his conclusion on the principle that the power to regulate did not connote the right to destroy nor was limitation the equivalent of confiscation. Under the pretense of regulating freights and fares, a State may not require a carrier to transport persons or merchandise without reasonable payment; nor can the State do that which legally amounted to the taking of property for public use without just compensation or without due process of law.

McKenna reasoned that the question of deciding the reasonableness of rates lay with the judiciary. The courts had always been vested with power to investigate allegedly extortionate or unjust rates and determine whether they infringed upon the constitutional or property rights of persons or corporations. No commission could substitute for a court in establishing the final judgment of the reasonableness of rates because such provision would deny judicial investigation by due process of law.

A test for railroad rates must be based on the fair value of the capital invested by the railroad for the convenience of the public. In keeping with later decisions of the Supreme Court he contended that a carrier was entitled to compensation for its service and to receive an adequate return upon its investment. To establish a fair rate, consideration must be given to the original cost of construction, the present value compared with the original cost, the comparative earning capacity under the proposed rates, operating expenses, cost of reasonable renewal and improvement of the roadbed, rolling stock and stationary equipment. All these matters were entitled to consideration and were to be given such weight as was just and right in each case. Since the railroad commissioners had not taken these factors into consideration when framing the table of rates, it must be concluded that the rates were unreasonable, confiscatory and hence restrainable.

No less important than the railroad cases were McKenna's decisions involving Chinese immigration. At the time that McKenna

---

[26] 68 F. R. 236 (Nov. 30, 1896).

took his position on the Ninth Circuit Court of Appeals, it was obvious that Chinese immigration problems would have to be shifted from the courts to immigration officials for adjudication. After Congress had authorized immigration officials to decide cases arising under the Chinese Exclusion Acts, Judge McKenna uniformly sustained these decisions when appealed to the Circuit Court.

In *United States v. Mock Chew*,[27] defendant was refused admission to the United States even though his certificate of identification had been signed by recognized officials in China, which in the eyes of the law was " prima facie evidence on the part of a person to establish a right of entry into the United States." McKenna, notwithstanding this stipulation, supported the immigration officials on the grounds that the law permitted them to refuse to accept any evidence presented by the immigrant. Since there was no allegation of improper hearing or irregularities on the part of the authorities, McKenna accepted their charge that investigation had established cause to suspect the authenticity of the defendant's certificate.

In sustaining his conclusion, McKenna explained that alien deportation proceedings were by their nature subjects for decision by executive officers. He reasoned that a sovereign nation had the power to forbid entrance of foreigners within its dominions, and that this power, being one affecting international relations, was vested in the political departments, that is the Executive and the Congress. Once the matter of immigration had been regulated by treaty or statute, it was to be administered by the executive authority according to the established regulations.

Thus it was the right of executive officials to determine the expulsion of a Chinese who appealed in *Lew Jim v. United States*.[28]

27 54 F. R. 490 (Jan. 30, 1893) ; "Jurisdiction of Executive Officers over Claims of Citizenship," *Columbia Law Review*, IV (April, 1904), 290; " Findings of Jurisdictional Facts by Administrative Officers," *Columbia Law Review*, V (Nov. 1905), 537.

28 66 F. R. 953 (Feb. 18, 1895). In *Lee Kan v. United States* 62 F. R. 914 (May 21, 1895), McKenna ruled that a Chinaman could be classified as a merchant if his name appeared in the articles of incorporation of a business. In 1882 Congress passed an act excluding Chinese laborers for a period of ten years and extended the life of the law for a like period in 1890 and

Appellant was refused re-admittance on the ground that he was a manual laborer and as such could not be re-admitted. McKenna sustained this regulation on the basis that it was an accepted maxim of international law that every sovereign nation had the power to regulate immigration. The Constitution clothed the national government with this power which could be exercised either by treaties made by the President and the Senate or through legislation enacted by Congress. The government possessed powers to be exercised for its protection and security, and was invested with the authority to determine the occasion on which these powers should be called forth. Its determination, so far as the persons affected were concerned, was conclusive upon all departments and officers.

If the Federal Government, through its legislative department, considered the presence of aliens dangerous to the peace and security, its decision was binding upon other departments. Chinese laborers residing in the United States, although entitled to the safeguards of the Constitution and to the protection of the laws, continued to be aliens, incapable of becoming citizens under the naturalization laws. They were therefore subject to the power of Congress, whenever in its judgment their removal or re-admission was deemed necessary or expedient for the public interest. According to the same principles McKenna determined *Lai Moy v. United States.*[29]

A survey of McKenna's opinions in Chinese exclusion cases indicated that he was convinced that the judiciary should cautiously approach the adjudication of political questions, the determination of which was entrusted by the Constitution to the political departments of the government. He believed that the decision of the constituted authorities was conclusive and, in the absence of flagrant violation of the Constitution, must be accepted as conclusive. The paramount power of the national government was the common idea which McKenna employed in sustaining congressional legis-

---

again in 1902. As a result of the exclusion policy the Chinese population in the United States declined rapidly.

[29] 66 F. R. 955 (Feb. 18, 1895); "Power of Administrative Officers," *Columbia Law Review,* V (Mar. 1905), 245; "Rights of Chinese within the United States," *Columbia Law Review,* V (Jan. 1905), 59.

lation aimed at averting an influx of undesirable aliens detrimental to the peace and security of the nation.

In addition to the railroad and Chinese cases McKenna wrote several significant opinions in the field of patent law. His thought in each case was usually based upon one or two of the following principles: that the fundamental reason for patent laws was to reward inventors with the exclusive enjoyment of their invention; that a patent was a contract between society and the inventor in which the former gave a privilege to the latter in return for his inventive contribution; that novelty, utility and exercise of the inventive faculty must be inherent in an invention; and that every improvement which rose to the dignity of an invention in a particular field was entitled to the protection of a patent.

In the mind of McKenna there was no precise rule by which to determine the presence or absence of invention. The existence of invention could only be determined by means of several negative rules which operated by a process of exclusion. Each rule applied to a large class of cases and were considered by McKenna sufficiently clear and authoritative to furnish a reasonable and fair basis of adjudication. For example, it was not invention to produce a machine which any skillful mechanic or electrician could make whenever required to effect a desired result.

Thus in *Butte City Railway Company v. Pacific Cable Railway* [30] McKenna ruled that no invention was involved in placing a gripping appliance, patented by another, on a dummy street car and attaching the combination to a standard passenger car. In supporting his conclusion McKenna reasoned that it was unjust in principle and injurious in consequences to grant a patent for every new application or slight advance on patented articles. The aim of the patent law was to reward those who made some substantial invention which materially added to human knowledge and marked a forward step in the useful arts. It was never the purpose of the law to grant a patent for every novel application of another's in-

---

[30] 60 F. R. 90 (Jan. 15, 1894); Thomas R. Powell, "The Nature of a Patent Right," *Columbia Law Review*, XVII (Dec. 1917), 665–667; "Improvement as a Ground for Patent," *Columbia Law Review*, XXIII (Feb. 1923); Edwin H. Abbot, "Patents and the Sherman Act," *Columbia Law Review*, XII (Dec. 1912), 709.

vention or for every slight improvement that naturally occurred to any skilled mechanic. To issue patents indiscriminately would obstruct rather than stimulate invention. Speculative schemers would be encouraged to derive an illegitimate profit from industry without contributing anything of real value and thereby impede the progress of business with threats of vexatious lawsuits and liabilities.

On the same principle, that slight improvements do not justify the issuance of a patent, McKenna in *Johnson v. Pacific Rolling Mills* [31] held that plaintiff was not entitled to monopolistic rights because he had made some inconsequential improvements in a contrivance in common use but not patented. Plaintiff charged infringements on a railway-coach chair which differed from previous models only in that the clips were riveted to the chair instead of being incorporated as integral parts. McKenna insisted that the contrivance of plaintiff was only a slight modification of an unpatented article and did not rise above the ordinary mechanical or engineering skill common among craftsmen.

Somewhat akin to the principle, that slight improvements were not inventions, was the doctrine that substitution of an equivalent element for one of the old elements in a patented article was not an invention. Thus in *Consolidated Piedmont Cable Company v. Pacific Cable Railway Company* [32] McKenna ruled that a patent for gathering slack in street railway cables had been infringed upon when a rival had substituted a gadget equivalent in function to one in defendant's machine.

McKenna explained that it was reasonable to conclude that one part was equivalent to another when it functioned in substantially the same way and accomplished the same result. It must be concluded that infringement existed when a machine differed from a patented contrivance only in an equivalent part. The substitution of an equivalent element did not produce a machine substantially

---

[31] 57 F. R. 242 (Nov. 27, 1893); "Nature and Validity of License Restrictions Imposed by a Patentee," *Columbia Law Review,* XII (May, 1912), 445–447.

[32] 53 F. R. 382 (Oct. 24, 1892); "Rights of a Patentee against Persons Infringing His Contract with the Government," *Columbia Law Review,* XVI (Jan. 1916), 53.

different in structure or purpose from the patented article. It did not differ in utility or novelty from its predecessor nor was it a product of the inventive faculty, hence the degree of distinction was not sufficient to justify protection of the patent laws. The same thought underlay McKenna's opinion in *Smith et al. v. Vulcan Iron Works* [33] when he declared that infringement existed in the case of a machine similar in all respects to a patented article except that it was cast in two pieces instead of one.

Another negative rule for testing the existence of an invention was applied by McKenna when he declared that a combination of old elements was not patentable if it consisted in a mere aggregate of several inventions each merely producing its separate effect. In *Butte City Street Railway Company v. Pacific Cable Railway Company* [34] McKenna ruled that the elements in a new invention had been used in bailing presses but that in applying these elements to track brakes, all the constituent parts interacted to produce a novel result. The old elements formed a new machine of distinct character and function, produced a single action different from the mere adding together of their separate contributions and was entitled to the protective guarantees of the patent laws.

In deciding cases involving patents, McKenna made few references to previous decisions, stated his thought in clear and precise language and made considerable contribution to the rules employed in deciding patent cases. In particular he confirmed the rules applicable to slight modification of patented articles, to the substitution of an equivalent element and to the combination of old elements. It was evident that he was reasonably well acquainted with the background, nature and development of the patent laws. The reasonableness and soundness of his opinions in patent laws was attested by the affirmance which the Supreme Court gave to all that were appealed.

On the Circuit Court, Judge McKenna was moderate as was fitting for a staunch supporter of the *status quo* and an advocate of the inviolability of the constitutional rights of liberty and property. Sustainer of duly constituted authority, he readily accepted

[33] 57 F. R. 934 (Dec. 5, 1892).
[34] 60 F. R. 90 (Jan. 29, 1894).

the decisions of immigration officials in cases involving the exclusion or deportation of aliens. His attitude toward the Southern Pacific Railroad was based on sound legal principles and did not justify the prediction that he would be a tool of that corporation. In supporting his opinions in patent cases he affirmed the principles that a patent was a contract between society and inventor by which the former rewarded the latter for his service; that a patent gave exclusive control over the invention; that novelty, utility and exercise of the inventive faculty were requisite characteristics of invention and that improvement on a patented contrivance which could be designated as a separate invention was entitled to the protection of a patent.

McKenna's opinions were not outstanding for their depth of thought, originality of interpretation or legal acumen, but they were sufficiently satisfactory to justify a friendly critic in concluding that while on the Circuit Court, McKenna had been

> a thoroughly honest man, an able, faithful and painstaking judge, who during his short incumbency of the office, has done some excellent judicial work.[35]

Upon William McKinley's election as President, names of potential cabinet members began to be bandied about. Those in the confidence of the President-elect surmised that one of the posts would go to a man from the Pacific slope. When questioned, Mr. McKinley, admitting several possible selections, emphasized that there was only one who would " not only be a credit to his official household . . . but would meet with the approval of the people of California." [36]

The promised honor to California aroused speculation but soon the possible appointees were reduced to three, namely Horace Davis, Judge Joseph Waymire and Joseph McKenna. In sifting the competency, ability and mental endowments of the three, political analysts placed Representative Davis as the least likely candidate, for, though he had the support of the entire California congressional delegation, his record had been " mediocre, frigid

---

[35] A. L. Jones, *American Law Review,* XXXVI (1902), 36.
[36] *Brown Scrapbook,* newspaper clipping, no name; Jan. 23, 1897.

and unemotional " and as a member of Congress he had " accomplished nothing." [37]   Judge Waymire, a recognized man of ability, was opposed by some of the most influential leaders of the Party and was thus classified as a " possible but not probable choice."

McKenna was considered the most likely contestant.  A close friend of the President-elect, his record in Congress and on the bench had been unblemished and conservative, and his numerous friends in the inner councils of the Republican Party made it appear that McKinley would select him.   McKenna acknowledged, when interviewed, that there might be some grounds for connecting his name with a cabinet assignment but he warned " there are some obstacles which may prevent my being chosen." [38]   The difficulties to which McKenna referred were his Roman Catholic faith and the lack of financial means to maintain his family in expensive Washington.[39]  The former difficulty was removed when McKinley proclaimed, very possibly in answer to charges of religious intolerance, that he would be " President of the whole American people and not of special groups—Protestant or Catholic, South or North, East or West." [40]

Originally McKinley intended to make McKenna Secretary of the Interior, but sensing opposition from anti-Catholic sources, he shrewdly shifted McKenna to Attorney General.   McKinley was keenly aware that the administration of Indian Schools by the Secretary of the Interior had been the cause of a bitter controversy

---

[37] *Woodland Democrat,* Jan. 19, 1897; *Biographical Directory of the American Congress* (Washington: 1928), p. 885 notes that Horace Davis was born at Worcester, Mass., Mar. 16, 1831.   A graduate of Williams College, he studied law at Harvard University, went to California in 1852 and was elected from that State to Congress in 1877 and 1879. Subsequently he became President of the Board of Trustees of Stanford University and President of the University of California.  He died in San Francisco in 1916.

[38] *Tulare Register,* January 19, 1897, hesitates to admit that McKenna would resign his position as Circuit Judge in exchange for a cabinet position.   It was predicted that if McKenna refused McKinley's offer, California would not have a representative in the cabinet.

[39] Duffield, *op. cit.,* p. 26.

[40] E. L. Pell, J. W. Buel, and J. P. Boyd, *McKinley and Men of Our Times* (Washington: 1901), pp. 140 f.

between Catholics and non-Catholics during the previous Republican administration and he wished to avoid such contentions.[41]

On January 13, 1897, McKinley summoned McKenna to his home at Canton, Ohio, where the President-elect ⁄reportedly greeted his visitor with " Well, Judge, they have been pretty busy with your name for a cabinet post." To this McKenna assertedly answered

> Yes, Governor, but I don't believe you realize what you are doing. I am a Roman Catholic, and the Protestants will never permit a Catholic to have charge of the Indian Missions.

Thereupon McKinley declared that he had in mind the Attorney Generalship which had nothing to do with the Indian Mission schools. McKenna agreed to accept this assignment if it were tendered. McKinley was supposed to have intimated that ahead there was an appointment to the Supreme Court and that if the Senate should fail to confirm nominee McKenna for the cabinet that he would continue to submit his name for some such position until it was ratified.[42] On the following day the press announced

---

[41] It was observed that McKinley had selected McKenna through a sense of gratitude to the Catholics who had supported him in the presidential campaign. Among the most prominent of these were Archbishop John Ireland of St. Paul, Senator Thomas H. Carter of Montana and Richard C. Kerens, father-in-law of McKenna's only son. Kerens (1842–1916) was an immigrant from County Meath, Ireland, promoter of the pony express, railroads, mines and lumber mills. A generous contributor to the Republican Party, he was rewarded with the patronage of Missouri from 1884 to 1900. After twice refusing diplomatic posts, he accepted the ambassadorship to Austria from President Taft in 1909. H. Edward Nettles, "Richard C. Kerens," *Dictionary of American Biography*, X, 353; Richard J. Purcell, "Archbishop Ireland," *Ibid.*, IX, 494.

[42] *Vallejo News*, January 19, 1897, reports that McKenna arrived in Canton at 3 A. M., began a conference with McKinley at 9, took luncheon and dinner at McKinley's home and left for the West the same evening. Cf., *San Francisco Call*, February 5, 1897; *San Diego Tribune*, January 20, 1897; *Bakersfield Echo*, January 14, 1897; *Oakland Enquirer*, January 16, 1897; *Oakland Tribune*, January 21, 1897; *Suisun Republican*, January 20, 22, 1897; *Marysville Appeal*, January 19, 1897; *Stockton Record*, January 20, 1897. *The San Francisco Chronicle*, February 6, 1897, predicts that McKenna would remain as Attorney General for six months and then succeed Stephen J. Field

that McKenna would be nominated for Attorney General.

When McKenna was confirmed as Attorney General on March 7, 1897,[43] he became the first Californian to occupy a Cabinet position and the first Catholic since the administration of Franklin Pierce to be so honored.  Prior to his departure for the national capital, the San Francisco Bar Association tendered him a banquet at which over three hundred guests from " all walks and parties, Governor Budd, Mayor Phelan, federal and state officials, navy and army representatives, professional and businessmen " attended.[44]  In his address, McKenna observed that " there was no greater discipline than the ambition of the bench to retain the respect of the bar . . . This has been my ambition and for this reason I value this testimonial tonight." [45]

A large group was present when McKenna entrained for Washington and when his train stopped momentarily at Suisun, a numerous delegation wished their former neighbor " God-speed." [46]

---

on the Supreme Court.  It cited the widely accepted report that William Warner of Missouri would be McKenna's assistant for the half year and then would succeed him.  *Woodland Democrat,* January 19, 1897, congratulates Mrs. McKenna, who " had done so much to aid his (McKenna's) ambition and encourage his aspirations . . . upon the probability that his honorable and illustrious career will be rounded out with the highest judicial honor ever conferred upon man."  Cf., *San Francisco Evening Post,* February 5, 1897; *Tulare Register,* January 19, 1897.

[43] *Ninth Circuit Court,* 1897–1901, contains the resignation of McKenna from the Circuit Bench which was dated Mar. 6, 1897.  *San Francisco Chronicle,* Mar. 8, 1897; *Berkeley Gazette,* Feb. 5, 1897; *Modesto Herald,* Feb. 4, 1897; *Yreka Journal,* Feb. 9, 1897; *San Francisco Wave,* Jan. 27, 1897; *Los Angeles Herald,* Feb. 9, 1897; *San Rafael Journal,* Jan. 21, 1897; *Weaverville Journal,* Jan. 23, 1897.  These papers carry commendations of the McKenna appointment.

[44] *San Francisco Call,* Feb. 27, 1897; *San Francisco Chronicle,* Feb. 27, 1897.

[45] *San Francisco Bulletin,* Feb. 21, 1897; *San Francisco Call,* Feb. 21, 1897, notes that when McKenna finished, Governor Budd jumped to his feet and invited all present to rise and give three cheers for " the pride of California —Joseph McKenna."  John P. Irish, a former opponent of McKenna in the Third Congressional District, was willing to predict that the " cabinet will be the best we ever had because in it are two men who have beaten me for Congress, Wilson of Iowa and McKenna of California."

[46] *Suisun Republican,* Feb. 23, 1897.

At Sacramento over a thousand citizens met and escorted McKenna to the State Capitol where the Legislature held a public reception in his honor.[47]  To this gathering McKenna professed that he went " into the cabinet as a Californian.  That is my highest title.  I go as the first Californian and that is my admonition and incentive." [48]

It was reported that McKenna would resign from the Circuit Court before the end of Cleveland's administration, but he was too well versed in the technique of political patronage to " permit the possibility of such a thought to enter my calculations."  When interrogated on his resignation, McKenna blandly replied, " I have no fear that President Cleveland would care to do anything that might be considered to savor of impropriety." [49]  However much he trusted Grover Cleveland's sense of propriety, Joseph McKenna did not resign from the Ninth Circuit Court until after the inauguration of President William McKinley.[50]

During the nine months that McKenna served as Attorney General, he proved a hard-working and exacting executive.  His interest in the duties of his office was well exemplified in the care which he took of federal prisoners.  At that time federal prisoners were lodged in State penitentiaries [51] and McKenna was careful to provide his charges with reasonably good food, living quarters,

---

[47] *San Francisco Chronicle,* Feb. 27, 1897; Statement by Mrs. McKenna Duffield, personal interview April 24, 1944; *San Francisco Call,* Feb. 27, 1897, pictures McKenna as entering the assembly hall in "evening dress, but illy [sic] concealed with a fawn-colored overcoat.  His ample shirt bosom blazed under the glare of the incandescent light chandeliers in the full glory of a French laundry."

[48] *San Francisco Call,* Feb. 27, 1897; *San Francisco Chronicle,* Feb. 27, 1897.

[49] *San Francisco Evening Post,* Feb. 5, 1897.

[50] File *Ninth Circuit Court, 1897–1901.*  The resignation reads " I hereby and respectfully resign the office of United States Circuit Judge for the Ninth Judicial Circuit to take effect immediately.

(Signed) JOSEPH McKENNA.

Accepted March 6, 1897.          (Signed) WILLIAM McKINLEY."

[51] National Archives, Department of Justice, *Letter-Press Copies of the Attorney General,* McKenna to J. S. Easby-Smith, Examiner of the Department of Justice, July 20, 1897.  Henceforth cited as *L.P.*

medical care, recreational facilities and occupations.[52]  McKenna
was especially interested in the care of the sick prisoners.[53]

In the case of a blind prisoner, whose sight could be restored
by a delicate operation, McKenna, after gathering pertinent data
on the cost and circumstances, ordered the operation at government expense.[54]  On another occasion at the request of a prisoner's
mother, McKenna ordered the transfer of an inmate from the
Illinois to the Ohio State Penitentiary on the grounds that the
change of climate would improve his health.[55]  A sympathetic
strain in McKenna's character was revealed when he was told that
a prisoner, eligible for discharge, was too ill to travel alone and a
friend, with whom he was going to live, too poor to come for him.
McKenna decided that "arrangements will be made by the Department to have him accompanied (by an employee of the department) to the place of his residence . . . the actual and necessary travelling expense . . . will be allowed by this department." [56]

In the care of insane prisoners the Attorney General was likewise kind and considerate and if their ailment was certified by

[52] *L.P.*, McKenna to Leo E. Bennett, Oct. 11, 1897; McKenna to R. V.
La Dow, July 8, 1897; McKenna to John R. Leonard, Warden, United States
Jail, Washington, D. C., Sept. 2, 1897; McKenna to S. W. Finch, Dec. 10,
1897.

[53] *Ibid.*, McKenna to R. V. La Dow, July 8, 1897; McKenna to E. S.
Wright, Warden, Western Penitentiary, Allegheny, Penn., Nov. 12, 1897;
McKenna to C. F. Dearstyne, Dec. 2, 1897; McKenna to R. J. Kirkwood,
Dec. 9, 1897; McKenna to J. W. French, Oct. 30, 1897; McKenna to Patrick
Hayes, Nov. 11, 1897; McKenna to J. B. Rutherford, Nov. 12, 1897; Mc-
Kenna to P. H. Dorn, Superintendent, House of Correction, Cleveland, Ohio,
July 28, 1897; McKenna to Samuel W. Welch, Assistant United States At-
torney, Buffalo, New York, June 7, 1897.

[54] *Ibid.*, McKenna to J. W. French, Oct. 30, 1897; McKenna to M. Tanner,
Warden, Southern Illinois Penitentiary, July 24, 1897; McKenna to Patrick
Hayes, Warden, Kings County Penitentiary, Brooklyn, New York, July 6,
1897.

[55] *Ibid.*, McKenna to E. G. Coffin, Warden, Ohio Penitentiary, Columbus,
Ohio, Aug. 17, 1897.

[56] National Archives, Department of Justice, *File No. 11112–1897;* Mc-
Kenna to Nathan Thompson, Superintendent, House of Reformation, Chel-
tenham, Maryland, July 23, 1897 and July 28, 1897, contains the final
arrangements for transporting the prisoner. Henceforth this will be cited
as *D. J. File.*

competent medical practitioners, they were removed quickly to a federal insane asylum.[57] Although McKenna was solicitous and thoughtful, he never allowed the prisoners to impose upon him. He always insisted that proper forms be observed and precautions taken to prevent subterfuge or imaginary illnesses being used as a means for obtaining lenient treatment.[58]

McKenna's emphasis on the importance of following the letter of the law was well illustrated in his replies to petitions for legal opinion. He insisted that a legal opinion would be given only in answer to a query made by the head of an executive department; that the desired information relate to the business of the department; and that it apply to actual, not theoretical problems.[59] If

---

[57] *D. J. File No. 8518;* McKenna to S. J. Barrows, United States Commissioner, International Prison Commission, State Department, June 8, 1897, explains that it was usual for the court to give a certified copy of the evidence taken in judicial investigation of the insane. After which a request was made by the Attorney General to the Secretary of Interior for authority to transfer the prisoner to the Government Hospital for the insane at Washington. Upon receipt of such permission the inmate was placed in the custody of the hospital officials "there to be detained until restored to sanity or otherwise disposed of according to the law." Cf., *D. J. File No. 2256,* McKenna to J. W. French, Warden, United States Penitentiary, Fort Leavenworth, Sept. 1, 1897.

[58] *D. J. File No. 11013-1897,* McKenna to James H. Southard, Aug. 6, 1897, contains McKenna's refusal to permit a change in place of confinement because a medical examination had not revealed any serious cause of illness; *L.P.,* McKenna to P. H. Dorn, July 28, 1897, orders the examination of the prisoner by an authorized physician and demands that the latter's report together with all documents pertinent to prisoner's case be forwarded to the Department of Justice; *ibid.,* McKenna to E. F. Coffin, Warden, Ohio State Penitentiary, Columbus, Ohio, June 11, 1897, expresses dissatisfaction with simple statement of warden that two physicians had declared prisoners to be insane. McKenna insisted that each doctor "sign a certificate declaring that each is insane because the mere statement, as contained in the letter of the physicians referred to, does not, as you will observe, at all comply with the requirements." Cf., *D. J. File No. 2256–1897,* McKenna to J. W. French, June 11, 1897.

[59] National Archives, Department of Justice, Files of the Attorney General, *Opinions, Sept. 1897–Aug. 1898;* McKenna to Secretary of the Interior, Mar. 25, 1897; McKenna to Secretary of War, Mar. 13, 1897; McKenna to Secretary of Navy, Mar. 23, 1897; McKenna to Holmes Conrad, Solicitor General, Mar. 26, 1897. Henceforth cited as *Opinions.*

any of these requirements were missing, the petitioner received a sharply worded explanation of the Attorney General's duties in respect to furnishing legal advice to government officials.[60]

Among the most significant opinions which McKenna wrote as Attorney General was that on Section 22 of the Dingley Tariff. Two questions were asked of the Attorney General, first, whether the discriminating duty of 10 per cent provided for in Section 22 applied to an invoice of tea shipped from China to Vancouver in British vessels and thence through Canada to Chicago. The second question was whether discriminating duties could be assessed against a cargo of manganese ore from Chile, recently arrived in Philadelphia aboard a British vessel.[61]

McKenna held that imports coming from foreign countries via Canadian ports and foreign goods shipped from countries other than British possessions in British vessels were not subject to the discriminating duty of 10 per cent provided for in Section 22. In both cases the goods were carried on British ships entitled, by the practice of reciprocity, to equal privileges in our ports with American ships. If the additional tax were levied in the present cases it would be tantamount to declaring that Congress had abolished the practice of reciprocity. But such was contrary to the intention of Congress because subsequent to the passage of Section 22, Congress had reaffirmed its support of reciprocity by extending the powers of the President in that very matter.[62]

---

[60] *Opinions,* McKenna to Secretary of Navy, Mar. 13, 1897; McKenna to Secretary of War, Mar. 13, 1897, in which McKenna bolsters his position by citing four decisions of predecessors to demonstrate that he was justified in refusing a legal opinion in a theoretical case.

[61] *D. J. File, Attorney General No. 11957–97; 30 U. S. Statutes 209.*

[62] *D. J. File, Attorney General No. 11957–97* notes that McKenna quoted Payton V. Moseley, 3 Monroe, to the effect that acts relating to a subject, passed during the same session of Congress, should be construed as one act and " the presumption of sudden change or revolution in the minds of the legislators ought not to be indulged between the two provisions, to authorize a court to say that the latter had repealed the former." Under Section 22, McKenna ruled that goods imported via Canada were subject to the extra tax because they were classified as retail trade and were not the manufacture of a country contiguous to the United States. James A. Finch, *Digest of Official Opinions of the Attorney Generals of the United States, 1881–1906* (Washington: 1908), p. 156.

Another significant opinion written by McKenna was that concerning revocation of a license for a Catholic Chapel at West Point.   On April 2, 1897, Secretary of War Alger authorized the Roman Catholic Archbishop of New York, Michael A. Corrigan,[63] to build a chapel for the exclusive and perpetual use of Catholics. In his opinion McKenna cited several licenses for construction of churches issued under Sections 161 and 217 of the Revised Statutes.[64] He demonstrated that neither the language nor reasonable interpretation of either section justified issuance of the permits.   The only law which could justify the license in question was that of July 22, 1892 [65] and it only authorized leases for five

[63] Michael Augustine Corrigan (1839–1902) was born in Newark, New Jersey of Irish immigrant stock. A graduate of Mount St. Mary's College, Emmitsburg, Maryland, he became one of the first seminarians at the American College at Rome where he was ordained in 1863. Bishop of Newark from 1873 to 1880, he was made coadjutor with the right of succession to Archbishop McCloskey of New York in the latter year. Beginning in 1885 as Archbishop of New York he was confronted with many difficult problems among which was his controversy with Father McGlynn, an advocate of progressive social ideas and a staunch supporter of Henry George. The Corrigan-McGlynn dispute resulted in the latter's removal from his pastorate and excommunication from 1887–1892. In the latter year Father McGlynn was restored to his priestly functions as the result of an exoneration that followed an investigation of his teachings by four theologians of the Catholic University of America. The publicity which Archbishop Corrigan's difficulties received has led many to overlook the consummate skill and ability with which he conducted the affairs of his office. Richard J. Purcell, " Michael Augustine Corrigan," *Dictionary of American Biography,* V. I, 450–452.

[64] *Opinions,* pp. 75–76. Sect. 161 reads: " The head of each Department is authorized to prescribe regulations not inconsistent with law, for the government of his Department, the conduct of its officers and clerks, the distribution and performance of its business, and the custody, use and preservation of the records, papers, and property appertaining to it." Sect. 217 prescribes that: " The Secretary of War shall have the custody and charge of all the books, papers, furniture, fixtures and other property appertaining to the department."

[65] The act of July 22, 1892 reads: " That authority be and is hereby given to the Secretary of War, when in his discretion it will be for the public good, to lease, for a period not exceeding five years and revocable at any time, such property of the United States under his control as may not for the time be required for public use . . . and such leases shall be reported annually to Congress."

years. Therefore the element of permanency in the license issued to Archbishop Corrigan violated the five year limitation in the statute and the Secretary of War was not justified in committing the government to a contract of perpetuity.[66]

In dealing with cases involving Chinese, McKenna uniformly insisted on strict observance of the law. For example, ten Chinese, allegedly of American birth, who returned to the United States after being deported to Canada, were ordered re-deported by McKenna without any investigation of their asserted right to remain in this country.[67] Likewise in strict accord with the letter of the law was McKenna's decision denying re-admission of a Chinese unavoidably delayed in returning to the United States.[68] Although only three days late, due entirely to delays occasioned by Canadian quarantine authorities, McKenna decided that the Chinese had overstayed the twelve-month period permitted for visits to China and therefore could not be re-admitted to the United States. The law allowed no inquiry into the causes of delay nor justified extension of time. No exceptions were to be allowed because if the present opinion sanctioned a three day concession then one could easily " envisage the impracticability of enforcing the treaty if such inquiries are permitted." [69]

[66] *Opinions,* p. 81 : Among the sharpest critics of McKenna's action in the West Point matter was Father Peter C. Yorke of San Francisco who considered McKenna to be "a nice little man with as much backbone as a plate of mush. He is the real original jellyfish . . . He therefore can be used by a stronger. Evidently the necessities of the Republican Party demanded that peace should be made with the preachers. McKenna's motto in such a case, even as a Catholic, would be 'surrender everything in sight.'" Frederic R. Coudert, a prominent member of the New York bar, declared "It amazes me to think that a public official holding an office of such responsibility could render a decision which seeks to deprive a number of his fellow-citizens of a right which belongs to every citizen of this country." *San Francisco Monitor,* June 12, 1897; cf. *The Church News,* May 29, 1897. For an account of an interview between McKenna and Cardinal Gibbons in which the latter relieved the conscience of McKenna with the observation that he had only done his legal duty, see Duffield, *op. cit.,* pp. 28–29.

[67] *D. J. File A. G. No. 10709–1894.*

[68] *D. J. File Solicitor General No. 7888–1896.* This letter was signed by John K. Richards, Solicitor General and approved by McKenna, July 16, 1897.

[69] *Loc. cit.* For further opinions of McKenna on enforcement of the immi-

The most important action during the Attorney Generalship of McKenna was his foreclosure of the Union Pacific Railroad. The Union Pacific was chartered by the United States Government in 1862 to construct a line from the Missouri River westward to meet the Central Pacific building eastward from California. To facilitate construction the government loaned the railroad large sums of money and when the corporation failed to repay the loan, it was forced into bankruptcy. When McKenna became Attorney General, the railroad was in the hands of receivers and a syndicate had been organized to bid on the property when it should be sold.[70] The United States held liens on the railroad which with interest amounted to about $58,000,000.

During the incumbency of McKenna's predecessor, Attorney General Judson Harmon, the United States had taken steps to foreclose its liens,[71] which were junior in first mortgages. The re-

---

gration laws, see *D. J. File A. G. No. 11247–97; D. J. File A. G. No. 2039– 1897;* and *D. J. File A. G. No. 10709–1894.*

[70] *D. J. Attorney General's Executive and Congressional Letter Book,* Vol. 30, McKenna to the President of the Senate, Mar. 22, 1897, is a reply to the Senate's request for information concerning the negotiations on the Union Pacific suit; cf., *Senate Doc. 83,* 54th Cong. 2nd Session, recites in great detail the history of this litigation; a copy of a number of the legal documents may be found in *D. J. Mail and Files Division No. 1203, " Union Pacific Indebtedness No. 9, 1900–1909,"* one of which notes, " the Union Pacific passed into the hands of receivers and became notoriously insolvent." A summary of the legal proceedings is in *D. J. Attorney General's Executive and Congressional Letter Book,* Vol. 33, McKenna to President of the Senate, Jan. 5, 1898. For the motives which prompted the institution of the suit, see *New York Herald,* Sept. 30, 1897; *San Francisco Examiner,* Sept. 7, 1897; *D. J. Mail and Files Division, File No. 1203–87,* contains a letter from George Hoadly to Attorney General Judson Harmon, July 16, 1896, in which the former contended that President Cleveland's action against the Union Pacific put " the administration in a pretty good position as against any complaint which populists might see fit to make." The members of the syndicate were General Louis Fitzgerald, President of the Mercantile Trust Co., Jacob H. Schiff, President of Kuhn, Loeb and Co., Chauncey Depew, representative of the Vanderbilt interests, and Marvin Hughitt, president of the Chicago & Northwestern Railroad. *Brooklyn Daily Eagle,* Oct. 18, 1897.

[71] As special assistant to the Attorney General in charge of the Union Pacific suit, President Cleveland appointed George Hoadly, Democratic governor of Ohio, 1883–1885. Hoadly continued to direct the government's

organization committee of the syndicate had guaranteed a bid of $45,000,000 over and above the first mortgages and the case came on for hearing before Judge Walter H. Sanborn at an informal session in Boston in June, 1897,[72] Sanborn rendered a decree of foreclosure for the United States, but to the disappointment of George Hoadly, special counsel for the government, the court pronounced a mortgage of over a million dollars on the Omaha bridge to be superior to the liens of the United States.[73]  Furthermore, it

case under McKenna. For further information on the history of the case prior to Mar. 1897, see *Senate Doc. 10,* 55th Cong. 1st session; *D. J. Attorney General's Executive and Congresional Letter Book,* Vol. 33, McKenna to President of the Senate, Jan. 5, 1898.

[72] *D. J. File A. G. No. 1203–1887,* Winslow S. Pierce (agent of the syndicate) to Judson Harmon, July 1, 1896. For the attempt of the government to increase the bid, see *ibid.,* Hoadly to Harmon, Jan. 15, 1897 which, after noting that Pierce had quoted the figure of $45,000,000, continues, " I believe him because it is the same figure that I have always heard from the beginning and . . . when we tried to get a raise, we failed—so badly . . . that it was the best that could be done." Hoadly protested that although his words might make it appear that he was making himself the advocate of the Reorganization Committee yet such was not his intention. He believed that if there was any possibility of enlarging the bid he would " stand for it strenuously." Judson Harmon to Cleveland, July 23, 1896 assured the President that " all who were familiar with the subject favored the acceptance of the bid. Cf., *D. J. File A. G. No. 1939–1897,* J. H. N. Patrick to Harmon, telegram, Jan. 4, 1897; *D. J. File A. G. No. 1203–1887,* E. Ellery Anderson to Harmon, Jan. 16, 1897; *ibid.,* contains a copy of the " Union Pacific Railway Co. Report of the Government Directors to the Secretary of the Interior." This document embodies a description of the attempts made in Congress to settle the Union Pacific indebtedness. It also enumerates several reasons for accepting $45,000,000 as a just price for the Government's lien against the Union Pacific; Hoadly to McKenna, Mar. 20, 1897; Hoadly to Harmon, Feb. 20, 1897; Feb. 17, 1897 and Mar. 1, 1897.

[73] For the details of the negotiations between Mar. 4, 1897 and June 1, 1897, consult *D. J. File A. G. No. 1203–1887,* John C. Coombs to McKenna, Mar. 5, 1897, May 12, 1897; H. W. Rosenbaum to President McKinley, Mar. 29, 1897, suggests that time be given in order to form another syndicate because the plan of the Reorganization Committee was " so unfair and unjust" that it will create a great scandal and bring discredit upon the administration; cf., *San Francisco Examiner,* Sept. 7, 1897; *D. J. Mail and Files Division, Union Pacific Indebtedness No. 5,* 1897; Josiah Reiff to President McKinley, July 15, 1897; Hoadly to McKenna, Mar. 20, 1897, encloses a copy of all correspondence pertinent to the commencement of the

was decreed that cash assets of two million dollars in the hands of the receivers should be sold along with the physical property of the railroad as integral parts thereof. This holding, of course, gave the committee two million dollars without additional payment, which they had not thought to get so easily. The government, under the close direction of McKenna, immediately prepared to take an appeal. However, the appeal was waived on the committee's undertaking to bid $50,000,000 at the foreclosure and the sale was set for November 1, 1897.[74]

The syndicate, who from the indication of the evidence, expected a large profit from its purchase, were confident that all details for their purchase were completed when McKenna announced that the United States had waived none of its rights except that of appeal and was prepared to protect its interests. A week before the foreclosure sale McKenna announced that he intended to seek a postponement of the sale until after Congress convened.[75] McKenna had intimated that the Government itself

---

foreclosure. Hoadly wrote "my purpose is to communicate to you all the information which is within my reach so as to enable you to have the same survey of the situation which your predecessor possessed." E. Ellery Anderson to McKenna, Mar. 20, 1897; Hoadly to McKenna Mar. 24, Apr. 8, 20, 21, 26, 30, May 3, 6, 8, 10, 12, 14, 1897. The letter of May 10, 1897 summarizes the principal events in the development of the Drexel–Morgan control over the Union Pacific after the railroad passed into the hands of receivers; cf., May 24, 1893; telegrams Hoadly to McKenna, May 22, 24, 25, 1897.

[74] *Op. cit.*, Hoadly to McKenna, Sept. 1, 1897, in which the writer reveals that, "The first thought that came to my mind . . . was to congratulate you upon your personal triumph in inducing the committee to increase its bid."

[75] For information on the opposition to the sale of the Union Pacific at less than $58,000,000, consult *D. J. File A. G. Union Pacific Indebtedness No. 6–1897;* Herbert C. Smith to McKenna, Oct. 16, 1897, encloses a twenty page discussion on the benefits of government ownership of the Union Pacific; ten men from Winchester, Mass., to McKenna Oct. 13, 1897; L. C. Blaisdell to McKenna, Sept. 30, 1897; J. C. Reiff to McKenna, Oct. 16, 1897, sent clippings from the *New York World, New York Herald, New York Journal* for Sept. 30, 1897 and remarks that it would be interesting to know by what authority the administration consented to accept anything less than the full amount of principal and interest without the consent of Congress; *Letter Press Copies of the Attorney General, Miscellaneous,* Vol. 81, McKenna to Hoadly, Oct. 22, 1897; *Town Topic Financial Bureau,* Oct. 26,

would bid on the Kansas Pacific, a subsidiary of the Union Pacific, if its sale were postponed, and none doubted his intention to do the same on the Union Pacific. The result was gratifying; the Reorganization Committee promptly guaranteed a bid which would cover the full amount of the government liens, principal and interest, if McKenna would allow the sale to be held on schedule.[76] The Attorney General accepted the offer and the sale took place on November 1, 1897.[77]

Joseph McKenna's accomplishments as Attorney General were such as demanded a considerable amount of courage, delicacy and skill and it was with some justification that he was rewarded with praise and commendation for his efforts. In spite of his reputation as a hard-working executive, it could be said that he spent,

---

1897; *Brooklyn Daily Eagle*, Oct. 18, 1897; *New York Journal*, Oct. 15, 1897, carries a cartoon of McKenna in the act of shovelling twenty million dollars of government funds into a sack held by J. P. Morgan and C. P. Huntington; *D. J. File A. G. Union Pacific Indebtedness No. 6–1897, 1203–87A*, telegrams Pierce to McKenna, Oct. 22, 1:06 P. M.; Hoadly to McKenna Oct. 22, 2:15 P. M.; McKenna to Pierce, Oct. 22, 3:00 P. M.; McKenna to Hoadly, Oct. 22, 3:05 P. M.; Hoadly to McKenna, Oct. 22, 5:34 P. M.; Hoadly to McKenna, Oct. 22, 5:55 P. M. These communications convey some of the anxiety experienced by McKenna in his desire to obtain the full amount of $58,000,000 owed to the United States.

[76] *Ibid.*, telegram, Pierce to McKenna, Oct. 25, 1897. One reason for the willingness of the syndicate to pay the full amount was the fear that a group of English capitalists would bid $58,000,000 and get control of the railroad. For information on the English opposition, see *ibid.*, Boies Penrose to McKenna, Oct. 25, 1897; McKenna to William Osborne, Consul General of the United States in London, Oct. 23, 1897; Andrews Orne to McKenna, Oct. 22, 1897, furnishes details of the plan proposed by the English financiers; Osborne to McKenna, cable, Oct. 25, 1897; Thompson to McKenna, Oct. 26, 1897.

[77] *New York Tribune*, Nov. 2, 1897, p. 4, describes the scene and events of the sale; *D. J. File A. G. Union Pacific Indebtedness No. 6—1897 1203–87A*, Cowin to McKenna, Nov. 1, 1897 notes that the bid on the railroad property was $39,800,000, the bid on the sinking fund was $12,645,000 and the cash $4,500,000 making an aggregate of $58,000,000. General Fitzgerald of the Reorganization Committee assured Cowin that readjustment could easily be made to meet the exact amount of the government lien. H. W. Rosenbaum to President McKinley, Jan. 11, 1898, estimated that the Reorganization Committee had profited to the extent of at least $20,000,000.

if not wasted, too much time in minutiae.[78]  His zeal for exactness
and compliance with trivial regulations became almost a pursuit
of the picayune and consequently detracted from his effectiveness
as an administrator.  Nevertheless he was regarded as the " hard-
est working Attorney General since Garland," [79] and devoted so
much time to his official duties that some of the Department of
Justice officials wondered why " he did not sleep in his office." [80]
McKenna's satisfactory administration of the Department of
Justice together with his warm personal friendship with President
McKinley contributed in a large measure to make him the logical
successor of United States Supreme Court Justice Stephen J.
Field of California who resigned from the bench in December,
1897.

On the resignation of Justice Stephen J. Field, President
McKinley nominated his friend McKenna as an associate Justice
of the Supreme Court (December 16, 1897) in the belief that he
was the most available sectional appointee.  It was intimated by
some Republican leaders that this had been anticipated for several
weeks and that it offered a means of relieving the administration
from a source of some anxiety.[81]  The nomination met with no
enthusiasm.  However, Republican Senators had no desire to

---

[78] *D. J. Letter-Press Copies of the Attorney General,* McKenna to E. L.
Hall, former United States Marshal, Santa Fe, New Mexico, Aug. 7, 1897,
demands that Hall make an exact account of expenses sustained from Mar.
28, to June 30, 1897, while engaged in pursuit of " Black Jack's gang of
desperadoes."  McKenna wished to know why Hall had not stated the price
of the first and last meals or " the charges for subsistence from dinner April
12th, to and including lodging, April 16, is $10.85.  As deputy marshals are
limited to $2.00 per day for subsistence, it will be necessary to furnish good
grounds for the above charge before a greater amount than $7.50 will be
allowed."  Other insignificant matters are the subject of letters from Mc-
Kenna to E. H. Bergmann, Warden, New Mexico Penitentiary; McKenna to
George Pfeiffer, former United States Marshal at Trenton, New Jersey,
Dec. 6, 1897; McKenna to Carter, Rice & Co., Dec. 29, 1897; McKenna to
E. J. Brooks, Dec. 29, 1897; McKenna to Herman Baumgarten, Dec. 17,
1897; McKenna to Messrs. Powers and Lyons, Dec. 17, 1897.

[79] *Brown Scrapbook,* newspaper clipping, n.n.; n.d.

[80] *San Francisco Call,* June 7, 1897.

[81] *New York Times,* Oct. 14, 15, Dec. 17, 1897; *Congressional Record,* 55th
*Congress,* 2nd Session, XXXI, 206.

appear critical of the President by voicing open and futile opposition.  Lawyers and judges in Portland and in San Francisco petitioned against the anticipated appointment before McKenna was
actually named.  He was described as " a small man in every way
and a cunning trimmer." [82]  A typical and careful Republican
Senator who preferred to be quoted anonymously maintained:

> It is the weakest nomination for the Supreme Court that
> has been offered to the Senate in many years, certainly
> the weakest in my recollection.[83]

However, there was little fear of the Nativist protests of the
violent but waning American Protective Association.  Indeed
there was a general belief that any such intolerant opposition might
be advantageous to McKenna when it came to a senatorial vote.
There was considerable opposition because of his railroad con-
nections, his conservative views, the rivalry of the Northern Pacific and Southern Pacific Railroads, and the hostility of certain
lawyers on the Pacific Coast who may not have been without
personal ambitions.[84]

While he was charged with insufficient legal attainments and
inherent vacillation or uncertainty, McKenna's decisions on the
Circuit Court were rarely reversed on appeal to the Supreme
Court, certainly not more than those of other judges of the Circuit
Court, according to Senator George C. Perkins of California
(Leland Stanford's successor) who spoke in defense of the appointment.  It was also charged before the Committee on the Judiciary that as Attorney General he had been " too reserved and
seclusive " with those who had important official business with his
office, due probably to a naturally reticent disposition.  As a recent
compiler of a slim volume on the Supreme Court has maintained
with some justification: " McKenna's being a Catholic did little to
popularize him with the Senate." [85]  Finally cleared by the Judi-

---

[82] *San Francisco Examiner,* Dec. 3, 4, 6, 1897.

[83] *New York Times,* Dec. 17, 1897.

[84] Davenport Brown, personal interview, January 4, 1944.

[85] Cortez Ewing, *Judges of the Supreme Court, 1789–1937* (Minneapolis,
1938), p. 124; cf., Sister M. Carolyn Klinkhamer, *Edward Douglas White,
Chief Justice of the United States* (Washington, 1944), p. 60.

ciary Committee, the nomination was considered in executive session. It was then that Senator William V. Allen of Nebraska, an aggressive Populist, spoke in opposition for three hours as he read at length resolutions and letters of protest from the Pacific Coast.[86] The Senate, however, unanimously confirmed the nomination (January 21, 1898).[87]

McKenna sat tight and stood on his record as he observed that the opposition of some men to his appointment might be expected and their motives might easily be guessed. In the meantime, he was said to have read some law at Columbia University. Five days after his confirmation, Justice McKenna was inducted in a ceremony requiring four minutes.

Thus he commenced a career of twenty-seven years on the Supreme Court where he evidenced loyal and fraternal responsibility, took special pride in the Court, and wrote some six hundred and fifty-six opinions.[88] His colleagues placed confidence in his uprightness and his independent ability suggested by his union with Justice Holmes in some dissents and he was frequently designated by various Chief Justices to write the Court's opinions in important cases under the Sherman Act, in insular matters, and involving taxation. Reasonably favorable to organized labor and rather nationalistic in his recognition of the growing federal power over men, States, and private business, he was regarded as somewhat slow in his mental processes, confused in his logic and lacking an easily definable legal philosophy, though the friendly testimonial of his brethren on his retirement generously described his style as characterized by clearness, force, and a grace of touch and aptness of phrase which stimulated a reader's interest.

---

[86] *New York Times,* Jan. 22, 1898.
[87] *Congressional Record,* XXXI, 824.
[88] United States Supreme Court *Reports,* Vols. 170–266.

# CHAPTER V

## McKENNA ON DUE PROCESS

The aim of the Fourteenth Amendment was to protect the civil rights of Negroes, but the realization of that purpose has not been achieved. On the other hand the Fourteenth Amendment, as a protection of property, has attained a role inferior to few others in the Constitution. Its general applications have not been challenged often; rather it has 'been questions of degree that the Supreme Court has been called upon to decide. Although the protective clauses of the Fourteenth Amendment have been invoked repeatedly and numerous decisions of moment have been written under its authority, yet the elementary conception of its scope has remained unchanged since the *Slaughter-house* and *Civil Rights* decisions in the last quarter of the nineteenth century.

In construing the Fourteenth Amendment, the Court has made it clear that the fundamental principles of the Constitution have remained unchanged, that the power of Congress was not extended over subject matter heretofore reserved to the States and the rights and privileges of citizens of the United States were not increased either in number or extent. However, the Fourteenth Amendment did amplify the power of the Federal Judiciary in reviewing the acts of the State legislatures and courts.

During his career on the Supreme Court, Justice McKenna made over one hundred opinions in which the due process clause was involved yet he never ventured to define the term. Rather he predicted that a precise definition of due process would never be framed. Instead of judging cases according to a preconceived standard of due process, Justice McKenna was wont to insist that the issue be decided in accordance with good sense and the general understanding of mankind. He had little patience with far-fetched and impractical applications of the Amendment and always insisted that the challenged law was constitutional unless it actually deprived one of acknowledged rights or property.[1] The duty of the Court, according to Justice McKenna, was to apply its conception of the due process clause in each case so that the rights of the citizen would be protected against arbitrary and unreasonable State action, yet without infringing upon the police power of the State.

One of the most frequent charges of unreasonable State action concerned the exercise of the taxing power. Practically any form of taxation could be condemned as appropriation without due process, if the meaning of that term were sufficiently expanded. Hence it was the degree to which the due process clause could be extended that became the point at issue. Although the Court was constantly criticized for the narrow interpretation which it gave due process, there were relatively few tax laws condemned on this score during Justice McKenna's term.[2] He and his brethren repeatedly rejected frivolous arguments of alleged sufferers and allowed the States to obtain revenue in any way that was reasonable and just.

Justice McKenna was persuaded that a plethora of taxation cases would flood the court calendar if trivial reasons were permitted to nullify State action. Consequently he never condemned tax legislation except for serious and manifest reasons. In a quotation from his fellow-Californian, Justice Field,[3] he informed petitioners that the Court was not to be considered as

---

[1] *Orient Insurance Co. v. Daggs,* 172 U. S. 559 (Jan. 16, 1899) ; *New York Life Insurance Co. v. Cravens,* 178 U. S. 389 (May 28, 1900) ; *Flannigan v. Sierra County,* 196 U. S. 553 (Feb. 20, 1905) ; *Bacon v. Walker,* 204 U. S. 311 (Feb. 4, 1907) ; *Bradford v. U. S.,* 228 U. S. 446 (Apr. 28, 1913) ; *Chicago Dock and Canal Co. v. Fraley* (May 26, 1913).

[2] Charles Warren, " The Progressiveness of the United States Supreme Court," *Columbia Law Review,* XIII (Dec. 1913), 294.

[3] Justice Stephen Johnson Field (1816–1898), born in Connecticut, admitted to the bar and went to California in 1849. He established a law office in Marysville, a mining town in the northern part of the State. In reward for his part in keeping California in the Union, President Lincoln appointed him to the tenth seat on the United States Supreme Court March 10, 1863. One of the most dramatic incidents in his life was the fatal shooting of David S. Terry by Field's bodyguard when the former attempted to assassinate Field. Lapsing into senility near the end of his life, Justice Field submitted his resignation to President McKinley in April, 1897, on condition that it would

a harbor in which can be found a refuge from ill-advised, unequal and oppressive state legislation or that a hardship, impolicy or injustice of state laws is necessarily an objection to their constitutionality.[4]

Justice McKenna held that the Fourteenth Amendment did not compel the States to " adopt an iron rule of taxation "[5] or in the language of Justice Bradley

All such regulations . . . so long as they proceed within reasonable limits and general usage, are within the discretion of the State legislature, or the people of the State framing their constitution.[6]

Justice McKenna's practice of solving taxation cases by applying the fundamental rules of good sense, reason and the universal understanding of man was well illustrated in his opinion in *Ballard v. Hunter*.[7] The litigation involved the foreclosure and sale of property for delinquent taxes. McKenna rejected the plaintiff's claim that he had been deprived of his property because he had not received proper notice of foreclosure.

In an opinion characterized by an extended and technical treatment of the subject, Justice McKenna asserted that since it was usual for men to be familiar with legislation adversely affecting their property, complainant was not entitled to relief. The custom of proprietors to keep abreast of tax measures was so widespread that it had become a rational basis upon which the legislature

---

not become effective until the following December when his term of office would have been two months longer than that of Chief Justice John Marshall. Edward S. Corwin, " Stephen J. Field," *Dictionary of American Biography,* VI, 372. For a more extensive treatment see Carl B. Swisher, *Stephen J. Field, Craftsman of the Law* (Washington: 1930), pp. 5, 21, 26, 29, 116, 348, 442.

[4] 170 U. S. 293. The statement of Justice Field was from *Mobile County v. Kimball.*

[5] *Magoun v. Illinois Trust and Savings Bank,* 170 U. S. 283.

[6] *Bell's Gap Railroad v. Pennsylvania,* 134 U. S. 232, quoted at 170 U. S. 295. For the significance of the opinion of Justice McKenna, see Thomas Reed Powell, " Extra-Territorial Inheritance Taxation," *Columbia Law Review,* XX (Dec. 1920), 8.

[7] *Ballard v. Hunter,* 204 U. S. 241 (Jan. 14, 1907).

might erect laws. Indeed it was imperative for the law-making body to accept such a hypothesis if " it would give efficiency to many of its activities."

It was to long standing practice, embedded in the common law, that McKenna again appealed in sustaining the Illinois Graduated Inheritance Tax.[8] Appellants, evidently despairing of persuading the Court that the tax deprived them of property without due process, claimed that they were denied equal protection of the laws. In the challenged statute, the first of its kind to be brought before the Court, the amount of tax was proportioned to the degree of relationship between the legatee and the testator and to the amount of the legacy. The first classification rested on manifest natural grounds while the second was based on economic principles long recognized by many countries.

The two principles which Justice McKenna employed in justifying the tax were: first, that it was a levy upon the right of succession and not upon property and, secondly, that the right to take property by devise or descent was not a natural right but one created or bestowed by the State. He considered that the first principle was easily acceptable but went into minute detail to explain the civil origin of the right of inheritance. He bolstered his thesis with numerous citations and lengthy quotations, yet was loath to admit the logical conclusion of his premise, namely, that if the State could create the right of inheritance, it could abolish that right.

Legislatures, according to this reasoning, possessed an absolute right over hereditaments and, if they so elected, could cause all estates to escheat.[9] It was this implied conclusion that prompted

---

[8] 170 U. S. 283.

[9] McKenna's contention that the right of inheritance was derived from the State was well supported by legal precedent, the only reported case in the United States specifically upholding the argument that inheritance was a natural right is *Nunnemacher v. Wisconsin*. The court in this case stated that the number of opinions to the contrary were only paralleled by the paucity of their thought. *Lawyers' Reports Annotated* (Rochester: 1907), IX, 121; for a list of cases supporting the view of McKenna, see *ibid.*, XLVIII, 1004. The natural law theory is presented by James T. Connor, " The Nature of Succession," *Fordham Law Review*, VIII (May, 1939), 151; Samuel Bornstein, " Statutes as the Source of Title in Descent and

Justice Brewer to write a vigorous dissent in which he maintained that the right of inheritance had its origin in the law of nature. He argued that a man had a responsibility to provide for his offspring not only during his own lifetime but also as far as possible after his death. Social progress and the stability of social institutions demanded protection for the right to transmit as well as the right to own property. Justice Brewer concluded

> the State may regulate, but has no arbitrary power in the matter. The property of a decedent does not at his death become the property of the State, nor subject to its disposal according to any mere whim or fancy.[10]

It was evident that Justice Brewer's dissent had some effect on Justice McKenna, for, eight years later, in two significant opinions on inheritance taxes, *Cahen v. Brewster* [11] and *Board of Education of the Methodist Episcopal Church v. Illinois,*[12] Justice McKenna based his argument solely on the power of the State to regulate the right of inheritance. There was some evidence that he had abandoned his position on the absolute right of the State over inheritances for he was careful to warn that challenged inheritance tax laws would be sustained only " if they had a reasonable regard to purposes of State and its legislation." [13]

---

Distribution in Wills," *Boston Law Review,* XV (Jan. 1935), 205; Charles Haines, " The Law of Nature in State and Federal Decisions," *Yale Law Journal,* XXV (June, 1916), 617; Edward S. Corwin, " The 'Higher Law' Background of American Constitutional Law," *Harvard Law Review,* XLII (Mar. 1929), 380.

[10] 170 U. S. 302. Justice Brewer's dissent supported a later dictum of McKenna's that due process " must not work a denial of fundamental rights." Haines, *op. cit.,* p. 634. For further comment on McKenna's decision, see *Chicago Legal News,* May 7, 1898; Thomas R. Powell, " Extra Territorial Inheritance Taxation," *Columbia Law Review,* XX (Jan. 1920), 8; " Recent Cases," *Harvard Law Review,* XII (Jan. 1898), 128.

[11] 203 U. S. 543 (Dec. 24, 1906).

[12] 203 U. S. 553 (Dec. 24, 1906). The principle enunciated was considered by some authors as a reliable guide to State action in framing inheritance taxes; Rodney L. Mott, *Due Process of Law* (Indianapolis: 1926), p. 376. In discussing the background of inheritance taxes, McKenna demonstrated that it was an ancient form of exaction and was equitable since there was no discrimination within a class.

[13] 203 U. S. 563.

If read alone, the Magoun decision might lead to the belief that Justice McKenna belonged to the Austinian school, but his expressions in the latter cases and his uniform opposition to confiscatory taxes belie such a conclusion.[14]

Additional weight to support the contention that Justice McKenna believed that the right of property, together with its transmission, had its source in the law of nature, rather than in the law of the state, was found in his rigid adherence to the principle that due process required compensation for property taken for public use. It was this doctrine that lay at the basis of his demand that assessments for public improvements be proportioned to the benefits received. That the property owner was to pay only for that portion of a public improvement which increased the value of his land was clearly explained by Justice McKenna in *Voight v. Detroit* [15] where he maintained that all the essentials of due process were found in that part of the contested statute which provided

> The amount of the benefit thus ascertained shall be assessed upon the owners or occupants of such taxable real estate, in proportion, as nearly as may be, to the advan-

---

[14] The Austinian School was named after an English jurist, John Austin, who maintained that political sovereignty was legally unlimited. The basis for this theory rests on two postulates, namely the State was superior to all other societies and the State had the physical power to compel all individuals and societies to obey its orders. John Austin (1790–1859) was born at Creeting Mill, Suffolk, England. Life-long friend of John Stuart Mill, Jeremy Bentham and Thomas Carlyle, Austin was a failure in law practice and teaching and when he turned to writing on the law he was equally unsuccessful. It was only after his death that attention was given to his *Province of Jurisprudence* and to the collection edited by his wife, *Austin's Introduction to Lectures on Jurisprudence.* John Macdonnell, "John Austin," *Dictionary of National Biography* I, 737–740.

[15] 184 U. S. 115 (Feb. 24, 1902). In this opinion McKenna repeated that if complainant had asserted and proved excessive taxation, relief would have been granted. In a similar case, *King v. Portland City,* 184 U. S. 61 (Jan. 27, 1902), he noted with evident satisfaction, "under the rule of the charter the opening and grading of streets has been done for years and the court has been watchful against abuse, watchful to protect the rights of property owners."

tage which such lot, parcel, or subdivision is deemed to acquire by the improvement.[16]

Even when necessity demanded a drainage system, Justice McKenna refused to permit the taxation of property which derived no benefit therefrom.[17]   On this point he declared that to include areas not benefited in drainage districts for the purpose of increasing the value of other parcels of land within the district was an abuse of power and confiscation of property.[18]   It was only natural that he refused to subscribe to the view that the legislature was the final arbiter of benefit conferred by the public improvements.  For he declared

> the Constitution . . . forbids an exercise of that power that would put upon private property the cost of a public work in substantial excess of the special benefits accruing to it from such work.[19]

During the first quarter of the present century, the muckrakers and purveyors of the literature of exposure found a plethora of material in the facts behind the ill-gotten franchises of municipal water companies, the sharp practices of insurance firms and the unfair methods of industrial giants.  As a result

---

[16] 184 U. S. 122.

[17] *Myles Salt Co. v. Board of Commissioners,* 239 U. S. 478 (Jan. 10, 1916).  The land in question was an island whose elevation was higher than surrounding drainage district, and the island's problem was to prevent erosion from the high rate of drainage, rather than artificial drainage of the water. For a review of McKenna's arguments favoring the establishment of drainage districts, see *Weyerhauser v. Minnesota,* 176 U. S. 550 (Feb. 26, 1900) and *District of Columbia v. Brooke,* 214 U. S. 138 (May 17, 1909).

[18] McKenna was likewise in favor of establishing limitations on the national government through the Fifth Amendment similar to those placed on the States by the Fourteenth Amendment.  For the consistency of his position in this matter, see *French v. Asphalt Paving Co.,* 181 U. S. 324 (April 29, 1901) ; *Wight v. Davidson,* 181 U. S. 371 (Apr. 29, 1901) ; *Tonawanda v. Lyon,* 181 U. S. 389 (Apr. 29, 1901).  In the Tonawanda case, a unanimous Court through Justice Shiras declared that the purpose of the Fourteenth Amendment was to extend the same protection against arbitrary State legislation as was afforded by the Fifth Amendment against similar legislation by Congress.

[19] 181 U. S. 350.

there was scarcely a State whose statutes did not reflect popular discontent and which did not attempt to establish more effective control over public utilities. The corporations, however, would not passively accept State control, and their opposition was amply illustrated in State and Federal court records. A standard defense was the liberty to contract under shelter of the due process clause.

Freedom of contract was not viewed by Justice McKenna as an absolute right. The State might validly limit and under some circumstances entirely prohibit its exercise. In practically all of his opinions he emphasized the dependence of the corporation upon the will of the State legislature. He stated that the corporation was the creature of the State and must conform its activities to the prescriptions established by that sovereignty.

In the conflict between due process and contractual relations, Justice McKenna refused to recognize implied obligations in franchises. He based this refusal upon the fact that a municipality enjoyed authority only by permission of a State, its charter ordinarily specifying in minute fashion what it might do, might not do or agree to do. Hence contracts let by municipalities must meet definite and specific standards, not required in other agreements. It was characteristic of Justice McKenna to demand proof of an exact bi-lateral agreement before he would acknowledge that the government had relinquished or allocated its power of regulation. Where any doubt existed, he favored the claims of the grantor.

Thus one month after he had ascended to the Supreme Court, he spoke for all his brethren in *Detroit Citizens' Street Railway Company v. Detroit*[20] and refused to support complainant's right to monopolize tram service. The opinion itself, although one of the first that Justice McKenna wrote, embodied in fully developed fashion some of the elements of his conception of " judicial tolerance of legislative policy." The issue in the case was whether the power of the city to grant charters was original and hence as extensive as that of the State, or delegated and thus limited by the terms of the delegation.

---

[20] 171 U. S. 48 (May 23, 1898). For a discussion of this case and its background see Herbert Pope, "Municipal Contracts and the Regulation of Rates," *Harvard Law Review,* XVI (Nov. 1902), 13.

114 *Joseph McKenna*

In answering plaintiff, Justice McKenna discussed the background and the significance of principles which he afterwards was to make more familiar: that a municipality might possess the plenary right to grant charters and hence be kept strictly to its contract as in *Los Angeles v. Los Angeles Gas Corporation;* [21] that the Court should yield to the judgment of the legislature on the expediency of local legislation as in *Bedford v. Eastern Building and Loan Association;* [22] and that the opinion of the State court be accepted as final if not repugnant to the Constitution, as he decided in *Lower Vein Coal Company v. Industrial Board of Indiana.* [23]

The absence of an exact bi-lateral agreement was the fundamental reason which again prompted McKenna to deny the right of a monopoly to plaintiff in *Shawnee Sewerage and Drainage Company v. Stearns, as Mayor of the City of Shawnee.* [24] Plaintiff claimed exclusive right to dispose of city's sewage but McKenna supported the right of the municipality to distribute the business of disposal to various firms. He argued that since it was accepted that government could regulate private property devoted to public use, it was reasonable to permit government to regulate the services of public service corporations. So precious was the right of regulation that Justice McKenna believed that its engrossment by a private corporation

> could not be assumed on any trifling pretext . . . for the future should not be committed and bound by the conditions of the present time and functions delegated for public purposes be paralyzed in their exercise by the existence of exclusive privileges. [25]

A monopoly of public service was to be sustained by the Court only when explicitly granted in the charter or implied in the presence of so strong a probability of intention that it could not

---

[21] 251 U. S. 32 (Dec. 8, 1919). Justices Pitney and Clarke dissented without comment.
[22] 181 U. S. 227 (Apr. 22, 1901).
[23] 255 U. S. 144 (Feb. 28, 1921).
[24] 220 U. S. 462 (Apr. 10, 1911).
[25] 171 U. S. 51.

be supposed "any other purpose was in the mind of the grantor." [26] Or as he was to observe in *Owensboro v. Owensboro Water Company* [27]

> power of regulation is a power of government continuing in its nature and if it can be granted away at all, it can only be by words of positive grant . . . If there is reasonable doubt it must be resolved in favor of the existence of the power.

The need for clear and definite relinquishment of power by the municipality was reiterated by Justice McKenna in 1901, when contrary to the dissent of Justices White, Brewer, Brown and Peckham, he ruled in *Freeport Water Company v. Freeport* [28] that plaintiff could not monopolize water service in the city. Complainant claimed he received his charter in virtue of authority granted by the State to the municipality to contract for water during a stated period and " to fix the rates by ordinance." The pivotal point as seen by Justice McKenna, were the words " to fix the rates by ordinance," which he interpreted as a power reserved to the city and acknowledged by the corporation which accepted the franchise. In its simplest terms, the grant to the corporation implied that the city reserved the right to readjust rates from time to time as justice to both parties would demand. On the same basic principle Justice McKenna sustained the reserved right of regulation by the municipality in *Danville Water*

---

[26] 171 U. S. 53.

[27] 191 U. S. 358 (Nov. 30, 1903). Although it has been questioned whether the regulatory power might be delegated to a municipality, Justice McKenna supported the view it might be and found no objection in the fact that it made the municipality judge in its own case in that it prescribed the rates of the utility which the municipality consumed. Cf. *Los Angeles v. Los Angeles Water Co.,* 177 U. S. 558 (Apr. 30, 1900) in which McKenna ruled that the municipality violated its contract when it reduced the rates for water.

[28] 180 U. S. 587 (Mar. 25, 1901). McKenna decided two other cases on the same principles, *Danville Water Co. v. Danville,* 180 U. S. 619 (Mar. 25, 1901) and *Rogers Park Water Co. v. Fergus,* 180 U. S. 624 (Mar. 25, 1901). For a discussion of Chief Justice White's dissent, see Sister Marie Carolyn Klinkhamer, *Edward Douglas White, Chief Justice of the United States* (Washington: 1943), pp. 148–150. For a critical evaluation of McKenna's opinion, see Pope, *op. cit.,* pp. 1–21.

*Company v. Danville*[29] and *Rogers Park Water Company v. Fergus.*[30]

Another application of the principle that only an explicit grant deprived a municipality of its right of regulation was found in McKenna's opinion in *City of Joplin v. Southwest Missouri Light Company.*[31] In this case he ruled that a municipality did not preclude itself from operating an electric plant merely because it had given a franchise to a corporation to do the same thing. The unreasonableness of complainant's position was demonstrated when McKenna noted that plaintiff had conceded the city had not exhausted its power to confer franchises but might invest one in some party other than plaintiff. In other words the city would create a private competitor but could not become a competitor itself.

The complaints of public service corporations against regulation of rates made little impression on Justice McKenna. He required the corporations to establish unquestionable evidence that the regulation was illegal and prevented a fair return. To declare legislative classification unconstitutional it was necessary to prove discrimination existed in the same class. The mere existence of discrimination among different classes was not sufficient to make a statute unconstitutional under the Fourteenth Amendment. In questions of a discriminatory law, the duty of the Court was not to condemn the discrimination *per se* but to discover whether or not there was a rational ground for the discrimination.[32]

[29] 180 U. S. 619.
[30] 180 U. S. 624.
[31] 191 U. S. 350 (Nov. 16, 1903).
[32] In *Muhlker v. New York and Harlem Railroad Co.,* 197 U. S. 544 (April 10, 1905), and in *Sauer v. City of New York,* 206 U. S. 536 (May 27, 1907) McKenna condemned statutes which deprived abutting property owners of easements without compensation. Piqued at the majority opinion in the latter case, he declared that he was not insensible to the strength of their reasoning "But certainly all lawyers would not assent to it. . . . At times there seems to be an antithesis between legal sense and common sense." For a discussion of the Muhlker case, see Frank M. Cobb, " Maximum Rates and Rate Regulation," *Harvard Law Review,* XXI (Jan. 1908), 184; Charles E. Carpenter, " Court Decisions and the Common Law," *Columbia Law Review,* XVII (Nov. 1917), 605; Robert H. Freeman, " Retroactive Operation of Decisions," *Columbia Law Review,* XVIII (Mar. 1918) 237; Wilbur

Justice McKenna's favorable attitude toward the regulation of public service corporations had much in common with his policy in respect to public businesses. Until McKenna's decision in *German Alliance Insurance Company v. Lewis* [33] in 1914, all callings designated as " public businesses " were related, directly or indirectly, to transportation. In the common law common carriers were the first to be termed " public businesses " and with them as a nucleus, the list of public businesses increased simply by adding those related to transportation, such as the transportation of water, gas, electricity, and intelligence through ditch, pipe, and wire.[34] To be classified as a public business subjected the corporation to stricter public control than those businesses not so identified.

In the German Alliance case, McKenna sustained a State law which regulated insurance rates. To justify this conclusion McKenna argued that since insurance was endowed with a public interest it could be recognized as a public business and as such subject to government control. Inasmuch as insurance had no relation with transportation its designation as a public business was an innovation.

---

Larremore, " Stare Decisis and Contractual Rights," *Harvard Law Review,* XXII (Jan. 1909), 182–189.

[33] 233 U. S. 389 (Apr. 20, 1914). Gustavus H. Robinson, " Public Utility Concept in American Law," *Harvard Law Review,* XLI (Jan. 1928), 281, 288; Edwin W. Patterson, " The Transfer of Insured Property in German and American Law," *Columbia Law Review,* XXIX (June, 1929), 698; Norman F. Arterburn, " The Origin and First Test of Public Callings," *University of Pennsylvania Law Review,* LXXV (June, 1927), 411; Breck P. McAllister, " Lord Hale and Business Affected with a Public Interest," *Harvard Law Review,* XLIII (Mar. 1930), 771–2; Samuel C. Wiel, " Public Service Irrigation Companies," *Columbia Law Review,* XVI (Jan. 1916), 44. John B. Cheadle, " Government Control of Business," *Columbia Law Review,* XX (May, 1920), 571; Maurice Finkelstein, " From Munn v. Illinois to Tyson v. Banton: A Study in the Judicial Process," *Columbia Law Review,* XXVII (Nov. 1927), 778; Alfred Hayes, " Partial Unconstitutionality with special reference to the Corporation," *Columbia Law Review,* XI (Jan. 1911), 129.

[34] 233 U. S. 426. Chief Justice White and Justice Van Devanter joined the dissent of Justice Lamar. They claimed insurance was not connected with transportation therefore should not be classified as a public business.

McKenna justified the classification of insurance as a public business and thus subject to regulation on the grounds that such regulation was imperative if government was to keep abreast of social and economic development. Numerous examples of state regulation of businesses, clothed with a public interest, demonstrated that the supervision of insurance was not revolutionary, but was necessary for the stability and welfare of society and was the universal desire of reasonable men. It could not be denied that

> a conception so general cannot be without cause. The universal sense of a people cannot be accidental; its persistence saves it from the charge of unconsidered impulse, and its estimate of insurance has substantial basis.[35]

This was a demonstration of a liberality of mind not generally associated with the era in which McKenna lived, an attitude which showed the man in sympathetic contact with the social problems of his time and anxious to solve them, even if he had to change long-established legal traditions.

Justice McKenna had made public realism, not historical practice, the basis for determining the distinction between private and public businesses. The wide latitude which McKenna's criterion permitted, at first sight, might appear to justify the fears of the dissenters. Yet a study of the method of McKenna's approach to the problem gives concrete evidence of the advantages of such a standard. That his thought was sound and his conclusion justified has been amply demonstrated by the practice of the Court in following his reasoning.

Justice Lamar's dissent on the grounds that the extension of regulatory powers had gone too far and that the principle was to have a " far-reaching effect " was realized by McKenna himself six months later.[36]  In the *Pipe Line Cases*,[37] Justice Holmes,

---

[35] 233 U. S. 412.

[36] *Tyson Brothers v. Banton,* 273 U. S. 418 (Feb. 28, 1927), was decided by a majority represented by Justice Sutherland who noted that McKenna's opinion was the "extreme limit to which this Court thus far has gone in sustaining price fixing legislation." Cf. Finkelstein, *op. cit.,* pp. 769–783.

[37] *United States v. Ohio Oil Co.,* 234 U. S. 548 (Oct. 15, 16, 1913); Felix

speaking for the majority, upheld an order of the Interstate Commerce Commission which compelled private pipe lines to carry the oil of competitors at specified rates. The regulation was upheld on the principle which Justice McKenna had enunciated in the German Alliance case, namely that a business endowed with a public interest was a public business and subject to regulation. Like a State legislature, Congress, within its field, might regulate any business having a " broad and definite public interest " or which operated to the detriment of the public under the guise of a purely private business.

In dissenting to Justice Holmes' opinion, McKenna insisted that his reasoning in the German Alliance case could not be construed to mean that the nature of the Government's power over a public carrier was essentially different from that over any other business that vitally affected the public interests. Even if it be admitted that the pipe line affected the public interest, yet, inasmuch as it was not employed in carrying oil for others as a business, it lacked the essentials of a public service company. McKenna explained that the practical result of the Holmes decision was to offer the pipe line owners the option of either serving the public in a capacity of a common carrier or of abandoning their business. Such compulsion had all the characteristics of taking property without compensation. It was conceivable for Congress to close the channels of interstate trade to an objectionable article but not to a legitimate enterprise.

In the course of his argument, Justice McKenna emphasized that the right of property had its source in the natural law. To him the private owner had certain definite rights, not only of management and administration, but also over the use, enjoyment and disposal of property. The right conferred an unlimited privilege of administering that object in any way that one saw fit, subject to the laws of society.

As if in refutation of Holmes' implication that the right of property originated in the State, McKenna contended

---

Frankfurter, " The Business of the Supreme Court of the United States," *Harvard Law Review*, XL (Mar. 1926), 595; Robinson, *op. cit.,* p. 297; Cheadle, *op. cit.,* p. 571.

Admitting that its possession of the pipe line gave its owner an advantage over his competitors, yet the very fact that it did give him an advantage was no reason to compel him to make it community property. One of the fundamental conceptions of property is exclusiveness, the right of exclusive possession, enjoyment and disposition, yet take away these elements and you take away all that there is of property.[38]

The principle that businesses clothed with a public interest were subject to government control caused Justice McKenna further discomfiture in 1921 when he dissented in the wartime rent cases of *Block v. Hirsh*[39] and *Marcus Brown Company v. Feldman*.[40] In the majority opinion Justice Holmes used the German Alliance opinion to support his conclusion that circumstances had clothed the business of renting houses in the District of Columbia with a public interest sufficiently great to justify regulation.[41]

Justice McKenna joined by Chief Justice White and Justices Van Devanter and McReynolds dissented on the ground that the regulation of rents was a violation of the Fifth Amendment. The

---

[38] 234 U. S. 575.

[39] 256 U. S. 135 (Apr. 18, 1921). Ray A. Brown, "Due Process, Police Power and the Supreme Court," *Harvard Law Review,* XL (May, 1927), 958; Henry Wolf Bikle, "Questions of Fact Affecting Constitutionality," *Harvard Law Review,* XXXVIII (Nov. 1924), 15; Felix Frankfurter and James Landis, "A Study in the Federal Judicial System," *Harvard Law Review,* XL (June, 1927), 1119; David Lilienthal, "Regulation of Public Utilities during Depression," *Harvard Law Review,* XLVI (Mar. 1933), 773. For a discussion of Justice Holmes' majority report and a criticism of Justice McKenna's dissent, see Max Lerner, *The Mind and Faith of Justice Holmes* (Boston: 1943), 278–285; the philosophic bases of Holmes' decisions are considered in Miriam T. Rooney, *Lawlessness, Law and Sanction* (Washington: 1937), 114–137.

[40] In reference to the rent cases, McKenna declared, "there is not a line in any of them that declares that the explicit and definite covenants of private individuals engaged in a private and personal matter and subject to an impairment by a state law . . . if the State have such power . . . it is superior to every other limitation upon every power expressed in the Constitution of the United States."

[41] In addition to McKenna's opinion in the German Alliance case, Holmes cited McKenna's argument in *North Carolina v. Perly,* 249 U. S. 510 (Apr. 21, 1919), which held that a State should keep a watershed clear of refuse and rubbish.

purpose of the statute was neither the improvement of public health nor the relief of administrative tension. McKenna was at a loss to know

> Of what concern is it to the public health or the operations of the Federal Government who shall occupy a cellar, and a room above it, for business purposes in the city of Washington? . . . Have conditions arisen, that are not amenable to passing palliatives, so that socialism or some form of socialism, is the only permanent corrective or accommodation? [42]

It was better, reasoned McKenna, to suffer temporary inconveniences than to undermine the prohibitions of the Constitution which were as " absolute as axioms."

Justice McKenna's opposition can be traced to an unwarranted fear of socialism. It was the word itself rather than its connotation that was abhorrent. The seventy-eight-year-old McKenna little realized that he had been in the vanguard of the crusaders for socialism when he handed down decisions sanctioning the milder forms of that theory. The rent case was merely another application of the postulates which he had uniformly supported. The principles of judicial tolerance of legislative discretion, liberal regulation of public businesses, and broad interpretation of health regulations, which had become an earmark of McKenna's opinions, were forgotten in his haste to meet the approaching threat of socialism.

The rent cases opened up a broad field of fearsome things. To permit a lessee to retain possession of property beyond the time specified by the lessor appeared to McKenna to be contrary to every conception of leases that the world had ever entertained. Complete breakdown of the economic structure was impending because

> if the public interest can extend a lease it can compel a lease; the difference is only in degree and boldness. In one as much as in the other there is a violation of the positive and absolute right of the owner of property. To regulate the business of mining, insurance and irrigation

---

[42] 256 U. S. 162.

is justified in order that they might not be used to the injury of others . . . To permit the government to regulate rents is to recognize its possession of a power over property that is unbounded and irresponsible.[43]

Justice McKenna's dissent in the rent cases was contrary to the principles which underlay practically all of his opinions involving contracts. The right to contract, unlike the right of property, was not envisaged as an absolute right. The State might validly limit and under some circumstances entirely prohibit its exercise.[44]

In the application of these principles, McKenna made a considerable contribution towards regulating corporations. Since *The Trustees of Dartmouth College v. Woodward*,[45] in 1819, the inviolability of charters or contracts had been established. Yet the courts and the legislatures had found means to impinge upon this inviolability. Justice McKenna aided this " chipping away " process by establishing the principle that corporations " doing business " in a State were proper subjects of regulation. As early as 1900, in *Waters-Pierce Oil Company v. Texas* [46] he held that a corporation was an artificial being, established by law and, as such,

---

[43] 256 U. S. 163. McKenna's contention was that constitutional clauses were " as absolute as axioms " and hence did not permit the violation of the right of contract. Yet those same constitutional clauses lost the quality of being "absolute as axioms" when the right of speech was violated by the State. McKenna supported the espionage act of Congress in *Schenck v. United States*, 249 U. S. 47 (Mar. 3, 1919) ; *Frowerk v. United States*, 249 U. S. 204; *Debs v. United States*, 249 U. S. 211 (Mar. 10, 1919) ; *Abrams v. United States*, 250 U. S. 616 (Nov. 10, 1919) ; *Schaefer v. United States*, 251 U. S. 466 (Mar. 1, 1920) ; *Pierce v. United States*, 252 U. S. 239 (Mar. 8, 1920). For a critical review of Justice Holmes' part in these cases, see Lerner, *op. cit.*, pp. 289–313. Zechariah Chafee, *Freedom of Speech* (New York: 1920), pp. 87–110, adversely criticizes the government's policy.

[44] *Kies v. Lowrey*, 199 U. S. 233 (Nov. 13, 1905).

[45] 4 Wheaton 518.

[46] 177 U. S. 28 (Mar. 19, 1900). William C. Coleman, " Constitutional Limitations upon State Taxation of Foreign Corporations," *Columbia Law Review*, XI (May, 1911), 402; Karl W. Kirchwey, " The Inter-state Commerce Commission and the Judicial Enforcement of the Act to Regulate Commerce," *Columbia Law Review*, XIV (Mar. 1914), 228; Elcanon Isaacs, " Federal Protection of Foreign Corporations," *Columbia Law Review*, XXVI (Mar. 1926), 285; " Notes," *Harvard Law Review*, XXXVIII (Mar. 1925), 965.

possessed only rights which the " charter of its creation confers upon it."

Prior to plaintiff's charter, the State had enacted a statute which prohibited foreign corporations from doing business if they became a party to illegal combinations in restraint of trade. McKenna held that the law imposed no conditions which were not within the State's power and since this was part of the agreement upon which defendant in error entered the State, there was no ground for complaint. In an *obitur dicta* McKenna asserted that the interpretation of statutory phrases, involving conditions for intra-state business, was a matter entirely for State decision and the rules thus established were binding on the Supreme Court.[47]

The doctrine of the pervading influence of a State decision on the Supreme Court was illustrated by Justice McKenna in *Chattanooga Building Association v. Denson.*[48] The opinion represents another incident in the struggle of McKenna for legislative regulation of charters. Alabama, faced by the growth of fly-by-night loan companies, attempted to regulate their activities. The issue was whether the law aimed at protecting the welfare and property of citizens or was an arbitrary regulation of foreign corporations. The Alabama courts had ruled that a foreign corporation doing a single act of business within the State violated the statute prohibiting any transactions prior to designating an agent. This definition was at variance with the accepted connotation of " doing business," that is, continuous prosecution of business or an act done in contemplation of that business.

In sustaining the action of the State, McKenna experienced no difficulty. He cited his Waters-Pierce opinion to the effect that a corporation was entirely dependent on a State for its existence. Since a State could prohibit all acts of a foreign corporation, it naturally could prohibit any act of that corporation. If the prohibition did not involve a violation of constitutional rights, then it was within the province of the State judiciary to determine the interpretation.

On the other hand Justice McKenna declared that the Supreme

---

[47] 177 U. S. 28.

[48] 189 U. S. 408 (Apr. 27, 1903). Justice Harlan dissented without comment. " Notes," *Columbia Law Review,* VII (Nov. 1907), 542.

Court had the right of explaining the phrase " doing business " in cases involving the validity of service. In *Conley v. Mathieson Alkali Works* [49] where, representing a unanimous Court, he condemned a New York statute which permitted service on the official of a corporation who merely resided in the State.

In establishing his thesis, Justice McKenna traced the steps which led to the abandonment of the inconvenient doctrine that a corporation could not be sued outside the State of its incorporation. Justice Field in *St. Clair v. Cox,* [50] abolished the doctrine that a service could be made wherever the agent of the corporation was found " doing business." However, permission to make service on a corporation's agent was not to be construed so as to

> encroach upon that principle of natural justice which requires notice of a suit to a party before he can be bound by it. It must be reasonable and the service provided for should be only upon such agents as may be properly deemed representatives of the foreign corporations. [51]

Thus the matter of service became one of due process and consequently subject to the Supreme Court. In these cases the Court had to be the final arbiter of when a corporation was " doing business " and disregard the ruling of the State court which did not insure a service, valid under the definition laid down by the Supreme Court. [52]

In the course of his discussions on the subject of when a corporation could be said to be doing business within a State, McKenna expressed his abhorrence of regulations resulting from impulse, emotion, passion, whim or caprice. However urgent the need for enactment or loud the clamor for repeal, the legislative act must be deliberate, rational, and objective. Convinced that the purpose of law was to promote the common good, he favored interpretations which would grant the individual all possible protection in the courts.

---

[49] 190 U. S. 428, (May 18, 1903).

[50] 106 U. S. 350.

[51] 106 U. S. 351.

[52] Coleman, *op. cit.,* p. 393; Isaacs, *op. cit.,* p. 263; " Recent Cases," *Harvard Law Review,* XXXV (Nov. 1921), 87.

During Justice McKenna's career on the Court there was a remarkable advance in sanitation as well as an ever-increasing tendency to submit every phase of life to legislative regulation which resulted in a vast amount of statutory law enacted in the interest of public health.[53] Justice McKenna recognized that the protection of health was a proper exercise of police power yet realized the need for constant alertness lest the police power of the States be employed as an excuse for infringement of constitutional rights. To Justice McKenna the essential idea in the adjudication of police power cases was that the judiciary was not to supplant the legislature in determining the need for action.

The willingness of Justice McKenna to concede that " some play must be allowed for the joints of the machine " was illustrated in his refusal to condemn legislation because it entailed the expenditure of money. In 1907 when speaking for a unanimous court in *Heath & Milligan v. Worst*,[54] he sustained the right of a State to compel paint manufacturers to identify the ingredients of their products even though it entailed financial considerations. Admitting that classification was based on arbitrary distinctions, yet the law could not be condemned as capricious, peremptory and unreasonable. The fact that the legislation was unwise, ill-advised, unequal and oppressive did not necessarily imply that it illegally impaired the property rights of complainants. It must be admitted that " exact wisdom and nice adaptations of remedies are not required by the Fourteenth Amendment."

The same principles underlay the thought of Justice McKenna eight years later in *Hadacheck v. Los Angeles* [55] when representing

---

[53] Charles Warren, " A Bulwark to the State Police Power—The United States Supreme Court," Columbia Law Review, XIII (Dec. 1913), 667; " The Progressiveness of the United States Supreme Court," *Columbia Law Review*, XIII (Apr. 1913), 298. For McKenna's attitude toward the need for health laws, see his opinion in *St. John v. New York*, 201 U. S. 263 (Apr. 16, 1906), where he sustained a law regulating the activities of milk dealers.

[54] 207 U. S. 338 (Dec. 9, 1907).

[55] 239 U. S. 394 (Dec. 20, 1915). For an evaluation of the case, see George W. Wickersham, " Government Control of Corporations," Columbia Law Review, XVIII (Mar. 1918), 199; Alfred Bettman, " Constitutionality of Zoning Laws," *Harvard Law Review*, XXXVII (May, 1924), 847;

all of his brethren he supported a city zoning ordinance. Complainant challenged the law on the grounds that it destroyed a large financial investment, which he had made in a brick works. The claim was rejected on the grounds that the removal of the plant was considered essential for the health of the community. Reasserting his belief in the competency and ability of local lawmaking bodies, McKenna declared that complainant was not entitled to relief because like restrictions had not been placed on other businesses equally amenable to control. It was to be remembered that the legislature, not the Court, decided when and to what extent the police power was to be employed.

In this discussion, McKenna framed his best known definition of police power. In the light of existing constitutional law, the scope would be too inclusive, yet it summarized McKenna's notion of its extent, a notion uniformly present in his opinions when sustaining social legislation. He deemed police power to be

> one of the most essential powers of government, one that is the least limitable. It may indeed seem harsh in its exercise, usually is on some individual but the imperative necessity for its existence precludes any limitation upon it when not exercised arbitrarily.[56]

The thread of this conception of police power was found repeatedly in McKenna's opinions from *Wilson v. Eureka City* [57] in 1899 to *Davis v. Manry* [58] in 1925.

---

"Public Health Laws Under the Police Power," *Columbia Law Review,* XVI (Mar. 1916), 239.

[56] 239 U. S. 410.

[57] 173 U. S. 32 (Feb. 20, 1899). Some of the cases in which McKenna sustained the exercise of police power were *Atchison, Topeka & Santa Fe Railroad v. Matthews,* 174 U. S. 96 (Apr. 17, 1899). *Deservant v. Cerillos Coal Co.,* 178 U. S. 409 (May 28, 1900); *District of Columbia v. Robinson,* 180 U. S. 92 (Jan. 7, 1901); *Cronin v. City of Denver,* 192 U. S. 115 (Jan. 4, 1904; *Flanigan v. Sierra County,* 196 U. S. 553 (Feb. 20, 1905); *Ah Sin v. Wittman,* 198 U. S. 500 (May 29, 1905); *Fifth Ave. Coach Co. v. New York,* 221 U. S. 467 (May 29, 1911); *Mutual Loan Co. v. Martell,* 222 U. S. 225 (Dec. 11, 1911); *Selover, Bates & Co. v. Walsh,* 226 U. S. 112 (Dec. 2, 1912); *Metropolis Theatre Co. v. Chicago,* 228 U. S. 61 (Apr. 7, 1913); *Heim v. McCall,* 239 U. S. 175 (Nov. 29, 1915).

[58] 226 U. S. 401 (Jan. 5, 1925).

It must not be assumed that Justice McKenna was willing to give *carte blanche* to State legislatures in the exercise of police power for in *International Harvester Company v. Missouri,*[59] he warned that the State had not the power arbitrarily to forbid the conduct of a business that was not detrimental to public welfare. In *Eubank v. City of Richmond* [60] he gave a clear-cut picture of the judicial check upon the illegal exercise of the police power, holding that

> It (police power) extends, . . . not only to regulations which promote the public health, morals, and safety, but those which promote the public convenience or the general prosperity . . . But in all cases there is constant admonition, both in their rule and examples, that when a statute is assailed as offending against the higher guarantees of the Constitution, it must clearly do so to justify the Courts in declaring it invalid.[61]

Justice McKenna's solicitude for the common welfare, as was patent in *German Alliance Insurance Company v. Lewis* and in *Chattanooga Building v. Denson,* finds form again when he introduced the principle that railroads are liable for injuries sustained by passengers in *Chicago, Rock Island and Pacific Railroad v. Zernecke,*[62] and in *Chicago, Rock Island and Pacific Railroad v. Eaton.*[63] Justice McKenna traced the common law doctrine of responsibility of common carriers, and explained the reasons for holding bailee responsible for damages to goods in transit. The rule applicable to cases of injuries to passengers came to be that the carrier should be held liable only if the injury was caused by negligence of an employee. As the law stood before McKenna's decision in the Zernecke and Eaton cases, a passenger in a train

[59] 234 U. S. 199 (June 8, 1914).

[60] 226 U. S. 137 (Dec. 2, 1912).

[61] 226 U. S. 142.

[62] 183 U. S. 582 (Jan. 6, 1902). Joseph H. Beale, "The Carrier's Liability," *Harvard Law Review,* XI (Oct. 1897), 158; Arthur H. Ballantine, "A Compensation Plan for Railroad Accident Claims," *Harvard Law Review,* XXIX (May, 1916), 717; "Notes," *Harvard Law Review,* XXXIX (Mar. 1926), 716.

[63] 183 U. S. 589 (Jan. 9, 1902).

which also carried his baggage might, if the train were wrecked, recover for the loss of his baggage by mere proof of his loss, but to recover for personal injuries, would have to prove the accident was caused by negligence. McKenna reasoned that if the legislature could subject railroads to absolute liability for damages to baggage, irrespective of negligence, it could likewise require reasonable sums for injuries to passengers.

The principle that the party better able to sustain the loss should be liable was only implied in the above opinion but it was given clearer acknowledgment in *Atchison, Topeka and Santa Fe Railroad v. Matthews*.[64] The Court, through Justice Brewer, held that a railroad was liable for damage to property by fire communicated by their locomotives. The common law permitted redress only when the fire was caused wantonly or through negligence, whereas the statute which the Court upheld, provided that the mere fact of setting fire to woods or fields by locomotives entitled the injured party to damages.

Justice Brewer claimed that the gist of the law was

> not to compel the payment of debts, but to secure the utmost care on the part of the railroad companies to prevent the escape of fire from their moving trains . . . Its monition to the railroads is . . . see to it that no fire escapes from locomotives, for if it does you will be liable, not merely for the damage it causes but also for the reasonable attorney's fees of the owners of the property.[65]

Had the law merely made the carrier responsible for fires started by their locomotives, McKenna would have upheld it but he dissented because, in addition to liability, the law granted attorney's fees to the injured property owner without granting the same concession to the carriers.[66] He contended that the Court was in-

---

[64] 174 U. S. 95 (Apr. 17, 1899). Charles W. Collins, " Stare Decisis and the Fourteenth Amendment," *Columbia Law Review*, XII (Nov. 1912), 610–611; " Notes," *Columbia Law Review*, V (May, 1905), 394.

[65] 174 U. S. 98.

[66] " Employer's Liability Based on Statutory Classification of Employees," *Columbia Law Review*, V (May, 1905), 394; " Preventing Litigious Delay in Payment of Insurance Claims," *Harvard Law Review*, XLVII (Dec. 1934), 322.

consistent with its ruling in *Gulf, Colorado and Santa Fe Railroad v. Ellis* [67] where it outlawed a similar statute, the only difference being that the railroad was made liable for the killing of stock.

McKenna's argument lacked strength for a reasonable distinction could be made between the two cases. The owner of real property adjacent to a railroad can do little or nothing to protect his property from fire communicated by locomotives. He was then entitled to a more secure protection than a livestock owner who was partially responsible for the loss of his animals when he neglected to prevent their trespassing upon the right of way of railroads.

A review of the due process decisions of McKenna illustrated that in spite of his temporary adherence to the tenets of the sociological school in his opinion in *Magoun v. Illinois Trust,* McKenna consistently supported the ideas of the Law of Nature School. He was thoroughly convinced that violations of the right of property would lead to the destruction of society. Socialism was no mere idle threat and his utterance in *Block v. Hirsh* as well as in *Schaefer v. United States* [68] demonstrated that he feared attacks upon the fundamental principles of society.

The cases in which due process of law was concerned composed the largest class of Justice McKenna's opinions. The principles which formed the framework for these expressions were: that the legislature's will was not to be upset without flagrant usurpation of rights, the universal practice of men was to be accepted as a basis for proper legislation, corporations were creatures of the law and subject to the absolute control of the State, classification was justifiable if all in the same class were treated alike, police power precluded any limitation when not exercised arbitrarily, and property was an inviolable right subject to regulation by the State but under all circumstances entitled to compensation if confiscated for public use.

---

[67] 165 U. S. 150.

[68] 251 U. S. 466 (Mar. 1, 1920). This was the only one of the espionage cases that McKenna wrote. Despite the dissent of Justices Brandeis, Holmes and Clarke, McKenna maintained the right of a State to punish inflammatory speeches during wartime.

# CHAPTER VI

## LABOR DECISIONS

In most cases involving a labor law there exists a conflict between society and the individual. The controversy concerns the amount of liberty which an individual may enjoy in the exercise of his right of contract. In a word, the problem in each case is to define " liberty of contract."

Down to 1898, when Justice McKenna was sworn in, the Supreme Court had held consistently that the liberty of contract was practically absolute. This concept meant that when two parties negotiated a contract, not contrary to public policy, the State could not interfere nor dictate the terms. Limitation of contract was permitted by the Court only when public necessity demanded it. The application of this highly individualistic interpretation of liberty of contract was the chief obstacle in the way of progressive labor legislation. It was somewhat naive for the Court to assume that the individual employee in a large industrial concern enjoyed full liberty of contract and could bargain on equal terms with his employer. Yet it was only during McKenna's term that a change in the Court's personnel, an infiltration of social ideas and a new concept of government responsibility that the Court gradually approved governmental control of contract rights in the interests of the laborer.

When Justice McKenna retired from the Court, in 1925, the social thought upon which the Court had rested its labor decisions a quarter of a century earlier had been materially altered. Individualism as expressed in the extreme laissez-faire doctrine had been repudiated and replaced by social responsibility and consciousness. The liberty of contract was hedged about with hour-laws for men and women, with prohibitions against tenement-house work, payment of wages in scrip and most of the common law defenses of the employer against liability for employee's injuries were whittled away.

130

Justice McKenna's share in this progressive development of labor law might be divided into two categories: first, stripping the employer of common law defenses against liability,[1] and, secondly, the enlargement of the national and State police power sufficiently to control labor conditions in the interests of society.

In the first category Justice McKenna urged the courts to abolish the rules of fellow-servant, contributory negligence and occupational risk as defenses of the employer against liability for injuries sustained by the employee in the course of his work. In short, he advocated a shift of the financial burden from employee to employer and a modification of the accepted interpretation of the law in order to protect those workers who, because of their financial or physical impoverishment, stood in special need of defense.

In the second category, he supported a gradually expanding list of industrial workers and conditions for whom the police power was to be exercised. Justice McKenna was among the first to advocate that consideration be given to the economic evils against which labor legislation was directed. The most progressive features in his labor views were a willingness to exercise tolerance of the legislature's discretion and attributing greater weight and authority to expert data and information than to legal precedent.[2]

It was on the need for judicial tolerance of legislative discretion that McKenna differed with his brethren most frequently, when it was a question of determining the values of constitutional rights involved in the freedom of contract. Labor legislation was directed at the elimination of conditions about which the Court

---

[1] For a discussion of the employers' common law defenses against liability for employee injuries, see John R. Commons and John B. Andrews, *Principles of Labor Legislation* (New York: 1920), pp. 387–392. McKenna's opinions on this point are found in *Deserant v. Cerillos Coal Company,* 178 U. S. 409 (May 28, 1900); *Texas and Pacific Ry. v. Dashiell,* 198 U. S. 521 (May 29, 1905); *Santa Fe Railroad v. Holmes,* 202 U. S. 438 (May 21, 1906); *Chicago, Rock Island and Pacific Railroad v. Zernecke,* 183 U. S. 582 (Jan. 6, 1902) and *Northern Pacific Railroad v. Dixon,* 194 U. S. 338 (May 16, 1904).

[2] See *Bunting v. Oregon,* 243 U. S. 426 (Apr. 9, 1917) for McKenna's expressions on the need for expert data. The decision sustained an hours-of-labor law for men.

could know but little and therefore should be extremely slow in condemning such acts as violations of constitutional rights.[3] McKenna admitted that labor laws restricted the freedom of contract but contended that the restriction was warranted inasmuch as the laws brought considerable benefit to society. Where it was a question involving the economic and industrial development of the nation, the rights of the individual must be subordinated to those of society.

The superior claims of the community over the individual right of freedom of contract was well illustrated by McKenna in his opinions on yellow-dog contracts, agreements by which an employee bound himself not to join a labor union.[4] In 1898, Congress attempted to abolish yellow-dog contracts because they were a means by which the employer destroyed the right of his employees to bargain collectively through their labor unions. Hence in the Erdman Act Congress made it criminal for a railroad to discharge or otherwise discriminate against an employee because of union affiliation. In brief it outlawed ratification of a yellow-dog contract as a condition of employment.

In 1906, the Erdman Act was attacked in *Adair v. United States* [5] and the Court, through Justice Harlan, held the act to be

[3] "Notes and Comments," *Michigan Law Review*, XIV (Feb. 1916), 325, remarks that in dealing with labor legislation "the court can make far less use of precedent than in ordinary cases . . . and that it was the realization of this which was a large factor in the establishment of the doctrine that all doubts must be resolved in favor of the legislation." Edward A. Adler, "Labor, Capital and Business at Common Law," *Harvard Law Review*, XXIX (Jan. 1916), 241; *Hadacheck v. Los Angeles*, 239 U. S. 394 (Dec. 20, 1915) ; *Bacon v. Walker*, 204 U. S. 311 (Feb. 4, 1907).

[4] Dale Yoder, *Labor Economics and Labor Problems* (New York: 1939), pp. 54, 543, 546, 547; Calvert Magruder, "A Half Century of Legal Influence Upon the Development of Collective Bargaining," *Harvard Law Review*, L (May, 1937), 1082; Osmond K. Fraenkel, "Recent Statutes Affecting Labor Injunctions and Yellow Dog Contracts," *Illinois Law Review*, XXX (Mar. 1936), 854–883; Homer F. Carey and Herman Oliphant, "The Present Status of the Hitchman Case," *Columbia Law Review*, XXIX (Apr. 1929), 440–460.

[5] 208 U. S. 161 (Jan. 27, 1908). For a favorable criticism of McKenna's dissent, see Richard Olney, "Discrimination Against Union Labor—Legal?", *American Law Review*, XLII (Apr. 1908), 884–890. Comments on the Adair

unconstitutional because it impinged upon the freedom of contract and therefore was a violation of liberty under the Fifth Amendment. The legislation could not be considered an exercise of the commerce power because labor relations had no actual or substantial relation to interstate commerce.

In his dissent, Justice McKenna made a careful analysis of the provisions of the statute, of which the challenged section, prohibiting yellow-dog contracts, was a part. He insisted that the yellow-dog section be considered in its relation to the whole law, not as an isolated unit. He contended that the aim of the statute was to prevent or settle disputes between common carriers and their employees. The contested section thereby obtained its justification. McKenna maintained that all material provisions of the disputed statute originated in the Pullman Strike of 1894 and that their purpose was to prevent a recurrence of the evils so emphatically impressed upon the public mind by that strike. All parts of the Erdman Act were aimed at the single end of preserving peace between interstate carriers and their employees.[6] The individual's freedom of contract must be limited in the interests of the community's right to uninterrupted railroad service.

McKenna went straight to the root of the matter when he claimed that there was a logical and legal connection between an employee's membership in a labor organization and the movement of interstate trade. He reasoned that since all courts took judicial notice of the prevalent conditions among the people, it was proper for the Court, in considering the relations between railroads and their employees, to recognize the relation of labor unions to interstate traffic.

It was naive for the Court to assume that an individual employee of a railroad was free to bargain on equal terms with his

decision are noted in Roscoe Pound, "Mechanical Jurisprudence," *Columbia Law Review*, VIII (Dec. 1908), 616; Jackson E. Reynolds, "Railway Valuation—Is It a Panacea?" *Columbia Law Review*, VIII (Apr. 1908), 275; Maurice Finkelstein, "Judicial Self-Limitation," *Harvard Law Review*, XXXVII (Jan. 1924), 361; Henry Wolf Bikle, "Judicial Determination of Questions of Fact Affecting the Constitutional Validity of Legislative Action," *Harvard Law Review*, XXXVIII (Nov. 1924), 22.

[6] *30 U. S. Statutes* 424.

employer. That equality of bargaining power was secured by the worker only when he joined a labor union. It was only through united and disciplined action that he could expect to cope with organized capital and obtain reasonable terms for his labor.[7] The union was the recognized agency which represented and furthered the economic interests of the worker. If justice demanded that the worker be made equal with his employer in bargaining, then it was logical to suppose that justice would support the only way of obtaining that equality, namely, membership in a union.

The government had learned that railroad strikes and interruption of interstate commerce had been frequently caused by the dismissal of employees solely on the grounds of union membership. To eliminate this cause of disturbance, it was provided in the Erdman Act that affiliation with a trade union could not be a cause for dismissal. This prohibition had a direct relation with the purpose of the act and was not a simple restriction upon liberty of the carrier for employing whomever he pleased. In the estimation of McKenna it was

> A provision of the law which will prevent or tend to prevent the stoppage of every wheel in every car of an entire railroad system . . . It was an oversight in the proportion of things that Congress may not prevent the discharge of an employee in order to prevent the disastrous interruptions of commerce, the derangement of business and even greater evils to public welfare.[8]

It must be concluded then that the prohibition of yellow-dog contracts was constitutional for it had a direct relation to the purpose which induced the act—elimination of labor disputes. It was a direct aid to the free flow of commerce and not a mere restriction upon the liberty to employ whomever it pleased or to have business relations with whomever it desired.[9]

---

[7] Olney, *op. cit.*, p. 886; Max Lerner, *Mind and Faith of Justice Oliver Holmes* (New York: 1930), pp. 150–151.

[8] U. S. 190. In a frequently quoted remark, McKenna declared that there was no worthier purpose to engage legislative attention or "be the object of legislative action" than the settlement of disputes between carriers and their employees.

[9] Thomas Reed Powell, "Due Process and the Adamson Law," *Columbia*

The line of reasoning which characterized McKenna's dissent in *Adair v. United States* was repeated nine years later when he concurred, in a written opinion, with the majority in *Wilson v. New*.[10] The Court sustained the validity of the Adamson Act which established an eight-hour day for employees of interstate carriers and fixed a scale of minimum wages with proportionate increases for overtime. Congress passed the Adamson Act in the face of a threatened strike of organized railroad employees during a time of peace and yet during a period of undeclared national emergency. An analysis of the majority opinion in *Adair v. United States* and in *Wilson v. New* demonstrated that the majority favored congressional action against a threatened interruption of commerce by a labor strike only when that strike was imminent. On the other hand, McKenna approved congressional action aimed at avoiding an interruption of commerce by labor strikes either remotely as in the Erdman Act or proximately as in the Adamson Act. He asserted that a distinction between a legal relation and factual relation in cases of this kind would not tend to promote a satisfactory result. The danger was that such differentiation might create the impression that the Court was

*Law Review*, XVII (Jan. 1917), 114–127, attempts to predict the position that McKenna will take toward the Adamson Law in the light of his arguments in the Adair case; Thomas Reed Powell, " The Constitutional Issue in Minimum Wage Legislation," *Minnesota Law Review*, II (Dec. 1917), 1–21; Maurice Finkelstein, " Judicial Self-Limitation," *Harvard Law Review*, XXXVIII (Jan. 1924), 361; Henry Bikle, " Judicial Determination of Questions of Fact Affecting the Constitutional Validity of Legislative Action," *Harvard Law Review*, XXXVIII (Jan. 1924), 22, discusses the power of Congress to stop strikes through an exercise of the commerce power.

[10] 243 U. S. 332 (Mar. 19, 1917) ; Arthur A. Ballantine, " Railway Strikes and the Constitution," *Columbia Law Review*, XVII (June, 1917), 502–22; Henry Hull, " Some Legal Aspects of Federal Control of Railroads," *Harvard Law Review*, XXXI (Apr. 1918), 862; Sidney Post Simpson, " Constitutional Limitations on Compulsory Industrial Arbitration," *Harvard Law Review*, XXXVIII (Apr. 1925), 792, supports McKenna's statement that compulsory investigation involving the prohibition of strikes pending award did interfere with liberty of contract but is justified under the police power.

proceeding upon artificial and academic assumptions rather than upon the facts of daily life.[11]

An important sequel to the Adair case was written in 1915 when a State law prohibiting yellow-dog contracts was declared unconstitutional in *Coppage v. Kansas.*[12] The statute involved was somewhat broader in scope than the Erdman Act in that it held an employer guilty of a criminal offense if he forbade employees to join a labor union. The Court, through Justice Pitney, ruled the statute unconstitutional on the ground that it infringed upon the right of the employer and the employee to contract freely.

Justice McKenna joined the majority only because he was convinced that the law merely aimed to restrict the liberty of contract, without any ulterior end in view, such as the prevention of strikes or walkouts. Furthermore, McKenna opposed the statute on the ground that it applied to all employers, not merely those engaged in business affected with a public interest. McKenna believed that

> There are rights, which when exercised in a private business may not be disturbed or limited. With them we are not concerned. We are dealing with rights exercised in a quasi-public business, and therefore subject to control in the interest of the public.[13]

A survey of the yellow-dog contract cases in which McKenna was concerned would show that the majority opinion was based on long-established understanding of the freedom of contract. The Court believed that the freedom of contract was to be pre-

---

[11] Henry Bikle, "Judicial Determination of Legislative Action," *Harvard Law Review,* XXXVIII (Jan. 1924), 22; Ray A. Brown, "Due Process, Police Power and the Supreme Court," *Harvard Law Review,* XL (May, 1927), 943–968 discusses the judicial problem of deciding between a personal view and the legislative discretion.

[12] 236 U. S. 1; Felix Frankfurter, "Mr. Justice Holmes and the Constitution," *Harvard Law Review,* XLI (Dec. 1927), 121–164 maintains that from 1908, the year of *Muller v. Oregon,* until after the First World War, the Supreme Court "allowed legislation to prevail which . . . curbed the freedom of enterprise and withdrew phases of industrial relations from the area of individual bargaining."

[13] 208 U. S. 190.

served by granting free reign to the individual's ability to secure advantageous terms. The State was to maintain a policy of non-interference, hence any laws restricting the conditions which an employer could demand of an employee were an infringement of the freedom of contract. This older view favored the employer and perpetuated the individualistic interpretation that the followers of Spencer and Bentham had established during the nineteenth century.[14] On the other hand, McKenna advocated a reasonable regulation of contract rights by the State, because it was the only way to establish the freedom and equality of the worker, in bargaining with employers.

The necessity of State intervention in modern industrial labor conditions was recognized by McKenna in his opinions on laws regulating the hours of labor. The struggle to shorten hours was a constant, dogged, frequently hopeless, insistence by one great part of society on the need for a shorter workday in the face of an equally determined resistance of a minority to every suggestion of change. The substance of the controversy was whether the individual was free to work as long as he desired or whether the State could limit his work-hours in the interest of society.

Justice McKenna favored the latter alternative. He believed that hour regulations were conducive to a better physical and political order, for by prohibiting the long, exhausting hours of work, the hour laws provided the leisure necessary to recuperate strength and preserve health. It was to the interest of the State to have a strong, robust, healthy citizenry, capable of bearing arms and adding to the resources of the nation. In order to establish an intelligent electorate, essential for the existence of democracy, leisure was needed to study, discuss and act rationally in political affairs.

In determining the constitutionality of hour laws, McKenna urged the Court not to cling to precedent and historic interpretation

---

[14] For a discussion of the Court's view toward state and congressional labor legislation, see Calvert Magruder, " A Half Century of Legal Influence upon the Development of Collective Bargaining," *Harvard Law Review*, L (May, 1937), 1071 ff.; Homer F. Carey and Herman Oliphant, "Present Status of the Hitchman Case," *Columbia Law Review*, XXIX (Apr. 1929), 440 ff.

of certain familiar constitutional phrases but to recognize the new conditions which the industrialization of the nation had wrought. He declared that a highly individualistic interpretation of constitutional rights was archaic in a civilization characterized by dependence of man on man and man on society. The simplicity and independence of past ages had been replaced by the complexity and interdependence of the contemporary age. Hence the acts of individuals had become matters of social concern and must be controlled in the interests of society.[15]

At first McKenna was somewhat hesitant to accept these principles but after he became convinced of their soundness, he adopted them wholeheartedly. In 1905 he joined the majority's opinion in *Lochner v. New York*[16] in condemning a ten-hour day for bakers because it was not a matter of " common understanding " that a longer workday was unhealthy. As employed by Justice Peckham, who wrote the majority opinion, the phrase " common understanding " meant the understanding of the Court, not that of the legislature or of the informed policy makers of the community.

The first indication of change in McKenna's thought came three years later when he supported Justice Brewer's opinion in *Muller v. Oregon*[17] which sustained a ten-hour day for women. It was of some interest to note that this case was presented in an entirely different manner from *Lochner v. New York*. Defendant presented expert opinion on the conditions of labor together with scientific conclusions of their effect on workers. The Court was convinced of the necessity of the ten-hour day for women and to justify its departure from *stare decisis* declared that the scientific information

> may not be, technically speaking, authorities . . . of the constitutional question presented to us . . . yet they are significant of a widespread belief that (the conditions of the case) justify special legislation.[18]

[15] Wladimir Woytinsky, " Hours of Labor," *Encyclopedia of the Social Sciences,* 1st ed., VIII, 478–493; T. N. Carver, " The Theory of the Shortened Working Week," *American Economic Review* (Sept. 1936), 451–462.

[16] 198 U. S. 45.

[17] 208 U. S. 412 (Feb. 24, 1908).

[18] 208 U. S. 420.

McKenna adopted two of the principles of this decision. First, that women were physically unable to endure the same exhaustive hours of labor as adult males and must be protected by legislation. Secondly, that a knowledge of industrial conditions, not legal precedent, should be the controlling factor in adjudicating hour laws. In short, the Court should base its decision on something more substantial than the " common understanding " employed in the Lochner case.

This movement, to consider laws as they applied to actual working conditions rather than merely as the judiciary thought they should, led McKenna in *United States v. Garbish* [19] to abandon legal precedent in interpreting the National Eight Hour Law in 1892. This law provided that, in all work done by, or in behalf of, the government, an eight-hour day was mandatory " except in cases of extraordinary emergency." By a narrow interpretation of this phrase, contractors flaunted the eight-hour provision by simply calling any work " an emergency." The American Federation of Labor had made repeated but fruitless efforts to eliminate this abuse but it did not succeed until 1911 when McKenna condemned this practice as a subterfuge aimed at emasculating the law.

Speaking for a unanimous Court, McKenna reversed the ruling of a Circuit Court that levee work on the Mississippi River presented " at all times an emergency." He declared that the phrase, " continuing extraordinary emergency," was self-contradictory and that, had the Congress desired to exempt levee work, it would have mentioned it in the bill.[20] He stressed the need of workmen for the paternal care of the government and emphasized the care that the Court should exercise in condemning legislation sanctioned by a well informed legislature. McKenna was becoming conscious of his power to frame an opinion in keeping with contemporary conditions and based on his own thought rather than upon *stare decisis*.

Fuller exposition of these principles was made by McKenna in

[19] 222 U. S. 257 (Dec. 11, 1911) ; Marion Cotter Cahill, *Shorter Hours* (New York: 1932), p. 74. For a short account of the trend toward a standard eight-hour day, see John R. Commons and John B. Andrews, *Principles of Labor Legislation* (New York: 1920), pp. 248–262.

[20] 222 U. S. 261.

*Riley v. Massachusetts*[21] when in the name of all his brethren
he upheld a ten-hour day for women. McKenna's opinion was
that women were so handicapped in the struggle for existence
that it was imperative for the State to protect them. He insisted
that the restrictions which the law placed upon their contractual
powers to bargain with their employers as to the number of hours
were not imposed exclusively on their behalf. They were established in part for the benefit of society.

The physical well-being of women was an object of prime importance to the State, for on the health of women depended the
existence of strong, robust and healthy citizens capable of defend-
ing and developing the nation. It was therefore an obligation on
the part of the State to safeguard the health of women by prohibiting conditions which destroyed this health.[22] Since continuous work for long hours tended to undermine the health of
women, it was obvious that to regulate the workday in the interest of females was a proper exercise of police power.

The inferior economic position of women was an additional
factor that made it obligatory upon the State to protect their freedom in making labor contracts. The restricted fields in which
women might labor, the keen competition therein, and the need for
remunerative employment compelled them to accept conditions in
the labor contract to which they would not otherwise submit. An
employer who utilized these conditions to dictate terms enjoyed
such an advantage in the negotiations of labor agreements that all
sense of equality was destroyed. Hence, the attempt of the State to
establish an equality of bargaining power between female workers
and their employers by limiting the hours of work must be conceded as wise and constitutionally sound.

It was natural therefore for McKenna in the following year to
join Justice Hughes in *Miller v. Wilson*[23] in sustaining a California eight-hour day for women. It was the most drastic legal
restriction of hours in private, " non-hazardous " industries sus-

21 232 U. S. 671 (Mar. 23, 1914) ; Cahill, *op. cit.,* p. 131 ; Felix Frankfurter
" Hours of Labor and Realism in Constitutional Law," *Harvard Law
Review,* XXIX (Feb. 1916), 353.
22 232 U. S. 674.
23 236 U. S. 373 (Feb. 23, 1915).

tained by the Court during McKenna's career. The act prohibited the employment of females more than eight hours a day or forty-eight hours a week. Without doubt McKenna was whole-hearted in his support of the measure for Justice Hughes' reasoning was based on the same principles that McKenna employed in *Riley v. Massachusetts* and in *United States v. Garbish,* particularly that classification was permissible if there was no discrimination within one of the established classes.

In line with McKenna's willingness to base his conclusions on data and information supplied by experts rather than on judicial precedent was the manner in which Justice Hughes upheld an hour law in *Bosley v. McLaughlin.*[24] The contested statute limited the working hours of student nurses but not those of graduate nurses. Against the claim that such regulations were discriminatory, Justice Hughes, supported by McKenna, utilized information contained in a bulletin of the United States Bureau of Education to demonstrate that the classification was based on fair, reasonable and widely recognized standards of employment.

The growing tendency of McKenna to look at actual conditions and find therein new application for old princples, was found again in his concurring opinion in *Wilson v. New.*[25] The majority opinion written by Justice Hughes, with Justices Pitney, Day, Van Devanter and McReynolds dissenting, supported a national statute which had established an eight hour day for railroad workers.[26]

---

[24] 236 U. S. 385 (Feb. 23, 1915) ; "Education Status of Nursing," Bulletin No. 7, United States Bureau of Education, 1912.

[25] 243 U. S. 332 (Mar. 19, 1917) ; Arthur A. Ballantine, " Railway Strikes and the Constitution," *Columbia Law Review,* XVII (June 1917), 502, 506; George W. Wickersham, "Government Control of Corporations," *Columbia Law Review,* XVIII (Mar. 1918), 205; Philip W. Lowry, "Strikes and the Law," *Columbia Law Review,* XXI (Nov. 1921), 785; Charles K. Burdick, "The Adamson Law Decision," Cornell Law Review, II (May, 1917), 320–324; Henry Hull, "Some Legal Aspects of Federal Control of Railways," *Harvard Law Review,* XXXI (Apr. 1918), 862; Sidney Post Simpson, "Constitutional Limitations on Compulsory Industrial Arbitration," *Harvard Law Review,* XXXVIII (Apr. 1925), 767; Thomas R. Powell, "Commerce Pensions and Codes," *Harvard Law Review,* XLIX (Dec. 1935), 216.

[26] In addition to establishing an eight-hour day for railroads, the Adamson Act provided the appointment of a commission to observe the effect of the

The dissenters maintained that the act actually fixed wages, not hours.  McKenna, however, declared that the wage provisions were merely incidental to the object of enforcing the hour provisions, and were not to be deemed as isolated units for

> it is the sense of the practical world that prescribing the hours of labor is not prescribing wages of labor and Congress has kept the purpose distinct.

As he dissented in the Adair case, McKenna again asserted that, since the right of Congress to regulate interstate commerce was plenary it must follow that Congress possessed the power to establish regulations which would facilitate the flow of that commerce.  Recent railroad history demonstrated that the movement of interstate commerce was not only impeded but brought to a standstill by strikes of railroad employees.  Therefore it was only logical that Congress aim at the elimination of such obstacles in the path of interstate traffic.  It did this by establishing an eight-hour day for railroad workers which could not be considered an illegal exercise of power nor an excessive interference with the liberty of contract for

> When one enters into interstate commerce one enters in a service in which the public has an interest and subjects one's self to its behests.  And this is no limitation of liberty; it is the consequence of liberty exercised, the obligation of his undertaking, and constrains no more than any contract constrains.[27]

The significance of this opinion in the history of hour laws was summarized by Professor T. R. Powell who declared

> The concurrence of five members of the court in the opinion that the Adamson Law is a regulation of commerce should definitely end any contention that such a regulation of the relations *inter sese* of persons engaged in commerce cannot be a regulation of the commerce in which they are engaged.[28]

---

new workday and that during the period of observation the wages of the workers were not to be reduced.

[27] 243 U. S. 364.

[28] "The Supreme Court and the Adamson Law," *University of Pennsylvania Law Review,* LXV (May 1917), 613.

McKenna's contention that wage provisions were merely incidental in laws which regulated the hours of work was the fundamental basis for his majority decision in *Bunting v. Oregon.*[29] In opposition to the dissent of Chief Justice White and Justices Van Devanter and McReynolds, McKenna declared that protective hour-legislation even for men was within the police power of the State, that its classification was reasonable and that it was not a wage-law but an hour-of-service aimed at preserving the health of male workers. The legislation furthered the welfare of the community and could not be considered a violation of the liberty of contract.

In arriving at this conclusion, McKenna relied neither on his own opinions in *Riley v. Massachusetts, Wilson v. New* nor on those in such leading cases as *Holden v. Hardy, Lochner v. New York* or *Muller v. Oregon,* but on the monumental brief prepared by Louis Brandeis and Josephine Goldmark.[30] This document gathered into more than a thousand pages the facts on hours regulations. It presented complete tables of American and foreign legislation and data from all over the world, illustrative of the necessity for shorter hours based on physiological, social and economic grounds.

In recognizing the power and importance of facts, McKenna asserted

> Particularly in the last decade science has given us the basis for judgment by experience to which, when furnished, judgment by speculation must yield . . . It is now demonstrable that the considerations that were patent

[29] 243 U. S. 426 (Apr. 9, 1917) ; Maurice Finkelstein, "Judicial Self-Limitation," *Harvard Law Review,* XXXVII (Jan. 1924), 362; Felix Frankfurter, "Mr. Justice Holmes and the Constitution," *Harvard Law Review,* XLI (Dec. 1927), 143; Ray A. Brown, "Police Power-Legislation for Health and Personal Safety," *Harvard Law Review,* XLII (May, 1929), 884; E. Merrick Dodd, "For Whom are Corporate Managers Trustees?" *Harvard Law Review,* XLV (May, 1932), 1151; Thomas R. Powell, "The Judiciality of Minimum Wage Legislation," *Harvard Law Review,* XXXVII (Mar. 1924), 557.

[30] Edward A. Adler, "Labor, Capital and Business at Common Law," *Harvard Law Review,* XXIX (Jan. 1916), 241 ff., stresses the need for more frequent presentation of briefs like those of Brandeis and Goldmark.

as to minors in 1898 are today operative, to a greater or less degree, throughout the industrial system . . . Inasmuch as the application of the contending principles must vary with the facts to which they are sought to be applied, of course, new facts are the indispensable basis to the determination of the validity of specific new legislation.[31]

This was one of the clearest statements that McKenna ever formulated as to the necessity of considering labor legislation in the light of its attending circumstances.

McKenna's opinion was noteworthy not so much as a landmark in the development of his own thought but in the history of hours' legislation. For the first time a law regulating the hours of both men and women was sustained as a health measure.[32] Thus hour-regulation was no longer limited to women as McKenna decided in *Riley v. Massachusetts* or to hazardous industries as in *Lower Vein Coal Company v. Cerrillos* but could be extended to both sexes in non-hazardous industries.

A survey of McKenna's opinions in hour-regulation cases showed that he recognized the power of the State to establish such laws for women as in *Riley v. Massachusetts* as a health measure and in *Wilson v. New* as a protection for their freedom of contract. Later he confirmed a virtual combination of the two principles when he sustained a State law in *Bunting v. Oregon* which gave positive protection to the health of workers and protected their freedom of contract at the same time. It was evident that McKenna recognized as fictitious the asserted equality of employer and employee and that he believed that such an error was the basis for the blind adherence to the doctrine that the right of contract was absolute.

Under modern industrial conditions, equality of employer and employee in a labor contract could be secured either by organization of the workers or by legislative enactment. It was obvious that the worker needed the paternal protection of the State to guarantee his right to join a union or to limit his hours of labor. The fact that the State and Federal Governments had enacted

---

[31] 243 U. S. 426.

[32] Cahill, *op. cit.*, p. 130.

protective measures for the benefit of the industrial worker was sufficient evidence for McKenna to believe that the object desired was reasonable and necessary.

His confidence in the discretion of legislative bodies prompted McKenna to support the First Federal Employers' Liability Act. In 1906 Congress passed this statute aimed at exempting railroad employees from the fellow-servant and contributory-negligence features of the common law. Under either, fellow-servant or contributory-negligence principle, an employer need not compensate an employee for injuries sustained in the course of employment.[33] In 1908, in the *First Federal Employers' Liability Cases* [34] the Court voted the act unconstitutional by a five to four decision on the grounds that the law applied to employees of interstate carriers even when they were employed in intrastate commerce. The two employments were so intimately blended in the statute that they were incapable of separation or distinction.

McKenna disagreed, joining Justice Harlan who asserted that if the legislation admitted of two interpretations, one of which brought the law within, while the other pressed it beyond the constitutional authority of Congress, it would be the duty of the Court to adopt the former construction. This obligation followed from the rule that it should never be presumed that Congress intended to exercise or usurp its authority unless that conclusion was forced upon the Court by direct and unambiguous language.[35] The law applied only to interstate commerce and should receive that interpretation.

Congress accepted the dictum of the Court, clarified the controverted sections and under this form McKenna and his brethren upheld it in the *Second Employers' Liability Cases.*[36] Once the

---

[33] John R. Commons and John B. Andrews, *Principles of Labor Legislation,* pp. 387–392, summarize the principles of fellow-servant and contributory negligence.

[34] 207 U. S. 463 (Jan. 6, 1908).

[35] 207 U. S. 540.

[36] 223 U. S. 1 (1912); Frank Warren, "The Federal Employers Liability Act of 1908," *Harvard Law Review,* XXII (Nov. 1908), 38–47; Ray A. Brown, "Police Power-Legislation for Health and Personal Safety," *Harvard Law Review,* XLII (May, 1929), 889; J. A. Fowler, "Federal Power to Own and Operate Railroads in Peace Time," *Harvard Law Re-*

constitutionality of the act was established, the Court was then asked, in a series of cases, to determine the conditions under which an employer was engaged in interstate commerce. The connection between certain occupations and the movement of interstate commerce was often difficult to determine precisely. The Court could only examine the circumstances of the case and endeavor to fit it into one of the accepted categories of employment or establish it as a new class.

In adjudicating cases under the Second Employers' Liability Law, McKenna clearly demonstrated his desire to ameliorate the conditions of the worker, expand the accepted interpretation of the law and shift the financial burden of the industrial casualty from the victim to his employer. As a general rule, McKenna held that all employments which facilitated the safety and speed of interstate transportation were included within the provisions of the Liability Act.

Such was the case of defendant in *Erie Railroad v. Collins*,[37] where McKenna, in face of the dissent of Justices Van Devanter and Pitney, held that an employee was protected by the act although he was injured while operating a gasoline engine used to pump water into a tank which serviced both interstate and intrastate commerce. McKenna ruled that, although not directly engaged in interstate transportation, the victim was engaged in work so closely connected with it as virtually to be a part of it. He maintained that when the work of the employee concerned motive power, his connection might be quite remote without removing him from interstate commerce.

On the same day in *Erie Railroad Company v. Szary*,[38]

---

*view*, XXXIII (Mar. 1920), 789; Felix Frankfurter and James M. Landis, "The Business of the Supreme Court of the United States," *Harvard Law Review*, XL (June 1927), 1122; Frederick H. Cooke, "Nature and Scope of the Power of Congress to Regulate Commerce," *Columbia Law Review*, XI (Jan. 1911), 59; Alfred Hayes, "Partial Unconstitutionality with Special Reference to the Corporation Tax," *Columbia Law Review*, XI (Jan. 1911), 124, 129–130.

[37] 253 U. S. 77 (May 17, 1920).

[38] 253 U. S. 86 (May 17, 1920); "The Meaning of Interstate Commerce in the Federal Employers' Liability Act," *Columbia Law Review*, XIX (Jan. 1919), 395; Lester P. Shoene and Frank Watson, "Workmen's Com-

McKenna, with only Justices Pitney and Van Devanter in opposition, extended the protection of the Employers' Liability Act to those engaged in the more menial tasks. He ruled that an employee drying sand for use by interstate and intrastate locomotives had a connection sufficiently important to classify him under the shelter of the act. The activities of the sandman were so interblended with interstate transportation that he should be considered an integral part of such traffic.

The following year with only Justice Clarke dissenting, McKenna wrote the decision in *Philadelphia and Reading Railroad v. Di Donato* [39] and established the principle that a watchman at a public crossing of a railroad track on which both interstate and intrastate trains ran was engaged in interstate commerce whether he was flagging an intrastate or interstate train.

Consistent in his benevolent attitude toward the employee was McKenna's dissent in *Northern Pacific Railway v. Dixon* [40] where the Court decided that in the case of a locomotive fireman's death that the negligence of a train dispatcher was not the negligence of a vice-principal for which the railway was liable in damages but the negligence of a fellow-servant, that is a risk assumed by the victim. McKenna contended that the train dispatcher was a vice principal for whose negligence the master, not a fellow servant, was responsible. McKenna's attempt to break down the atrocious fellow-servant doctrine of the common law bore fruit two years later when the Court accepted his reasoning in *Santa Fe Railroad Company v. Holmes.* [41]

The principles which underlay McKenna's reasoning in the adjudication of cases under the Federal Employers' Liability Act were that an employer was liable for damages unless his agent acted as a reasonable man would have acted under like circumstances, that the employer could easily transfer to the customer

---

pensation on Interstate Railways," *Harvard Law Review,* XLVII (Jan. 1934), 389 ff., traces the development of the philosophy that became the basis for the Federal Employers' Liability Act.

[39] 256 U. S. 327 (May 16, 1921) ; " Recent Decisions," *Pennsylvania Law Review,* LXX (Jan. 1922), 115–118.

[40] 194 U. S. 338 (1904).

[41] 202 U. S. 438 (May 21, 1906).

the necessary pecuniary equivalent of the cost of the risk and that employment was undertaken primarily in the interest of the employer and as the receiver of the largest share of the profits he should be obliged to assume the risks of the business.

In the light of this liberal attitude it was reasonable to suppose that McKenna would be a staunch supporter of Workmen's Compensation Acts but such was not the case. His reputation as an opponent to workmen's compensation and in fact the entire anti-labor mark attached to his name, might be traced to the vigorous dissent which he wrote against the widely publicized Arizona Compensation Act as upheld by the Court on June 9, 1919. The conclusion that he was opposed to labor unions and labor laws was unjustified, for a brief review of his record in these cases demonstrated the contrary. The Arizona case was the exception, not the rule of his attitude. Thus the only time that McKenna favored the principle " no liability without fault," was in the case which curiously became the accepted criterion of his stand toward labor.

Until the Arizona Compensation case, McKenna had consistently favored the employee by supporting exceptions to the principle, " no liability without fault," which was the fundamental basis for his opposition to the Arizona Compensation law. As early as 1899 in *Atchison, Topeka and Santa Fe Railroad v. Matthews* [42] he asserted that the doctrine, " no liability without fault," was not universal even in common law for the master was liable for the tort of his servant and the obligations of innkeepers and common carriers were universally recognized. Therefore it was logical and reasonable to conclude that railroads, although without fault, should be held liable for damage to property caused by fire communicated by its locomotives.

Three years later McKenna added another exception to the principle of " no liability without fault " when he declared in *Chicago, Rock Island and Pacific Railroad v. Zernecke* [43] that the carrier of passengers could be held to the same liability that the common law had placed on the carrier of goods. In *Northern Pacific Railroad v. Dixon* he attempted further to weaken the prin-

---

[42] 174 U. S. 96 (Apr. 17, 1899).
[43] 183 U. S. 582 (Jan. 6, 1902).

ciple by declaring a train dispatcher to be a vice-principal for whose negligence the master was liable. Without hesitation he supported Justice Lurton's opinion in *City of Chicago v. Sturges* [44] which held that a city could be made liable for property damage inflicted by a mob.

A great advance was made in the process of abandoning the doctrine of " no liability without fault " when the New York Compensation Act was upheld in *New York Central Railroad Company v. White* [45] and again McKenna was on the side of those who were willing to impinge upon the principle. The law at issue imposed liability upon the employer in various groups of hazardous employments for all injuries of employees sustained in the course of their employment in lieu of the common law liability confined to cases of employer-negligence. In return for the imposition of absolute liability and the loss of common law defenses, the employer gained limitation on the loss of jury-assessed damages. On the other hand the employee procured certainty of recovery in practically all cases.

Thus in four noteworthy cases, including one on compensation, McKenna sustained the basis on which compensation acts were erected. He repeatedly favored interpretations of the law which protected the industrial casualty and hence it might appear somewhat of an anomaly that he would oppose the most adequate and efficacious remedy for the evil of disability among industrial workers.

Justice McKenna was conscious of his long pro-labor record and felt impelled to give substantial reasons for his reversal of position in the *Arizona Employers' Liability Cases.* [46] He main-

---

[44] 222 U. S. (Dec. 18, 1911) ; Ray A. Brown, " Police Power-Legislation for Health and Safety," *Harvard Law Review,* XLII (May, 1929), 866 ff.

[45] 243 U. S. 188 (Mar. 6, 1917).

[46] 250 U. S. 400 (June 9, 1919) ; Brown, *op. cit.,* p. 890; John B. Cheadle, " Government Control of Business," *Columbia Law Review,* XX (May, 1920), 573; " Notes," *Columbia Law Review,* XXI (Feb. 1921), 174; E. Merrick Dodd, " The New Doctrine of the Supremacy of Admiralty over the Common Law," *Columbia Law Review,* XXI (Nov. 1921), 660; " Comments," *Yale Law Journal,* XXIX (Dec. 1919), 225–227; " Juristic Theory and Constitutional Law—Liability without Fault," *Harvard Law Review,*

tained that in *New York Central Railroad v. White* the compensation law had been sustained because it had required both employers
and employees to relinquish certain advantages under the old laws
for new gains under the compensation law.  In the Arizona case
the Court had maintained a law which placed on the employer,
irrespective of negligence, liability for all injuries to employees
incident to their employment.  It abolished the defenses of the
fellow servant rule, assumption of risk and contributory negligence and, in addition, left to jury determination the assessment
of damages.  This to McKenna was giving all of the concessions
to the employee and placing all of the burdens on the employer.
It meant the complete abandonment of the principle, " no liability
without fault," and socialization of the property of the employer.
He declared that

> It seems to be of the very foundation or right—of the es-
> sences of liberty as it is of morals—to be free from lia-
> bility if one is free from fault.  It has heretofore been
> the sense of the law and the sense of the world . . . that
> there can be no punishment where there is no blame; and
> yet the court now by its decision erects the denial of these
> postulates of conduct into a principle of law and govern-
> mental policy.[47]

Not only did McKenna repudiate the exceptions that he had
made to the principle " no liability without fault " but he had permitted himself to forget that trover, trespass, slander and libel
were ancient parts of the law and moral wrong-doing was not
essential to any one of them.  What McKenna probably meant
in declaring that the law should not create liability without fault
was that no employer should be forced to pay compensation to an
employee injured outside of his immediate employment.  Yet an
employer under modern industrial conditions was definitely within
the chain of causation which resulted in the casualty.  In the light
of the compensation movement, in which almost all the chief
nations of the world participated, McKenna's statement that such

XXXIII (Nov. 1919), 87, sharply criticizes the economic and legal grounds
of McKenna's dissent.
[47] 250 U. S. 438.

laws "inverted the conception of mankind of the relation of right and wrong," was inaccurate and unfounded.

No other opinion of McKenna's was so vigorously and widely criticized. Not only on economic grounds but also on legal principles was his reasoning found to be faulty.[48] His insistence that the Arizona law was contrary to the fundamental elements of justice led one authority to state

> there are few more striking examples in the judicial literature of the relation between a mystical absolutism of natural rights and the practice of laissez faire.[49]

In subsequent cases on compensation laws, McKenna demonstrated that he was not wholeheartedly in agreement with the social and economic theories on which such laws were based. Nevertheless, he supported the Court in *New York Central Railroad v. Bianc*[50] which held that under an amendment to the New York Compensation Act the award of compensation was not dependent upon the actual impairment of the employee's earning power but might be made for mere disfigurement.[51] The Indiana Compensation Act was sustained by McKenna in *Lower Vein Coal Company v. Industrial Board of Indiana*[52] where he maintained that there was a sufficient difference between coal mining and other hazardous occupations to justify the application of compensation to the former occupation and not to the others. Nor could it be accepted that the law was arbitrary because it extended benefits to all employees of coal mines irrespective of the danger of their employment.

Really indicative of McKenna's thought toward compensation laws was his dissent in *Ward & Gow v. Krinsky*[53] where the

[48] "Juristic Theory and Constitutional Law," *Harvard Law Review,* XXXIII (Nov. 1919), 86–88.

[49] Max Lerner, *The Mind and Faith of Justice Holmes,* p. 162.

[50] 250 U. S. 596 (Nov. 10, 1919).

[51] This ruling was similar to the decision of McKenna in 253 U. S. 77, *Erie Railroad Company v. Collins* in which he held that an employee was entitled to damages for "shame, humiliation and personal disfigurement" suffered while in the course of his employment.

[52] 255 U. S. 144 (Feb. 28, 1921).

[53] 259 U. S. 503 (June 5, 1922). Roy A. Brown, "Legislation for Health

Court upheld an amendment to the New York Compensation Law which designated as "hazardous," and thus subject to the compensation provisions, all employments in which four or more persons were engaged in manual labor. While Justice Pitney's majority opinion was not altogether clear, the apparent result of it was to justify the extension of the compensation principle to all employments regardless of the existence of hazards.

With evident querulousness, McKenna, joined by Justice McReynolds, was at a loss to know

> What possible reason is there for imposing liability in favor of the one hundred employees otherwise outside of the compensation statutes, simply because their employer has found it desirable to hire four men to do manual work in a shop, or dig trenches, miles away from the only place where the hundred serve.[54]

It was evident that McKenna had been convinced of the justice of workmen's compensation after the Arizona case and was willing to extend their benefits to hazardous employments but he was unwilling to include non-hazardous occupations within the scope of those laws. He was unable to perceive that his position was at variance with the facts of industrial life; that the worker did not receive sufficient wages to cope with accident expenses; that the burden of the casualty if placed primarily on the victim was borne by his dependents, by charitable neighbors or by public charities and eventually, in one way or another, was thrust upon the public, that is, the general public, not those who, as consumers, were peculiarly benefited by the low-cost product of the underpaid and inadequately protected worker.

However strong his opposition to workmen's compensation laws, the general tenor of McKenna's philosophy toward the laborer and laboring conditions might be recognized as sympathetic and progressive. He contributed materially to abolish the highly individualistic interpretation of freedom of contract by opposing yellow-dog contracts, supporting hour-laws for men and women,

and Safety," *Harvard Law Review*, XLII (May, 1929), 892; *American Law Reports Annotated*, XXVIII (*Rochester:* N. Y. 1924), 1222.
[54] 259 U. S. 529.

and stripping the employer of common law defenses against liability for employee injuries. His uniform support and expression of views which established exceptions to the principle, " no liability without fault," aided considerably in bolstering the argument of the court when it upheld workmen's compensation laws, the very grounds on which McKenna was reputed to be anti-labor.

# CHAPTER VII

## FEDERAL POWER OVER COMMERCE

During the first quarter of the twentieth century the Supreme Court sanctioned a wide expansion of the powers of Congress under the Commerce Clause. The decisions defining the powers of the national government over interstate commerce resulted in the establishment of federal control over those matters generally associated with the police power, namely the morals, health, safety and welfare of the citizenry. In addition, the Court's favorable interpretation of congressional commerce legislation sanctioned and promoted the trend toward increased centralization of control in the national government permitting it to expand its powers at the expense of the state governments.

The Court justified the exercise of this so-called federal police power on the grounds that the industrialization of the nation necessitated such an exertion of power if legislation was to keep abreast of economic and social development. Since the Constitution did not specifically grant the national government control of those matters under police power, it required a goodly amount of ingenious reasoning on the part of the Court to establish a right of the Congress to do so by means of its interstate commerce power.

Congress, for example, could not directly protect the health of the people by prohibiting the adulteration of food, but it could indirectly do so by prohibiting the transportation of this adulterated food in interstate commerce. Justice McKenna materially contributed to the development of this new field of congressional legislation by uniformly sustaining the acts of Congress even when the majority of the Court was convinced that Congress had exceeded its authority under the Commerce Clause. The extent of the interstate power in such matters was announced with particular

154

clarity by McKenna in *Hoke and Economides v. United States* [1]
to be

> complete in itself, and . . . Congress, as an incident to it,
> may adopt not only means necessary but convenient to its
> exercise, and the means have the quality of police regula-
> tions.

One of the earliest attempts of Congress to close the stream
of interstate commerce to objectionable articles was in 1895 when
it forbade interstate transportation to lottery tickets. In *Champion v. Ames*,[2] the Court held that lottery tickets were articles of
commerce and Congress was justified in protecting society from
the " widespread pestilence of lotteries " by preventing their transmission across State lines.

Once its so-called police power was recognized, Congress was
not slow in exercising it. In 1906 the Pure Food and Drug Act [3]
was passed which prohibited the interstate transportation of adulterated food or drugs. In *Hipolite Egg Company v. United
States*,[4] Justice McKenna speaking for a unanimous court sustained the constitutionality of this act.

McKenna reasoned that Congress had acted within its constitutional powers in forbidding the carriage of impure food in interstate commerce. He argued that since regulation meant the prohibition of something, in the regulation of interstate commerce,
Congress had the unlimited right to prohibit any part of that com-

---

[1] 227 U. S. 308 (Feb. 24, 1913). Max Farrand, *Framing of the Constitution of the United States* (New Haven: 1913), p. 7, describes the conditions
which existed as the result of a lack of central power over commerce prior
to the adoption of the Constitution.

[2] 188 U. S. 321 (1903).

[3] *34 U. S. Statutes* 768, c. 3915. The Pure Food and Drug Act was
passed by Congress as the result of information brought to light by investigations conducted by Federal and State agencies. Upton Sinclair's *The
Jungle* aroused public support for the act.

[4] 220 U. S. 45 (Mar. 13, 1911). Henry Wolf Bikle, " The Silence of
Congress," *Harvard Law Review*, XLI (Dec. 1927), 218, discusses the con-
flicting views of the Court as to the nature of the essential test of a regulation of commerce. The present case was determined by the objective test
" that is the field of operation of the law." The subjective test being the
purpose or motive which the law was believed to disclose.

merce for, as the Court ruled in *Champion v. Ames,* the regu-
lative power of Congress extended to the absolute prohibition of
any article in interstate commerce.

Having thus established to his own satisfaction that the Pure
Food Law, in its immediate operation, was within the constitutional power of Congress, McKenna discussed its possible infringement of the powers of the States. To the contention that articles
could be seized only while in transit or before they had become
part of the general mass of property in the State, McKenna replied

> The contention misses the question in the case. There
> is here no conflict of national and state jurisdiction over
> property legally articles of trade. The question here is
> whether articles which are outlaws of commerce may be
> seized wherever found, and it certainly will not be con-
> tended that they are outside the jurisdiction of the na-
> tional government when they are within the borders of a
> state.[5]

There was no denial of the fact that the purpose of the Pure
Food Act was to stamp out the vicious practices connected with
the preparation of food. McKenna recognized and sustained this
purpose. He was convinced that Congress had no direct power
to prohibit the preparation of adulterated food, but under the
Commerce Clause it could deny food processors the use of the
facilities of interstate commerce. McKenna's reasoning pointed
the way to further extension of federal supervision and the principles which he announced were utilized in upholding the constitutionality of the Mann White Slave Act.[6]

The Mann White Slave Act, which prohibited the interstate
transportation of women for immoral purposes, was similar to
the Pure Food Act in that it aimed at protecting the health and
morals of society and prohibited interstate commerce as a means
of accomplishing an evil. In *Hoke and Economides v. United
States,*[7] *Harris and Green v. United States,*[8] and *Bennett v. United*

---

[5] 220 U. S. 55.

[6] *36 U. S. Statutes* 825, c. 395.

[7] 227 U. S. 308 (Feb. 24, 1913). Thomas I. Parkinson, "Congressional
Prohibitions of Interstate Commerce," *Columbia Law Review,* XVI (May,
1916), 370, 372, 375, 378, supports the reasoning of McKenna; "The Power

*States,*[9] Justice McKenna spoke for a unanimous Court in sustaining the constitutionality of the Mann White Slave Act.

In refutation of the charge that the statute infringed upon the powers of the States, Justice McKenna replied that the act did not interfere with any matter subject to State authority, nor attempt to regulate intrastate commerce. The act simply established the policy that the facilities of interstate commerce could not be utilized to promote commercialized vice. The public policy of the nation, which the Congress had the right to express, was formulated with the purpose of benefiting the entire nation and Congress had the power to further that policy by all available means.[10]

It logically followed that, if Congress could exclude lottery tickets, diseased cattle and adulterated food from interstate commerce, it could also forbid the use of interstate commerce to facilitate commercialized vice.

The unique feature of this opinion was the amount of space and reasoning which McKenna devoted toward establishing the pre-eminent position of Congress in the matter of interstate commerce. As a supplement to his previous arguments, he declared that the right of Congress to prohibit articles in interstate trade could be adduced from an analysis of the Ninth Section of the First Article of the Constitution which reads

> The migration or importation of such persons as any of the states . . . shall think proper to admit, shall not be prohibited by the Congress prior to 1808.

Such prohibition by the Congress was based on the power to regulate commerce. The power to regulate included the power to prohibit, otherwise this express restriction, on the power to prohibit such migration of commerce, was superfluous.

The principles of the Hoke case were extended by Justice McKenna in *Athenasaw and Sampson v. United States* [11] to those

---

of Congress to Regulate Child Labor through Interstate Commerce," *Harvard Law Review,* XXXV (May, 1922), 863; " Recent Cases," *Harvard Law Review,* XXVI. (May, 1913), 657.

[8] 227 U. S. 340 (Feb. 24, 1913).

[9] 227 U. S. 333 (Feb. 24, 1913).

[10] 227 U. S. 322.

[11] 227 U. S. 326 (Feb. 24, 1913).

who transported women for the perpetration of acts which might ultimately lead to prostitution. The term "debauchery" was employed in the statute to include any vice or offense against morality as well as illicit sexual intercourse. McKenna contended that the law aimed to eliminate commercialized vice, not isolated, individual, immoral acts.

In this sense his dissent with Chief Justice White and Justice Clarke in *Caminetti v. United States* [12] was entirely consistent. The majority of the Court sustained the conviction of a couple who had voluntarily crossed a State border and committed an act which in their own State would have been immoral but not criminal. McKenna contended that the Court should look beyond the letter of the statute to the aim of Congress which was to strike at commercialized vice. Even a close study of the wording of the act would not justify the interpretation given by the Court, because the interpretation was so comprehensive that it would include every form of conduct contrary to good order. The decision under the facts of the instant case would encourage blackmail which was already prevalent, and give to the Department of Justice, as it desired, a wider scope in the enforcement of the law. Thus the minority called attention to the necessity of amending the Mann Act which encouraged extortion and blackmail and which probably no jury would enforce unless a violation of the law was proved to be connected with white slavery.[13]

In all of the above cases the evil which Congress sought to eliminate had been accomplished with the aid of interstate commerce, the evil was consummated through the instrumentalities of interstate commerce, hence the prohibition of such articles from interstate channels was sufficiently close to the regulation of com-

---

[12] 242 U. S. 470 (Jan. 15, 1917). Frank L. McCarthy, "White Slave Traffic Act," *Yale Law Journal,* XXVI (Apr. 1917), 501–502, 509–510; "Scope of the White Slave Traffic Act," *Virginia Law Review,* IV (May 1917), 653–660; "Note and Comment," *Michigan Law Review,* XV (Mar. 1917), 425; Max Radin, "Statutory Interpretation," *Harvard Law Review,* XLIII (Apr. 1930), 883; Robert L. Stern, "That Commerce Which Concerns More States than One," *Harvard Law Review,* XLVII (June, 1934), 1355; John E. Hallen, "Comment on Omissions in Testimony," *Yale Law Journal,* XXVI (Apr. 1917), 501.

[13] Stern, *op. cit.,* p. 1355.

merce to justify the action of Congress. However, in *Hammer v. Dagenhart* [14] the Court was asked to sustain the Keating-Owen Act which prohibited interstate transportation of products produced by child labor. The Court ruled that the evil of child labor ended before the goods were offered for transportation and the connection between accomplishment of the evil and interstate commerce was not sufficiently close to justify regulation.

Justices McKenna, Brandeis and Clarke joined Justice Holmes in opposing the holding of the Court. To McKenna, it was sufficient that Congress had judged it expedient to abolish the evil of child labor by a proper exercise of its commerce power. As he had stated in *Hoke and Economides v. United States,* if the statute was a proper exercise of the commerce power, it was immaterial how it affected the persons or the property within the States. He was convinced that the commerce power was sufficiently broad to prevent evils occurring before, as well as after, interstate transportation.

In these decisions McKenna was more consistent than the majority of his brethren who, in one case, would look beyond the letter of the law, and in another would look through the form to the substance, through words to the meaning, through the law's alleged purpose to its actual aim.

In the same general category of trade laws was the Sherman Anti-Trust Act of 1890 by which Congress sought to impede the concentration of great wealth by outlawing contracts and combinations.in the form of trusts or conspiracy in restraint of trade among the States or with foreign nations. The Supreme Court had declared the act constitutional before Justice McKenna came to the bench but during the period of his justiceship the interpretation of the Sherman Act was a subject of prime importance in the economic life of the nation.

The first important case under the Sherman Act in which McKenna participated was *Northern Securities Company v.*

[14] 247 U. S. 251 (1918). McKenna believed that Congress could exclude products produced by child labor from interstate commerce by exercising its commerce powers but Congress could not do the same thing in virtue of its taxing powers hence his opposition to the exercise of the tax powers in *Bailey v. Drexel Furniture Company,* 259 U. S. 20 (1922).

*United States.*[15]   He supported the Court in holding that the Northern Securities Company, organized for the purpose of acquiring the stocks of the Northern Pacific, Great Northern, and Chicago, Burlington and Quincy Railroads, was an illegal combination.   The acquisition of the railroad stocks was an act tending to restrain trade, throttle competition and create a monopoly, hence it violated the Sherman Act.

Six years later Justice McKenna in *Standard Oil of New Jersey v. United States* [16] supported the ruling that plaintiff's combination was illegal in that it monopolized and unduly restrained the interstate trade of petroleum and its products.   A similar decision in *United States v. American Tobacco Company* [17] dissolved the combination formed to monopolize and restrain the interstate trade in tobacco.   In each of these cases, stress was laid upon the illegal acts of the promoters prior to the formation of the combination, upon the continuance of the illegal acts subsequent thereto, and upon the actual dominating control and influence of the combinations in question.   The performance of acts which illegally restrained interstate trade was the basis for the court's decisions. It was the exertion of the power to restrain trade or to monopolize an industry that was condemned, not the mere possession of the power.

This distinction was made by Justice McKenna in *United States v. United States Steel Corporation* [18] when, despite the dissent

---

[15] 193 U. S. 197 (1904).   Justice White read the dissent in behalf of four justices and declared that Congress was without power to regulate the acquisition and the control of stock and if there were any such power, Congress had not exercised it in the Sherman Act.

[16] 221 U. S. 1 (1911).

[17] 221 U. S. 106 (1911).

[18] 251 U. S. 417 (Mar. 1, 1920).   Francis Rooney, "The Legality of Combinations in Foreign Trade," *Columbia Law Review,* XVII (May, 1917), 405, 407, 408, 414; Gilbert H. Montague, "Anti-trust Laws and the Federal Trade Commission," *Columbia Law Review,* XXVII (June, 1927), 670, 672; Mathew O. Tobriner, "Cooperative Marketing and the Restraint of Trade," *Columbia Law Review,* XXVII (Nov. 1927), 834; Milton Handler, "Industrial Mergers and the Anti-trust Laws," *Columbia Law Review,* XXXII (Feb. 1932), 219–224; Myron W. Watkins, "The Change in Trust Policy," *Harvard Law Review,* XXXV (May, 1922), 815; Felix Frankfurter and James M. Landis, "The Business of the Supreme Court of the

of Justices Day, Pitney and Clarke, he maintained that the mere size of a corporation, or the existence of unexerted power to restrain competition or interstate commerce, was not of itself a violation of the Sherman Act. The existence of a combination *per se* was not illegal. McKenna admitted that the Steel Corporation had the same intent to monopolize and restrain trade as had Standard Oil, American Tobacco and Northern Securities. Unlike them it had not acquired the monopoly it sought and that, great as was its capability to dominate the iron and steel trade, it had not attempted to exercise that power.

As if to emphasize the distinction between the Steel Corporation and the condemned combinations, McKenna stressed the fact that the conduct of the promoters and managers of the former was not characterized by the " brutalities and tyrannies which, it is charged, were practiced by the promoters and managers of the Standard Oil and Tobacco Companies." McKenna went to the full limit of holding broadly that mere size or the mere existence of the power to dominate trade did not constitute an offense against the law, unless that power was exercised and manifested in overt acts.

The toleration of " good " combinations which underlay McKenna's support of the United States Steel Company manifested itself again in *American Column Company v. United States*.[19] This was called the " Hardwood Case," because it concerned " open price reporting " among the hardwood lumber firms of the nations. " Open price reporting " was a method of exchanging price and other industrial information among the mem-

---

United States—A Study in the Judicial System," *Harvard Law Review*, XL (June 1927), 1120; Louis L. Jaffe and Mathew O. Tobriner, " The Legality of Price-Fixing Agreements," *Harvard Law Review*, XLV (May, 1932), 1164, 1181; William W. Gager, " Efficiency or Restraint of Trade," *Yale Law Journal*, XXVII (June, 1918), 1060–1068, 1085.

[19] 257 U. S. 377 (Dec. 19, 1921). Herman Oliphant, " Trade Associations and the Law," *Columbia Law Review*, XXVI (Apr. 1926), 386, 389; Milton Handler, " The Constitutionality of Investigation by the Federal Trade Commission," *Columbia Law Review*, XXVIII (Nov. 1928), 934; Malcolm P. Sharp, " Movement in Supreme Court Adjudication," *Harvard Law Review*, XLVI (Jan. 1933), 396; Max Lerner, *The Mind and Thought of Justice Holmes* (New York: 1939), pp. 246–249.

bers of a trade association.  During the first World War this practice was permitted and even encouraged by the government, but,
in 1919, the government sued the Hardwood Association, pointing to the high lumber prices which were ascribed to the collusive
price practices of the Association.  In a six to three decision,
Justice Clarke held that the Association had violated the anti-trust
laws by means of this open conspiracy to fix prices.  There was
evidence that the Association, which controlled about a third of
the hardwood production, had urged limitation of production and
publicized the production of individual members.

McKenna objected, maintaining that the Sherman Act prohibited only unreasonable restraints of trade, and that good combinations, not oppressive toward competitors but aiming at constructive social results, were legal.[20]  With Justice Brandeis he
believed that rational competition among keen business rivals was
possible only when there was cooperative exchange of trade information.  Since the Court already held it legal to vest fifty per
cent of the steel industry in a single corporation and to entrust
one company with practically the whole machinery industry, it
would not then be illegal to confide one third of the hardwood
industry to one business group.

The basic concern of Justice McKenna in the Hardwood Case
was for the small businessman, for he feared if small independent
owners who had formed a trade association were not permitted
to act together reasonably for common economic purposes they
would be inclined to consolidate their holdings and the result
would be a trust with all the consequences of concentration of
power.

The determination of McKenna to condemn unreasonable restraints of trade was the fundamental idea behind his most notable
opinion under the Sherman Act.  In *Standard Sanitary Manufacturing Company v. United States*[21] commonly known as the

---

[20] President Theodore Roosevelt first spoke about the distinction between
good and bad trusts which distinction McKenna makes in the United States
Steel cases.  Justice Holmes in a dissent against the Northern Securities
decision noted that the ability to do wrong, the possession of the power to
monopolize and restrain trade, was in itself not illegal.

[21] 226 U. S. 20 (Nov. 18, 1912).  Edwin P. Grosvenor, "The 'Rule of

"Bathtub Case," McKenna spoke for a unanimous Court in outlawing an agreement whereby a patentee licensed 85% of the manufacturers of sanitary enameled ironware to use certain patents in return for a promise to observe fixed prices and to deal only with specified jobbers.

Justice McKenna went to the core of the problem by pointing out that a legitimate patent license could not be made a shelter for a violation of the Sherman Act. He maintained that, under the pretense of exercising the monopolistic rights of a patent, the combination disguised an agreement to fix prices and interfere with interstate commerce. After demonstrating that the agreements at issue had frequently been condemned by the Court in similar cases, he continued

> The agreement clearly, therefore, transcended what was necessary to protect the use of the patent or the monopoly which the law conferred upon it . . . The added element of the patent in the case at bar cannot confer immunity from . . . condemnation . . . Rights conferred by patents are indeed definite and extensive, but they do not give . . . a universal license against positive prohibitions.[22]

One important feature of the opinion was the clear decision that the patents applied only to a tool employed in the manufacture of ironware, not the ironware itself. The patents covered the tool, but not the ironware trade which plaintiff in error attempted to monopolize. McKenna might have decided the case on that distinction without any consideration of patent rights, but he expressly refused to base it on such narrow grounds. He insisted

Reason' as applied by the United States Supreme Court to Commerce in Patented Articles," *Columbia Law Review,* XVII (Mar. 1917), 208, 212; "The Acquisition of Patents as a Restraint of Trade," *Columbia Law Review,* XXIV (June, 1924), 657; "Control of Patentee over Unpatented Articles," *Harvard Law Review,* XXV (May, 1912), 641; Amos J. Peaslee, "The Effect of the Federal 'Anti-trust Laws' on Commerce in Patented and Copyright Articles," *Harvard Law Review,* XXVIII (Feb. 1915), 394. On the same principles of his Standard Sanitary decision, McKenna decided *Virtue v. Creamery Package Manufacturing Company,* 227 U. S. 8 (Jan. 20, 1913).

[22] 226 U. S. 20.

on placing his conclusions upon the broad principle that patent rights, though extensive, did not give a universal license against positive prohibitions.[23]

He analyzed and distinguished between the rights inherent in a patent and rights granted by law to the patentee. The right to make, use and vend the patented article had its origin in the common law, and existed independently of the statute law. The only right granted by patent laws was that of excluding all others from making, using or vending the thing patented without permission of the patentee.

This doctrine, that patent rights were not a universal license against prohibitions, was the grounds of Justice McKenna's dissent in *United Shoe Machinery Company v. United States*.[24] The Court, through Justice Day, held that a combination of non-competing companies in the shoe machinery business was not a violation of the Sherman Act. McKenna dissented without a comment, yet it can reasonably be supposed that his opposition was similar to that in the Bathtub Case, since the United Shoe Company compelled customers to use certain unpatented auxiliary machines in conjunction with their patented article. If the auxiliary machines were obtained from another source, the patented machine was withdrawn and the customer was forced to go out of business.

These circumstances were similar to those on which the Court had condemned the Standard Sanitary Manufacturing Company for it appeared to McKenna that the United Shoe Machinery Company was employing its patent rights to restrain trade and establish a monopoly and hence should be held a violator of the Sherman Act.

Unreasonable restraints of trade were not only attributable to

---

[23] McKenna's decision has become a leading case on the subject of the relation between the Sherman Act and the Patent Law. It has been cited five times by the Supreme Court and in at least eighteen reported cases in the lower Federal Courts.

[24] 258 U. S. 451 (Apr. 17, 1922). William W. Gager, "Efficiency or Restraint of Trade," *Yale Law Journal*, XXVII (June, 1918), 1064; Edwin P. Grosvenor, "The 'Rule of Reason' as Applied by the United States Supreme Court to Commerce in Patented Articles," *Columbia Law Review*, XVII (Mar. 1917), 218; "Rights of Licensee Against Third Parties," *Columbia Law Review*, XVII (June, 1917), 546.

combinations of capitalists but also to associations of workers, and Justice McKenna believed that acts in restraint of interstate commerce by labor unions were likewise amenable to the Sherman Act. He was convinced that justice should be administered impartially to combinations of employers and employees and hence supported the Court in *Loewe v. Lawlor* [25] or the Danbury Hatters case, which held that an interstate boycott by a labor union fell under the ban of the Sherman Act. A similar decree was handed down with McKenna's approval in *Duplex Printing-Press Company v. Deering* [26] where the boycott was against printing presses manufactured by a Michigan corporation for out-of-state customers.

The consistency of Justice McKenna toward illegal restraints of interstate commerce by boycotts was illustrated in his dissent with Justice Pitney in *Paine Lumber Company v. Neal.* [27] Plaintiffs, non-union manufacturers, sought to enjoin defendants, members of a labor union, from continuing a secondary boycott which restrained plaintiff's interstate trade. Justice Holmes, speaking for the majority, held that an act, although a violation of the Sherman Act, could not be enjoined at the instance of a private party even though it had suffered special damage therefrom, the remedy by injunction being available only to the government.

Justice McKenna maintained that, under the equity doctrine, a private person was entitled to an injunction under the circumstances and apart from any express right granted by the Sherman Act. This act undoubtedly gave the federal courts jurisdiction in such an action and the fact that the district attorneys were charged with a duty to institute equity proceedings to restrain violations of the act, did not in any way interfere with the right

––––––

[25] 208 U. S. 274 (1908). This case dragged along for fourteen years, reached the Supreme Court three times and was finally settled when the unions paid $235,000.

[26] 254 U. S. 443 (1921).

[27] 244 U. S. 459 (June 11, 1917). Thomas Reed Powell, "Commerce, Congress and the Supreme Court," *Columbia Law Review*, XXVI (May, 1926), 547; Albert M. Kales, "The Sherman Act," *Harvard Law Review*, XXXI (Jan. 1918), 445; Harris C. Lutkin, "The Sherman Anti-Trust Act, Injunction not Available to Private Party," *Illinois Law Review*, XII (Jan. 1918), 435–437; "Recent Cases," *Minnesota Law Review*, II (Mar. 1918), 306–307.

of a private person to proceed in this way, but merely supplied a remedy where no private person was suffering a special damage by reason of the violation of the act.

The most significant contribution which he made to the doctrine that Congress should exercise unfettered jurisdiction over inter-state and foreign commerce was in the Insular Cases. In these cases the Court was faced for the first time in its history with the problem of determining whether territory annexed to the United States immediately became an integral part of the United States or could be held merely as a dependency. The question arose as the result of our annexations of the Philippines, Porto Rico and the Hawaiian Islands.

The first of these cases came before the Court in *De Lima v. Bidwell*.[28] The majority concluded that Porto Rico, annexed in 1898, had not become an integral part of the Federal Union by mere annexation, yet it not being foreign territory, duties could not be placed on its exports to the United States. In dissent, Justice McKenna, speaking for Justices White, Shiras, and Gray, contended that the island occupied a status midway between a domestic and foreign territory and that unless Congress expressly gave the harbors of the island the character of domesticity, duties on exports from Porto Rico to the United States must be collected.

McKenna preferred to treat the question of the status of the island pragmatically, insisting that not sovereignty, but reasons of policy, as embodied in legislative utterances, were the real test. In treating the status of Porto Rico to be in a twilight zone be-tween domestic and foreign territory and emphasizing the right of Congress to deal with it in a manner not foreseen by the framers

[28] 182 U. S. 1 (May 27, 1901). Carman F. Randolph, " The Insular Cases," *Columbia Law Review*, I (Nov. 1901), 436; Edward B. Whitney, " The Insular Decisions," *Columbia Law Review*, II (Feb. 1902), 88; Paul Fuller, " Expansion of Constitutional Powers by Interpretation," *Columbia Law Review*, V (Mar. 1905), 207; Frederic R. Coudert, " The Evolution of the Doctrine of Territorial Incorporation," *Columbia Law Review*, XXVI (June, 1926), 824; Emlin McClain, " The Hawaiian Case," *Harvard Law Review*, XVII (Apr. 1904), 388; E. F. Albertsworth, " Judicial Review of Administrative Action by the Federal Supreme Court," *Harvard Law Review*, XXXV (Dec. 1921), 147; Malcolm P. Sharp, " Movement in Supreme Court Adjudication," *Harvard Law Review*, XLVI (Mar. 1933), 808.

of the Constitution, McKenna established the fundamental basis for the principle of incorporation, later more fully developed by Justice White in *Downes v. Bidwell.*[29]

After the decision in *De Lima v. Bidwell,* Congress modified the tariff statutes but retained the duties upon imports from Porto Rico and the Philippines. In *Downes v. Bidwell* the tariff law was challenged as a violation of the constitutional provision which required " all duties, imports and excises shall be uniform throughout the United States." The issue was whether Porto Rico had become a part of the United States within the meaning of this provision. The Court held, through Justice Brown, that it had not. A lengthy concurring opinion was written by Justice White and supported by Justices McKenna and Shiras.

Justice White fully expressed the thought of McKenna when he divided all annexations into incorporated and unincorporated territories. By this principle the former became an integral part of the nation by action or implied intention of Congress, whereas the latter were possessions not entitled to equality under the tariff laws unless Congress specifically extended that concession. Thus Congress under the Commerce Clause had the sole right to determine the status of acquired possessions.

In view of McKenna's staunch advocacy of unfettered congressional control of interstate commerce, it was natural that he would reject any attempt on the part of the States to interfere directly with the flow of that commerce. Hence he ruled as void a State law in conflict with congressional control of interstate commerce. In *Erie Railroad v. New York,*[30] speaking for a unani-

---

[29] 182 U. S. 244 (May 27, 1901). Frederic R. Coudert, " Our New Peoples : Citizens, Subjects, Nationals or Aliens," *Columbia Law Review,* III (Jan. 1903), 25; Percy Bordwell, " The Function of the Judiciary," *Columbia Law Review,* VII (Nov. 1907), 521 Charles E. Littlefield, " The Insular Tariff Cases in the Supreme Court," *Harvard Law Review,* XV (June, 1901), 164; Emlin McClain, " The Hawaiian Case," *Harvard Law Review,* XVII (Apr. 1904), 388.

[30] 233 U. S. 671 (May 25, 1914). Charles W. Needham, " Exclusive Power of Congress over Interstate Commerce," *Columbia Law Review,* XI (Mar. 1911), 251. The same rule was applied to *Southern Railway Company v. Reid,* 222 U. S. 424 (Jan. 9, 1912), and to *Southern Railway Company v. Reid and Beam,* 222 U. S. 444 (Jan. 9, 1912).

mous Court, McKenna maintained that, in the presence of a federal hours-law for employees of interstate railroads, a State was precluded from acting even though its law imposed more drastic restrictions than those imposed by Congress. In summarizing his conclusion McKenna declared

> the right of a State to apply its police power for the purpose of regulating interstate commerce . . . exists only from the silence of Congress on the subject, or manifests its purpose to call into play its exclusive power . . . as the enactment by Congress of the law in question was assertion of its power, by the fact alone of such manifestation that subject was at once removed from the sphere of the operation of the authority of the State.[31]

The principal idea which McKenna stressed was that, when Congress acted, it occupied the whole field. The supremacy of congressional power admitted of no division nor supplement; it was the prescribed measure of what was necessary and sufficient for the regulation of the working hours of interstate railroad workers. In its presence State legislation was not permissible.

This principle that such Congressional regulation thus precluded State regulation in the same realm was the basis for two other decisions of McKenna. In *Texas and New Orleans Railroad Company v. Sabine Tram Company*[32] and *Railroad Commission of Louisiana v. Texas and Pacific Railroad Company*,[33] he sustained the position of the carriers who had charged a higher rate set by the Interstate Commerce Commission than that set by the State. In the former case the shipper sued to recover the difference between the Interstate Commerce Commission rates and lower ones fixed by the Texas Commission; in the latter the carrier sued the Louisiana Commission to enjoin enforcement of its orders and the imposition of penalties for their violation. The Sabine Company shipped lumber from interior Texas to Gulf ports where

---

[31] 233 U. S. 682.
[32] 227 U. S. 111 (Jan. 27, 1913). Thomas R. Powell, "Supreme Court Decisions on the Commerce Clause and State Police Power," *Columbia Law Review*, XXI (Dec. 1921), 742; "Recent Cases," *Harvard Law Review*, XXVI (Apr. 1913), 554.
[33] 229 U. S. 336 (June 10, 1913).

it was placed on ships destined for foreign ports. Sabine Company's concern ended when the lumber reached the docks.

In sustaining the carriers, McKenna laid down the principle that merchandise marked for export acquired the character of foreign commerce as soon as it began its journey or was delivered to an interstate carrier. In distinguishing other cases, cited by defenders of State rates, McKenna insisted that in those cases there was only local movement of freight, whereas in the case at bar the freight had acquired the character of foreign commerce at the initial point of its journey and hence was a matter for congressional control.

The doctrine that congressional legislation precluded State regulation was strengthened and confirmed by McKenna in *Southern Railway Company v. Reid* [34] and in *Southern Railway v. Reid and Beam*.[35] The carriers refused to accept and ship, contrary to State law, but in obedience to congressional statute, freight for which no rate had been fixed and proclaimed. Thus the State law penalized refusal to ship although the federal law forbade shipping in the absence of established rate. In outlawing the action of the State, McKenna emphasized his belief that the absence of congressional action did not justify the State in exercising control of interstate commerce. The unexerted right of the Congress to fix a rate in interstate commerce could not justify a State in establishing that rate.

In addition to condemning State laws which conflicted with or were made in the absence of congressional legislation, McKenna established certain principles which could be employed in determining when a State regulation imposed direct and unconstitutional burdens on interstate commerce. In *Seaboard Airline Railroad v. Blackwell*,[36] Chief Justice White and Justices Pitney, Clarke and

[34] 222 U. S. 424 (Jan. 9, 1912). Henry Hull, " Jurisdiction and Causes of Action Arising Under the Act to Regulate Commerce," *Columbia Law Review*, XXII (Jan. 1922), 33; " Recent Decisions," *Columbia Law Review*, Decisions on the Commerce Clause and State Police Power," *Columbia Law Review*, XXII (Jan. 1922), 33; " Recent Decisions," *Columbia Law Review*, XII (Feb. 1912), 167.

[35] 222 U. S. 444 (Jan. 9, 1912).

[36] 244 U. S. 310 (June 4, 1917). Henry Wolf Bikle, " Judicial Determination of Questions of Fact Affecting the Constitutional Validity of Legisla-

McKenna decided that a State law compelling railroad trains to check speed when approaching crossings was a direct interference with interstate commerce. It was so in the sense that it made the conduct of railroads more expensive and more difficult with the result that either a smaller amount of the commerce was carried or that some of it was diverted to other channels.

McKenna's predilection for opposing undue interference with interstate commerce by State laws was again demonstrated in *Chicago, Burlington and Quincy Railroad v. Railroad Commission of Wisconsin* [37] when he held, as an unconstitutional burden on interstate commerce, a State law which provided that every village of 200 or more inhabitants should be served by at least one train a day in each direction, and by two trans if four or more were operated. McKenna contended the railroad already furnished facilities adequate to care for the local traffic and there its obligations ceased. To compel interstate trains to stop at villages was a direct burden in that it demanded increased speed between stops with corresponding danger to passengers, if the trains were to meet the competition of other lines. On the same principle, McKenna held a similar State regulation unconstitutional in *St. Louis, San Francisco Railway Company v. Public Service Commission of Missouri*.[38]

The principles which formed the framework of McKenna's decisions were that a State was competent to demand adequate railroad facilities for local traffic even to the stoppage of interstate trains or the rearrangement of their schedules; that when these demands had been met, the unnecessary stoppage or impeding of interstate trains became an illegal and improper interference with interstate commerce and that the Supreme Court had the right to determine the conditions of local service and whether that demand involved a direct and arbitrary burden on interstate commerce.

Likewise frustrated, as a direct burden on interstate commerce, was the Oklahoma law which attempted to keep natural gas from being piped to points outside the State. In *West v. Kansas Nat-*

tive Action," *Harvard Law Review,* XXXVIII (Nov., 1924), 10; "Notes," *Columbia Law Review,* XXVII (May, 1927), 575.

[37] 237 U. S. 220 (Apr. 12, 1915).
[38] 261 U. S. 369 (Mar. 19, 1923).

*ural Gas Company,*[39] McKenna, over the dissent of Justice Hughes, Holmes, and Lurton, ruled that the State could not permit domestic corporations to pipe unlimited quantities of gas to different points in the State and simultaneously prohibit foreign corporations from pumping gas outside the State. Hence foreign corporations could not be forbidden to run interstate pipe lines over privately purchased rights-of-way and to cross over or under public highways. The permission to use the highways longitudinally could not be withheld from those intending to construct an interstate pipe line when it was granted to those engaged only in intrastate transportation.

No State, in the opinion of McKenna, could by its action or inaction unreasonably burden, discriminate against, directly regulate interstate commerce or the right to engage in interstate commerce. From such a statement it followed that a State could not forbid a corporation from carrying on intrastate commerce in connection with interstate commerce if such refusal unreasonably burdened the latter.

Although Justice McKenna was a consistent supporter of the paramount power of Congress over interstate commerce, he did not stubbornly oppose the incidental regulation of that commerce by State law. He was convinced that the State control of intrastate commerce was as absolute and sovereign as that of Congress over interstate commerce. In the exercise of their particular power, either government might reasonably burden, but not destroy, the commerce of the other. In adjudicating State laws which were allegedly direct regulations of interstate commerce, McKenna believed that recourse must be had to reason and practical appreciation of the circumstances under which the regulation was made. To condemn laws merely because of their incidental effect on interstate commerce would bring many salutary legislative activities to a standstill. There was need for " freedom

---

[39] 221 U. S. 229 (May 15, 1911). Thomas R. Powell, " Supreme Court Decisions on the Commerce Clause and State Police Power," *Columbia Law Review,* XXI (Dec. 1921), 749; Thomas R. Powell, " Indirect Encroachment on Federal Authority by the Taxing Powers of the States," *Harvard Law Review,* XXXI (Mar. 1918), 750; " Recent Cases," *Harvard Law Review,* XXV (Nov., 1911), 90.

of action in the joints of the machine" of government if legislation was to keep abreast of industrial and social development.

These principles were the basis for McKenna's decision in *Smith v. St. Louis Southwestern Railroad* [40] in which he upheld a Texas law prohibiting interstate shipment of diseased cattle. The gravity of contagious cattle diseases to the economic life of Texas was sufficiently cogent for McKenna to uphold the regulation, despite the dissent of Justices White and Harlan. He traced the cautious policy of the Court in forestalling attempts on the part of the States in the exercise of their police power to encroach upon the domain of interstate commerce. In the instant case, however, regulation was justified since the aim of the law was to localize animal diseases, the State thereby closing the channels through which disease was ordinarily transmitted. If there was interference with interstate commerce it was only incidental to the proper exercise of the police power and would have to be borne by interstate commerce until Congress regulated the matter.

Practical considerations again entered largely into Justice McKenna's thought when he spoke for a unanimous court in *Mutual Film Corporation v. Industrial Commission of Ohio* [41] and *Mutual Film Corporation v. Hodges, Governor of Kansas.* [42] Ohio and Kansas demanded the censorship of films before exhibition. Plaintiffs in error challenged the laws on the ground that the films were delivered to consignees in the original package and to subject them to censorship in the original package was an undue interference with interstate commerce. [43]

In conjunction with common sense and public opinion, McKenna maintained that there was need for censorship of films if the pruriency of human nature was not to be unduly excited and appealed to by situations presented in the cinema. The laws were a proper and reasonable exercise of the police power and were not

---

[40] 181 U. S. 248 (Apr. 22, 1901). Thomas R. Powell, "Commerce, Pensions and Codes," *Howard Law Review,* XLIX (Dec. 1935), 194.

[41] 236 U. S. 230 (Feb. 23, 1915). "Recent Cases," *Columbia Law Review,* XV (June, 1915), 546.

[42] 236 U. S. 248 (Feb. 23, 1915). "Recent Decisions," *Columbia Law Review,* XV (June, 1915), 546.

[43] 236 U. S. 242.

aimed as direct restraints of interstate commerce. In refutation of the original package doctrine McKenna noted

> the films were mingled as much as from their nature as they can be with other property of the State and subject to its otherwise police regulation even before consignee delivered them to exhibitors.[44]

While McKenna recognized that State regulations of interstate commerce were to be sustained only when the commerce in question was of the type that satisfactorily admitted of diversity of treatment in different localities, he decided that not all State laws which bore on interstate commerce were thereby rendered inapplicable. State police measures derived their sanction from the general authority enjoyed by the State and were sustained as an exercise of that authority up to the point where, in application to interstate commerce, they entered the field in which Congress had exclusive control. McKenna sustained the principle that as to interstate commerce which is national in character and required uniformity of regulation, State laws were allowed to apply if they fell short of regulating interstate commerce.

In *Western Union Telegraph Company v. Commercial Milling Company* [45] Justice McKenna, with only Justice Holmes dissenting, permitted the State of origin of an interstate message to apply a statute forbidding the telegraph company to limit its liability for negligent delivery. McKenna distinguished the case at bar from one in which a statute of the State of origin, penalizing negligent delivery in another State, was considered a regulation of interstate commerce. McKenna considered that the condemned statute had imposed affirmative duties in another State, ignored the requirements of the laws of that State and gave " action for damages against the permission of such laws for acts done within its jurisdiction." The present statute had no such objectionable qualities. He maintained:

---

[44] *Ibid.,* 243.

[45] 218 U. S. 406 (Nov. 28, 1910). Edward P. Buford, " Assumption of Risk under the Federal Employers' Liability Act," *Harvard Law Review,* XXVIII (Dec. 1914), 172; Thomas R. Powell, "Supreme Court Decisions on the Commerce Clause and State Police Power," *Columbia Law Review,* XXI (Dec. 1921), 745.

It imposes no additional duty. It gives sanction only to an inherent duty. It declares that in the performance of a service, public in its nature, that it is a policy of a State that there shall be no contract against negligence. The prohibition of the statute, therefore entails no burden. It permits no release from that duty in the public service which men in their intercourse must observe, the duty of observing the degree of care and vigilance which the circumstances justly demand, to avoid injury to another.[46]

McKenna was not willing to restrict the State in such an important duty as protecting its citizens from negligent public service, nor was he willing to restrain the State in the collection of debts when there was no legislative act directly affecting interstate commerce. In *Davis v. Cleveland, Cincinnati, Chicago & St. Louis Railway Company*[47] Justice McKenna, in a unanimous Court decision, sustained an Iowa statute which permitted writs of attachment to be levied upon certain railroad cars employed in interstate commerce. The writs were levied upon empty cars in possession of a domestic company under an agreement providing that such companies should forward, reload and return them to an Indiana corporation. The garnishment and attachment, in so far as they did not tie up interstate commerce, were not a regulation of that commerce, their real and proper purpose was to secure payment of debt.

In addition to conflicts between the exercise of State police power, and the congressional control of interstate commerce, there were frequent controversies over the State right to tax interstate carriers. In *Diamond Match Company v. Ontonagon*[48] Justice McKenna spoke for a unanimous court in upholding the right of a State to tax goods before interstate movement began. In discussing the right to tax property of plaintiff, McKenna made a detailed study of the exact time that interstate commerce came

[46] 218 U. S. 416.

[47] 217 U. S. 157. " Notes," *Harvard Law Review,* XX (Feb. 1907), 319; " Recent Cases," *Harvard Law Review,* XXIII (June, 1910), 643.

[48] 188 U. S. 97 (Jan. 19, 1903). William Cullen Denis, " Notes on Some Recent Supreme Court Cases Relation to the Situs of Intangible Personal Property," *Columbia Law Review,* XV (May 1915), 378; " Notes," *Harvard Law Review,* XVI (Apr. 1903), 441.

into being. He maintained that neither the character of the merchandise nor the intention of the owner created interstate commerce. It began only when delivery was made to a carrier for interstate carriage and ended when the commodity arrived at a place " where intended that it should finally halt."

The most significant difference between McKenna's ideas and those of his colleagues on the relation of State police power to interstate commerce was exemplified in cases where the States attempted to tax foreign corporations doing intrastate business. In *Western Union Telegraph Company v. Missouri*[49] (1903) McKenna, with only Justices White and Peckham dissenting, upheld the right of a State to tax property and equipment of plaintiff in error. In refuting the claim that the tax was an illegal burden on interstate commerce, McKenna cited a number of decisions which held companies doing business in virtue of a congressional act were not exempt from ordinary taxation. McKenna admitted that the State could not prevent the telegraph company from doing what the national laws warranted but the State could tax the corporation for furnishing protection to its property. McKenna referred to the principle he had explained in *Waters-Pierce Oil Company v. Texas*,[50] *Chattanooga Building Association v. Denson*[51] and *Conley v. Mathieson Alkali Works*[52] that a State had the right to prohibit a foreign corporation from doing business within its confines. The State simply sought to regulate the activities of a foreign corporation doing interstate business. It did not tax nor burden interstate commerce. The State had exercised a right in a field in which it was sovereign and absolute and its exertion could not be considered a burden on interstate commerce.

These principles became one of the bases for his dissent with Justice Holmes in *Western Union Telegraph Company v. Kansas*[53] in which the Court held as unconstitutional a State law taxing foreign corporations. The statute provided that foreign corporations engaged in intrastate business were to pay, in addition

---

[49] 190 U. S. 412 (May 18, 1903).
[50] 177 U. S. 28 (Mar. 19, 1900).
[51] 189 U. S. 408 (Apr. 27, 1903).
[52] 190 U. S. 406 (May 18, 1903).
[53] 216 U. S. 1 (Jan. 17, 1910).

to a privilege tax, a fixed percentage of their total authorized capital, wherever located.   In the case at bar the law applied to an interstate carrier which was taxed for its intrastate business.

The Court, through Justice Harlan, held that the tax was an impediment to and burden on interstate commerce.   The maxim, that States might regulate the right of foreign corporations to do local business, did not justify a regulation of a firm doing interstate business.

Justice McKenna and Chief Justice Fuller joined Justice Holmes in maintaining that the power of a State to exclude foreign corporations from doing business included the right to tax those corporations.   There was no attempt to impede the flow of interstate commerce; the State merely declared a tax would have to be paid before intrastate business could be carried on.   There was no compulsion for

> The whole matter is left in the Western Union's hands. If the license fee is more than the local business will bear, it can stop that business and avoid the fee.   The State seeks only to oust the corporation from that part of its business that the corporation has no right to do unless the state gives leave.[54]

Justice McKenna questioned the conclusion that the right of a corporation to remain untaxed for its interstate business precluded a State from regulating or prohibiting the corporation's intrastate business.   The State had the power of giving or withholding the right of doing local business and to withhold or regulate that right could not be unconstitutional since the Constitution granted the State exclusive power over that business.

In rejecting the right of States to tax the local business of interstate carriers, the Court was convinced that it was more salutary to eliminate the vicious habit of discriminatory taxation of interstate carriers than to maintain the absolute power of the States over foreign corporations.   Justice McKenna believed that the latter alternative was not only intrinsically more important but also had the weight of precedent in its favor.   He was unwilling

---

[54] *Ibid.* 53.

to sanction the impingement of a recognized power merely because it had been abused on occasion.

The opinions on the Commerce Clause contained cogent expression of principles which Justice McKenna advocated not only in their adjudication but in the consideration of all constitutional law. They contained a clear indication of the importance which he gave to history, precedent, reason and the universal consent of man. Underlying the reasoning in practically every case, was the pervading idea of the exclusive and plenary power of Congress over interstate and foreign commerce. It was the kernel and core of McKenna's arguments which supported the significant " incorporation " doctrine proposed by him in nuclear form in *De Lima v. ·Bidwell*, formed the framework for support of an expanding federal police power, extended jurisdiction of the Interstate Commerce Commission and induced liberal interpretation of the Sherman Anti-Trust Law. The exclusive character which McKenna attributed to national power left no room for a collateral power of the States in the regulation of interstate commerce and as a consequence his opinions in commerce cases were completely logical in distinguishing between the exercise of State and national power in this sphere.

# CHAPTER VIII

## PERSONAL CIVIL RIGHTS AND POLICE POWER

The Supreme Court has usually given a strict interpretation to the personal civil rights guaranteed by the Constitution. The Court asserted that the first eight Amendments to the Constitution, which safeguarded these rights, were framed for a specific purpose. It was the duty of the Court to make this purpose the criterion by which to judge laws involving personal civil rights. The only exception to the practice of strict interpretation was in respect to the personal civil rights under the First and Fifth Amendments where the Court vacillated in the definition and extent of the constitutional guarantees.

This uncertainty was particularly noticeable when the constitutional right of freedom of speech was involved in cases under the Espionage Acts of 1917 and 1918. These laws severely punished anyone guilty of interference with the draft, encouraging disloyalty, criticizing the army, navy or government or in any way impeding the war effort.

The six leading cases under these acts were decided in 1919 and 1920 and in each Justice McKenna supported the right of the government to limit the freedom of speech during the time of war.[1] He maintained that freedom of speech and press were not absolute and that restrictions upon them were justifiable and necessary for the protection of public safety and welfare. All in-

---

[1] *Frohwerk v. United States,* 249 U. S. 204 (Mar. 3, 1919); *Debs v. United States,* 249 U. S. 211 (Mar. 3, 1919); *Schenck v. United States,* 249 U. S. 575 (Mar. 3, 1919); *Abrams v. United States,* 250 U. S. 616 (Nov. 10, 1919); *Schaefer v. United States,* 251 U. S. 468 (Mar. 1, 1920); *Pierce v. United States,* 252 U. S. 239 (Mar. 8, 1920). For a favorable review of the government's position in all these cases, see J. P. Hall, " Free Speech in War Time," *Columbia Law Review,* XXI (Mar. 1921), 526. An adverse criticism of the government's position is, in Zechariah Chafee, *Free Speech in the United States* (Cambridge, Mass.: 1942), 80 ff.

fluences which might delay or prevent victory were to be averted and all utterances and statements critical of the aims and efforts of the government suppressed.  Even though enforcement of the laws was accompanied by mistakes and abuse, yet the social benefit derived from such laws was sufficient compensation for tolerating such inconveniences.  Just as circumstances in wartime justified a modification of the interpretation given to the right of due process of law so wartime permitted qualification in the connotation given to the right of freedom of speech.

McKenna justified the limitations of speech by Congress on the grounds of the war power.  Since Congress could declare war and raise armies, it could facilitate its work by punishing those who either directly kept men out of the service by starting a draft riot or indirectly by persuading men not to register or not to enlist.  In addition to punishing overt acts, which impeded the draft, Congress could forestall such acts by punishing the mere intent to interfere with the draft.  It was immaterial whether the intent was manifested by words or acts, if the intent were present, it was punishable.

In the light of these views it was reasonable to suppose that McKenna would support Justice Holmes in upholding convictions under the Espionage Act in *Schenck v. United States,*[2] *Frohwerk v. United States*[3] and *Debs v. United States.*[4]  In all three cases the Court decided that Congress had the right to punish utterances which were reasonably likely to interfere with the effective conduct of the war.

It was natural that when McKenna represented the majority of

---

[2] In the Schenck case, defendants had mailed circulars to men accepted for service by the draft boards. The men were urged to assert their constitutional rights on the grounds that the draft was unconstitutional despotism.  The Court decided that circulation of the circulars was a direct and dangerous interference with the right of Congress to raise armies.

[3] Defendants in the Frohwerk case had published anti-army, pro-German propaganda in a German language newspaper.  The court upheld conviction for interfering with the draft although no special effort had been made to reach men subject to the draft.

[4] Eugene Debs, five time Socialist candidate for the presidency, was released by President Harding after serving two years and eight months of a ten year sentence.

the Court in *Schaefer v. United States* [5] he would uphold a verdict against five officers of the *Philadelphia Tageblatt,* convicted of violating the first clause of the Espionage Act of 1917, which prohibited the publication of

> false reports and statements with intent to interfere with the operation of the military or naval forces of the United States or to promote the success of its enemies.

In sustaining the power of the Congress to regulate the freedom of speech, McKenna first demonstrated that the government could forbid direct and intentional incitation to crime as well as the commission of crime itself. For example, the State could punish those who encouraged as well as those who actually committed arson, robbery or treason. Since impeding the war was a crime it logically followed that the government could punish those who encouraged as well as those who created impediments.

In short McKenna argued that during war, Congress possessed the power to punish direct or indirect obstruction of the prosecution of the war. Hence language intended to impede or hinder any of the multifarious activities connected with the war effort was criminal. Achievement of the desired result need not be proved for the Espionage Act punished conspiracies to obstruct as well as the actual obstruction and as the tendency and the intent were the same whether the result was realized or unrealized, there was no reason to hold that success was needed to make the act criminal.

The same principles underlay the arguments of McKenna in *Gilbert v. Minnesota* [6] where the problem of freedom of speech

---

[5] 251 U. S. 466 (Mar. 1, 1920). For a comparison of McKenna's reasoning and that of Justice Brandeis, see Chafee, *op. cit.,* pp. 86–91; Thomas F. Carroll, "Freedom of Speech and of the Press in War Time: The Espionage Act," *Michigan Law Review,* XVII (June, 1919), 621; M. G. Wallace, "Constitutionality of the Sedition Laws," *Virginia Law Review,* VI (Mar. 1920), 385 ff.; John H. Wigmore, "Freedom of Speech and Freedom of Thuggery in Wartime and Peacetime," *Illinois Law Review,* XIV (Mar. 1920), 539.

[6] 254 U. S. 325 (Dec. 13, 1920). Zechariah Chafee, *The Inquiring Mind* (New York: 1928), 40–54; Charles Warren, "The New 'Liberty' under the Fourteenth Amendment," *Harvard Law Review,* XXXIX (Feb. 1926), 456; Ray A. Brown, "Due Process of Law, Police Power and the Supreme

was presented to the Court from a new viewpoint. The issue was the constitutionality of a State statute prohibiting public utterances against enlistment in the armed forces or against aiding the war effort. The decision was significant in the light of the numerous and drastic character of the State sedition laws enacted during and after the First World War.[7]

The case was primarily concerned with the conflict of State and federal powers in respect to the freedom of speech. McKenna contended that defendant in error's conviction did not violate the constitutional guarantees of freedom of speech. He bolstered his arguments on this point by quoting, among other cases, *Schenck v. United States,* where the Court asserted that the words uttered must be used under such circumstances and be of such a nature as to create a clear and present danger and that they will result in the evils which Congress may prevent.

Although Justice Brandeis, who dissented, held that defendant in error's speech did not create a clear and present danger, Mc-Kenna insisted that Gilbert's speech

> had the purpose they (the words of the Minnesota statute) denounce. The nation was at war with Germany, armies were recruiting, and the speech was the discouragement of that—its purpose was necessarily the discouragement of that. The war was flagrant; it had been declared by the power constituted by the Constitution to declare it . . . This was known to Gilbert . . . and every word that he uttered in denunciation of the war was false, was deliberate misrepresentation.[8]

McKenna quoted Justice Holmes' words in *Frohwerk v. United States* to the effect that the meaning to be placed upon words, and the effects to be feared from their utterance, depended largely upon

---

Court," *Harvard Law Review,* XL (May, 1927), 963; Felix Frankfurter, "Mr. Justice Brandeis and the Constitution," *Harvard Law Review,* XLV (Nov. 1931)), 90; "Recent Cases," *Michigan Law Review,* XIX (June, 1921), 871; Zechariah Chafee, "Freedom of Speech and States' Rights," *New Republic,* XXV (Jan., 1921), 259.

[7] For summary of State laws affecting freedom of speech, see Zechariah Chafee, *Free Speech in the United States,* pp. 575–597.

[8] 254 U. S. 325. For a comment on these words, see Chafee, *op. cit.,* p. 297.

182        *Joseph McKenna*

the circumstances under which they were spoken.  Although the
facts disclosed no effective interference with the enlistment, yet
defendant in error spoke in a region and under conditions " where
a little breath would be enough to kindle a flame."

On the issue of conflict between State and federal powers it was
of interest to note that the nationalistically minded McKenna
ruled that a State could constitutionally regulate a national problem
even after Congress had legislated upon it.  The basic idea in his
reasoning which reconciled national and State exertion of power,
was that the State law was in aid of, not in conflict with, federal
law.  He maintained that State and federal citizenship were
complementary, not antagonistic and that the interests of the
United States are those which a State should cherish and foster.
The war powers of Congress were exclusive yet it did not follow
that the nation and the States could not cooperate against a
common enemy.

The difference between victory and defeat depended on the
morale of the States as well as the nation, the outcome of the
war rested on

> the spirit and determination that animates them, whether
> it is repellent and adverse or eager and militant; and to
> maintain it eager and militant against attempts at its
> debasement and in aid of enemies of the United States is
> a service of patriotism; and from the contention that it
> encroaches upon or usurps any power of Congress, there
> is an instinctive and immediate revolt.[9]

A survey of McKenna's position and expressions in the above
opinions demonstrated that he believed the right of speech was not
absolute but subject to limitation and restriction.  He approached
the problem from a practical point of view and insisted that from
a social standpoint a quick victory justified limitation of the
freedom of speech.  The right of the nation to exist was paramount to the right of any individual to discuss the means employed
to continue that existence.  A government faced with a clear and
present danger might conclude that suppression of a divergent
opinion was imperative and that force and compulsion must be
employed in the emergency.

9 254 U. S. 329.

However laudable were the motives of McKenna in supporting the limitation of speech, it was evident that his expressions were influenced by the anti-Communist movement that agitated the United States after the first World War. Most of the defendants in the speech cases were asserted to be Communists or preached communistic doctrines and McKenna had an unreasonable fear of Communism. This fear first appeared in 1919 in his dissent in *Arizona Employers' Liability Cases,*[10] where he condemned a State workmen's compensation act. It asserted itself again in the spring of 1920 in the cases under the Espionage Act and in the winter of the same year in support of the drastic Minnesota " gag law." Finally in 1921 in *Block v. Hirsh,*[11] he was convinced that his fears had been realized when the Congress regulated rents in the District of Columbia and that, in spite of all his efforts, the government had finally succumbed to the blandishments of Communism and to the arguments of those whose speech McKenna sought to suppress.

If Justice McKenna can be considered as a staunch supporter of the State against the individual in the case of freedom of speech, it must be admitted that he was a consistent protector of the individual against the Federal Government in respect to other civil rights included within the first eight amendments to the Constitution. McKenna's deep respect for the Constitution was evidenced in *Lang v. New Jersey* [12] when speaking for a unanimous Court, he upheld a State statute which provided that any grand juryman over 65 years might be challenged, but that such challenge must be taken before the impaneling of the grand jury. Plaintiff in error had been indicted for murder by a grand jury, containing two over-aged members, impaneled prior to his imprisonment, and therefore he claimed that he was deprived of equal protection of the laws because he was unable to challenge the two grand jurors over 65.

---

10 250 U. S. 400 (June 9, 1919). For a discussion of this dissent see, pp. 148–151; Max Lerner, *The Mind and Faith of Justice Oliver Holmes* (New York: 1939), 150–151.

11 256 U. S. 135 (Apr. 18, 1921) ; Lerner, *op. cit.,* p. 279.

12 209 U. S. 467 (Apr. 27, 1908). " Recent Decisions," *Harvard Law Review,* XXII (Dec. 1908), 142.

In rejecting complainant's argument McKenna had recourse to the principle which he had explained in *Hadacheck v. Los Angeles* and *Waters-Pierce Oil Company v. Texas* that equal protection of the laws simply required that all persons in the same class be treated alike, and that classification based on a real difference was not prohibited. In the case at bar there was classification between two types of offenders, those committing crime before and those committing crime after the impaneling of the grand jury. The distinction was based upon the time of committing the crime and since a difference of the time was one upon which classification might reasonably be based for the more efficient administration of justice, defendant was not denied equal protection of the laws.

In another civil rights case McKenna wrote one of his most vigorous dissents. The issue involved the question of double jeopardy. In *Kepner v. United States*,[13] which was similar to *Trono v. United States* [14] in which McKenna wrote a dissent, the plaintiff in error had been tried in the Philippine Islands for embezzlement, and acquitted in the court of the first instance, but was convicted upon appeal by the Government. The majority of the Supreme Court held that this proceeding was contrary to the guarantee against double jeopardy as conceived by the American courts. One trial constituted one jeopardy, and a defendant after acquittal in one court could not be tried again for the same offence.

Justices McKenna and Hughes speaking through Justice Holmes, dissented and declared that within the meaning of the Constitution there was but one jeopardy in one entire cause as carried through to its termination in the court of last resort. From this point

---

[13] 195 U. S. 100 (May 31, 1904). Ralph F. Colin, "The Evolution of the Doctrine of Territorial Incorporation," *Columbia Law Review*, XXVI (Nov. 1926), 843; "Double Jeopardy," *Harvard Law Review*, XVIII (Jan. 1905), 216; "Current Legislation," *Columbia Law Review*, XXVI (June, 1926), 752.

[14] 199 U. S. 521 (Dec. 4, 1905). McKenna's interest in the personal civil liberties of the citizen may be gauged in his remark, "The life and liberty of the citizen are precious things—precious to the State as to the citizen, and concern for them is entirely consistent with a firm administration of criminal justice." 199 U. S. 539; "Notes," *Columbia Law Review*, VI (Apr. 1906), 261; "Recent Cases," *Harvard Law Review*, XIX (Feb. 1906), 300.

of view the jeopardy was a continuing one from trial court to the highest court and did not end with the verdict of the trial court or become double when the highest court ordered a new trial. Either party was permitted to appeal except in cases where there was a trial on a new indictment for an offense of which the defendant had already been tried.

In *Trono v. United States* the controverted " once in jeopardy " rule was again involved. Plaintiff in error had been indicted for murder in the first degree and convicted of assault in a lower court. He appealed and was found guilty of murder in the second degree. The issue therefore was whether plaintiff in error's appeal had started a new trial and in a five to four decision the Supreme Court of the United States held that it had.

McKenna dissented and asserted that accused waived the plea of former jeopardy only to that part of the judgment which convicted him of guilt. McKenna believed that to hold that the plea was also waived as to the acquittal of any higher grades of crime included in the indictment would clearly subject the accused to double jeopardy without his consent. It was quite clear that defendant had not the slightest intention of appealing from a judgment of acquittal in his favor and

> a citizen should not be required to give up the protection of a just acquittal of one crime as the price of obtaining a review of an unjust conviction of another.

In conclusion, McKenna noted that if the language used in the Kepner case cited by the majority expressed

> a proper and determining test of once in jeopardy against the appeal of the United States, it must also be the test of once in jeopardy against the appeal of the accused in the case at bar.[15]

The immunity against self-incrimination like that against double jeopardy was protected by the Fifth Amendment and McKenna demonstrated that he was keenly concerned about its preservation. In *Burdick v. United States*,[16] McKenna speaking for a unanimous

---

[15] 199 U. S. 540.

[16] 236 U. S. 79 (Jan. 25, 1915). McKenna's argument for immunity against self-incrimination that, " in this as in other conflicts between personal

Court, held that a witness did not lose his privilege against self-incrimination by refusing an unconditional pardon. Plaintiff in error, city editor of the New York Tribune, refused to testify before a grand jury on the grounds that he would incriminate himself, even though he was offered a presidential pardon granting full and unconditional pardon for all offenses committed in connection with any matter to which he might testify. Upon refusal he was forthwith held in contempt and fined.

In supporting the position of the plaintiff in error, McKenna reasoned that the validity of a pardon depended upon acceptance; that the witness was consequently not technically free from danger of punishment, although he had the means at hand to remove that danger; that he could not be compelled to relinquish the right to refuse the pardon and avoid possible disgrace, and that therefore his right against self-incrimination continued to exist.

McKenna entered into a lengthy discussion in an effort to distinguish between a pardon and legislative immunity. The latter was non-committal and tantamount to silence of the witness while the former carried imputation of guilt and to accept it was to recognize the existence of that guilt. Therefore to accept a presidential pardon would be an acknowledgment of guilt even though the receiver were innocent of any crime. To refuse a presidential pardon was permissible and left untouched the right of protection against self-incrimination.

On similar grounds, Justice McKenna vigorously upheld the right of an individual to be protected from illegal seizure of incriminating evidence. In *Wilson v. United States*,[17] he dissented

---

rights and the powers of government, technical—even nice, distinctions are . . . to be regarded," is somewhat diminished when balanced against the basis employed by Judge Learned Hand in the lower court who declared, "Legal institutions are built on human needs and are not merely arenas for the exercise of scholastic ingenuity." *United States v. Burdick,* 211 F. R. 494.

[17] 221 U. S. 361 (Apr. 15, 1911). McKenna's language gives some indication of his regard for personal civil rights. He declared, "If the government had no other concern, short-cuts to conviction would be justified and commendable in proportion to their shortness . . . Is it possible that a written constitution is more flexible in its adaptations than an unwritten one and that the spirit of English liberty is firmer or more consistent than that of American liberty? . . . *Obsta principiis,* withstand beginnings . . . against the

and upheld the right of the plaintiff in error to refuse access to the books of a corporation of which he was an official, on the ground that they contained information which would incriminate him. The central thought in his opposition was that the information was sought primarily to incriminate the plaintiff in error rather than the corporation. He sharply criticized judicial sanction of what he considered a violation of personal civil rights, condemned the official action of the Government in the case at bar and compared it to the arbitrary investigations of the British in the colonies prior to the Revolutionary War. To McKenna the present case was another attempt of officialdom to obtain evidence at the expense and destruction of individual security.[18] His reasoning did not find favor in later decisions for the rule of *Wilson v. United States* was followed in *Essgee Company of China v. United States* [19] and was frequently cited by authorities as the governing rule in such controversies. However, there was a faint echo of this thought when Justice Holmes characterized such official investigations as " dirty business " in *Olmstead v. United States.*[20]

The privilege against self-incrimination was staunchly supported by McKenna when it concerned an individual but the same privilege, in his mind, did not protect a corporation. In *Hale v. Henkel* [21] he wrote a concurring opinion in which he contended

---

attempt of the government to break down the constitutional privileges of the citizen." Arthur M. Allen, " The Opinions of Mr. Justice Hughes," *Columbia Law Review,* XVI (Nov. 1916), 573–574; Joseph M. Proskauer, " Corporate Privilege Against Self Incrimination," *Columbia Law Review,* XI (May, 1911), 451; Osmond K. Fraenkel, " Concerning Searches and Seizures," *Harvard Law Review,* XXXIV (Feb. 1921), 374; " Recent Decisions," *Columbia Law Review,* XVI (Feb. 1916), 158.

[18] 221 U. S. 394.

[19] 262 U. S. 151.

[20] 277 U. S. 438 (1928). The majority ruled that tapping telephone wires and listening in on conversations was not illegal search and seizure though such acts were criminal and invasions of the right of privacy.

[21] 201 U. S. 45 (Mar. 16, 1906). Henry W. Taft, " The Tobacco Trust Decisions," *Columbia Law Review,* VI (June 1906), 375; Frederic C. Coudert, " Constitutional Limitations on the Regulation of Corporations," *Columbia Law Review,* VI (Nov. 1906), 492; Proskauer, *op. cit.,* p. 450; George F. Canfield, " Corporate Responsibility for Crime," *Columbia Law Review,* XIV (June, 1914), 478; Milton Handler, " The Constitutionality of

that an official of a corporation could not invoke his personal immunity against self-incrimination in order to prevent investigation of the corporation's books.

McKenna first distinguished between the case at bar and *Wilson v. United States* by demonstrating that it was the corporation, not its official, that was being investigated. An official was immune from self-incrimination as far as he himself was concerned but he could not plead that immunity in behalf of a corporation of which he was an official. The official was possessor of all the rights of citizenship, he was entitled to conduct business in his own way, and possessed an unlimited power of contract. His rights existed by the common law prior to the organization of the State and could be curtailed only by due process and according to the Constitution.

On the other hand a corporation was the creature of the State, incorporated for the benefit of society and exercised its rights according to the laws of the State and the prescriptions of its charter. McKenna referred to the reasoning he had employed in *German Alliance Insurance Company v. Kansas* to demonstrate that a corporation's powers were created and could be limited by a State. It was recognized that an individual might decline to produce incriminating evidence but it did not follow that a corporation, endowed by a State with special privileges and rights, might refuse to permit investigation of its records when charged with an abuse of those privileges and rights.

Not so partial to the individual yet in strict accord with the law, were his opinions in *Brown v. Elliot* [22] and *Hyde v. United States.* [23] Despite the dissent of Justice Holmes, Lurton, Hughes, and Lamar, McKenna held that a conspiracy begun in one federal district and completed in another was punishable in either. In

---

Investigations by the Federal Trade Commission," *Columbia Law Review,* XXVIII (Nov. 1928), 917, 918; "The Immunity of Corporations Under the Fourth and Fifth Amendments," *Columbia Law Review,* VI (May, 1906), 344; Osmond K. Fraenkel, "Concerning Searches and Seizures," *Harvard Law Review,* XXXIV (Feb. 1921), 374.

[22] 225 U. S. 392 (May 1, 1912).

[23] 225 U. S. 347 (June 10, 1912). "Recent Decisions," *Columbia Law Review,* XII (Dec. 1912), 743.

rejecting the argument of the dissenters, McKenna admitted that the Sixth Amendment to the Constitution provided that a trial must be by jury and " of the State and district wherein the crime shall have been committed."

McKenna admitted that conspiracy, of which plaintiffs in error were guilty, could consist simply of an unlawful agreement to menace the State without any ensuing act. However, it was not compulsory to localize the secret meeting in which the conspiracy was evolved because the agreement was not to be considered as a single act but as a " continuing active accord between the minds of the conspirators which is punishable wherever this fact is evidenced by an overt act." Furthermore, the statute under which the indictment was brought provided that there should be no liability without an overt act. Therefore since there was no liability under the statute prior to the overt act it was logical to conclude that the act was necessary for the crime, and that it could be punished either in the district of origin or of completion. McKenna's opinion was significant in the fact that it arrested the inclination of the Court to hold to the judicial definition that conspiracy was punishable only in the place of origin.

McKenna's deep respect for the Constitution and desire to interpret strictly its provisions was manifested in his vigorous dissent in *Pettibone v. Nichols* [24] and *Haywood v. Nichols*.[25] Pettibone and Haywood, officials of the Western Federation of Miners, were indicted and convicted of hiring an assassin to murder Frank Steunenberg. The latter, as governor of Idaho, had strongly opposed labor activities in the Coeur d'Alene strike

---

[24] 203 U. S. 192 (Dec. 3, 1906).

[25] 203 U. S. 221 (Dec. 3, 1906). William Dudley Haywood, born Salt Lake City, Utah, Feb. 4, 1869, was elected secretary-treasurer of the Western Federation of Miners in 1900. From 1901 to 1906 Colorado and Idaho mines were frequently disturbed by strikes, marked by acts of savage violence on both sides. Frank Steunenberg, former governor of Idaho, was murdered and Haywood and Pettibone were accused of instigating the act. A period of excitement followed the imprisonment and thousands of dollars were raised throughout the country for their defense. Haywood's trial on July 28, 1907, attracted wide attention and resulted in an acquittal. Pettibone was later tried and acquitted. W. J. Ghent, " William Dudley Haywood," *Dictionary of American Biography,* VIII, 467–469.

of 1899.   Plaintiff in error in both cases contended that their constitutional rights had been violated in that they had been forcibly removed from one State to another without recourse to habeas corpus.   The majority of the Court decided in both cases that plaintiff in error was not entitled to habeas corpus though they had been removed from one State to another through the connivance of officers of both States rather than through the regular constitutional proceedings.   Liberal and protective of proper constitutional forms was McKenna's dissent and observation thereupon:

> The foundation of extradition between the States is that the accused should be a fugitive of justice from the demanding state, and he may challenge the fact by habeas corpus immediately upon his arrest.   If he refute the fact he cannot be removed . . . The right to resist removal is not a right of asylum . . . it is the right to be free from molestation.   It is the right of personal liberty in its most complete sense . . . It is to be hoped that our criminal jurisprudence will not need for its efficient administration the destruction of either the right or the means to enforce it.   The decision in the case at bar, as I view it, brings us perilously near both results.[26]

The decisions rendered by McKenna on personal civil rights indicated that, with the exception of the right to freedom of speech, he consistently defended the individual against encroachments of the government.   As demonstrated in *Weems v. United States, Trono v. United States, Burdick v. United States* and *Pettibone v. Nichols,* McKenna refused to sustain any infringement upon rights guaranteed by the first eight amendments to the Constitution.   Even his uniform opposition to complete freedom of speech and press were not without reasonable foundation, for it was apparent to thoughtful men that untrammeled right of speech and press could materially impede the war effort.   Throughout these opinions it was evident that McKenna endeavored to guide his thoughts according to the primary purpose of the constitutional right rather than by strict precedent and accepted interpretation.   He adapted his conclusions to changing social and

---

[26] 192 U. S. 218.

economic conditions and aimed at modifying the interpretation of the Constitution rather than the Constitution itself.

Frequently involved in cases in which personal civil rights were at issue, was the authority of the State to exercise its police power. Admitting that the fields of personal civil rights and police power are somewhat remote from one another, yet there was sufficient relation between the two in McKenna's mind to justify consideration of them in the same chapter.

The first eight amendments to the Constitution protected the fundamental rights of the individual and in McKenna's mind the police power protected the fundamental rights of society. The police power was the inherent right of the State to protect itself and all its constituents in so far as necessity required. Society's desire to protect itself and the individual's desire to exercise his rights inevitably caused conflicts. Hence McKenna's opinions in such conflicts not only reflected his attitude toward the police power but shed additional light upon his conception of individual rights as viewed from the standpoint of society. They furnished a clear picture of McKenna's general policy in respect to the individual's position in society and of his belief in the attitude the Court should take in striking a balance between the rights of the citizen and those of the State.

In the era of Justice McKenna on the Supreme Court, extensive use of police power was made by the States in order to cope with the problems created by rapid industrial expansion. State laws were frequently contested as the Court was asked to decide their constitutionality in over four hundred cases during the three decades prior to 1918. Since the Court condemned only about ten per cent of these laws, it has been asserted that adjudication of police power cases " has been one of the most remarkable features of its career." [27]

Justice McKenna considered the police power to be among the most extensive enjoyed by the State on the grounds that

> It is subject only to constitutional limitations which allow a comprehensive range of judgment, and it is the province

[27] Charles Warren, *Supreme Court in United States History* (Boston: 1922), II, 741.

of the state to adopt by its legislature such policy as it deems best.[28]

In a word, he believed that it was the right of the State to protect the health, morals, safety and welfare of its citizens. He consistently supported the exercise of police power on the principles that there should be judicial tolerance of legislative discretion; that legislative judgment was binding when no palpable violation of the Constitution existed; that personal civil rights must be controlled for the benefit of the community and that economic and social changes demanded and justified new exercises of power.

In one of his most important rulings on the State police power, he upheld the blue sky laws of Ohio, Michigan and South Dakota. With only Justice McReynolds dissenting, McKenna held in *Hall v. Geiger-Jones Company*,[29] *Caldwell v. Sioux Falls Stock Yards Company* [30] and *Merrick v. Halsey* [31] as constitutional, laws which prohibited the sale of securities within a State unless the broker gave evidence of good reputation and soundness of his securities.

---

[28] *Hadacheck v. Sebastian, Chief of Police, City of Los Angeles*, 239 U. S. 394 (Dec. 20, 1915). George W. Wickersham, "Government Control of Corporations," *Columbia Law Review*, XVIII (Mar. 1918), 199; "Public Health Laws under the Police Power," *Columbia Law Review*, XVI (Mar. 1916), 239; Alfred Bettman, "Constitutionality of Zoning," *Harvard Law Review*, XXXVII (May, 1924), 847, notes that both the State Supreme Court and the United States Supreme Court upheld the zoning law even though plaintiff in error's property was worth $800,000 for brick-making purposes and only $60,000 for residential purposes.

[29] 242 U. S. 539 (Jan. 22, 1917). Harold D. Saylor, "Blue Sky Laws," *University of Pennsylvania Law Review*, LXV (June, 1917), 785–787; Clarence D. Laylin, "The 'Ohio Blue Sky' Cases," *Michigan Law Review*, XV (Mar. 1917), 369–385, gives lengthy treatment of McKenna's reasoning; J. Edward Meeker, "Preventive Punitive Security Laws," *Columbia Law Review*, XXVI (Mar. 1926), 320; "Uniform Sale of Securities Act," *Columbia Law Review* XXX (Dec. 1930), 1189.

[30] 242 U. S. 559 (Jan. 22, 1917). Saylor, *op. cit.*, p. 786; "Recent Decisions," *Columbia Law Review*, XVII (Mar. 1917), 244.

[31] 242 U. S. 568 (Jan. 22, 1917). The decision of McKenna was declared to be important to the stock and bond business and represented an interesting but not new development of the law, except in one respect. The Ohio law, supported in *Hall v. Geiger-Jones* provided for the issuance of licenses at the direction of a single official, instead of commissions, and therefore went further than previous State enactments.

In *Hall v. Geiger-Jones Company,* he held that the Ohio law, aimed at preventing deception in the sale of securities, was within the police power of the State and that the grant to the commissioner of authority to issue, refuse or revoke licenses was a proper method of executing the conferred power. Under the Fourteenth Amendment the exemptions in the statute were reasonable. Indeed he stressed his belief that individual rights must yield to public necessity when he remarked

> Inconvenience may be caused by supervision and surveillance but this must yield to the public welfare; and against counsel's alarm of consequences, we set the judgment of the States.

Although the South Dakota statute questioned in *Caldwell v. Sioux Falls Stock Yards Company* differed in many details from that of Michigan, challenged in *Merrick v. Halsey,* McKenna decided both cases upon the principle that interstate commerce was not unduly burdened even if the law affected foreign corporations. He rejected the argument that the laws conferred an arbitrary power on the licensing officials or that the rights of contract or property as guaranteed by the Fourteenth Amendment were arbitrarily regulated. In characteristic language McKenna insisted that a proper sense of duty must be accorded State agents who would presumably exercise their functions reasonably and fairly and for the public interests. To deny discretion to the commissioners would deprive the government of one of its most essential agencies of which State and national commissions were instances.

Equal protection of the laws was not denied because there was discrimination between cases where more or less than fifty per cent of the bonds was sold to a single person. McKenna referred to his decision in *Hadacheck v. Los Angeles* [32] where he gave a clear exposition of the right of a State to classify. It must be assumed that police power was exercised for the public welfare and no class legislation existed when laws were directed against particular wrongs. There was always an ulterior public purpose, although it seemed that the statute wilfully attacked a particular

---

[32] 239 U. S. 394 (Dec. 20, 1915).

group. In a statement which significantly reflected his idea that private rights should be subordinated to those of society and the discretion which the latter may use in establishing its right, he noted that a State

> may direct its law against what it deems evil . . . without covering the whole field of possible abuses . . . If a class is deemed to present a conspicuous example of what the legislature seeks to prevent, the 14th Amendment allows it to be dealt with.[33]

In a word, classification as established by the State to protect itself need not be ideal, precise nor convenient; if reasonably included within the scope of the police power, it was constitutional.

In a similar case, *La Tourette v. McMaster*,[34] McKenna speaking for a unanimous court, upheld the right of a State to discriminate between domestic and foreign insurance brokers. The law provided that brokers' licenses would be issued only to residents of the State with two years' experience. McKenna based his conclusion on the principles that a State had the obligation to protect the welfare and security of its citizens, that the right of a State to insure this security was superior to the individual right to property or to contract and that the legislature acted for what was right and for what made for the public well-being. It was important for the interests of the public that insurance business be in the hands of competent and trustworthy persons and this result

> can be more confidently and completely secured through resident brokers, they being under the inspection of the commissioner of insurance. The motive of the statute, therefore, is benefit to insurer and insured and the means it provides seem to be appropriate.[35]

Similar principles were employed by McKenna in *Lehon v. City*

---

[33] 239 U. S. 410.

[34] 248 U. S. 465 (Jan. 20, 1919). John B. Cheadle, "Government Control of Business," *Columbia Law Review*, XX (May, 1920), 567; "Comments," *Yale Law Journal*, XXVIII (Apr. 1919), 601.

[35] 248 U. S. 468.

*of Atlanta* [36] where he sustained a State law which regulated the licensing of private detectives.

The right of the State to establish classifications was again the principle upon which McKenna sustained a State law requiring mine operators to establish and maintain wash houses for miners. In *Booth v. Indiana* [37] contention was made by plaintiff in error that the law discriminated between surface and sub-surface employees and therein violated the equal protection clause of the Constitution. To McKenna the argument was unreasonable; since the police power of the state included regulation of coal mines, it logically followed that that power was not limited by time nor circumstances for the conditions encountered by miners were reasonable grounds upon which to establish a distinction between them and other employees.

As has been stated, McKenna firmly supported the plenary power of Congress to control interstate commerce; nevertheless he did not stubbornly insist that all State laws which impinged upon that commerce were thereby unconstitutional. He recognized that a State's desire to protect the health, safety, morals and welfare of its citizens must be given consideration if the federal system was to operate efficiently. Thus in speaking for a unanimous court in *St. Louis, Iron Mountain and Southern Railroad v. Arkansas,* [38] McKenna upheld a State law which prescribed a minimum crew for interstate trains. Complainant claimed that the law made an unjustifiable distinction between roads over and under one hundred miles in length.

In justifying the law, McKenna maintained that the State had the right to establish classification providing no discrimination was permitted between members of the same class. It was impossible for the legislature to make all the delicate distinctions demanded. Police laws otherwise constitutional might contain classifications based on practical and local considerations. It was within the power of the legislature to compel interstate trains to carry larger crews for safety. Particular emphasis was given to the fact that the State did not attempt to regulate directly inter-

---

[36] 242 U. S. 53 (Dec. 4, 1916).
[37] 237 U. S. 391 (May 3, 1915).
[38] 240 U. S. 518 (Apr. 3, 1916).

state trains but merely sought to protect the lives of its citizens. The burden thereby placed on interstate commerce was so remote as to be inconsequential and a necessary incident to the exercise of a recognized power of the State.

The incidental effect on interstate commerce did not invalidate a State law which ordered the semi-monthly payment of workers on interstate railroads. In *Erie Railroad Company v. Williams* [39] McKenna supported the statute on the grounds that its primary purpose was to further the welfare of the workers by giving them the advantage of buying with cash rather than credit. The financial cost and inconvenience to the railroad were not sufficient to justify nullification; nor did the regulation impinge upon its charter rights; nor was its freedom of contract arbitrarily limited. Police regulations, made for the welfare of the citizenry, were matters of policy to be determined by the legislature and in the absence of flagrant constitutional violation must be considered as conclusive.

The right of a person to carry on his business unimpeded by a State law was the basis for litigation in *Chicago, Burlington & Quincy Railroad Company v. Cram.* [40] Plaintiff in error contended that the Nebraska act which regulated the minimum speed of interstate cattle trains and imposed a scale of damages for infraction thereof was an infringement upon interstate commerce and an unconstitutional deprivation of property. In refutation McKenna asserted that a railroad was clothed with a public interest and must submit to public control in those matters that vitally affected the economic welfare of the community.

The purpose of the law was to prevent depreciation in the value of cattle during transportation by compelling carrier to maintain a reasonable speed between ranch and market. It did not demand unreasonable service of the railroads; the scale of damages was commensurate with the loss and the Court must assume that the legislature acted with wisdom and moderation in framing the legis-

---

[39] 233 U. S. 685 (May 25, 1914). In addition to the advantages which cash payment of bills would bring to workers, supporters of the law argued that the statute would also prevent unfair and perhaps fraudulent methods in the payments of wages.

[40] 228 U. S. 70 (Apr. 7, 1913).

lation. The legislature was cognizant of the difficulties faced by cattle men and it properly exercised police power to solve these difficulties in so far as delinquent transportation service was concerned.

This wide discretionary power which the State could exercise in the formulation of public policy was recognized again by McKenna in *Chiles v. Chesapeake & Ohio Railroad Company* [41] when he upheld a State law which compelled colored passengers to ride in cars reserved for their use. Plaintiff in error contended that he was subject to discrimination and that his rights under the Fourteenth Amendment were violated. Pillaring his arguments on the conclusions in *Plessy v. Ferguson*,[42] McKenna ruled that the State could oblige common carriers to provide separate but equally comfortable compartments for white and colored passengers. Such requirements were in harmony with the established usage, custom and tradition of the community and were aimed at the promotion of public peace and order. There was no attempt to deprive persons of color of transportation. The express requirements were for equal though separate acommodations for the white and colored races. The liberty to ride was not restricted; the most that was done was to require a member of a class to conform to reasonable rules in regard to the separation of the races.

It would not be reasonable to suppose that in view of McKenna's repeated assertion of the paramount power of Congress over interstate commerce, he would allow unnecessary infringement of that power by the States. As has been observed, he condemned the Georgia " blow-post " law in *Seaboard Airline Railway Company v. Blackwell* and rejected the attempt of North Carolina to regulate interstate rates in the absence of congressional regulation in

[41] 218 U. S. 71 (May 31, 1910). Warren B. Hunting, " The Constitutionality of Race Distinctions and the Baltimore Negro Segregation Ordinance," *Columbia Law Review*, XI (Jan. 1911), 24–35, discusses the background and constitutionality of separate compartments for colored people on railroad cars; " Separate Accommodations for Negroes," *Columbia Law Review*, XV (Jan. 1915), 185.

[42] 163 U. S. 537 upheld a Louisiana statute requiring railway companies to provide equal but separate accommodations for white and colored passengers.

*Southern Railroad Company v. Reid.* Therefore when Wisconsin sought to compel interstate trains to make unnecessary stops, it was natural that McKenna would condemn such action in *Chicago, Burlington and Quincy Railroad Company v. Railroad Commission of Wisconsin.*[43] The State law was a direct and unconstitutional burden on interstate commerce in that it demanded service beyond the needs of the community, endangered the lives of interstate passengers by requiring increased speed of trains, subjected interstate carriers to disadvantages, not borne by intrastate carriers, and was a measure of convenience, not necessity, in the life of the community.

The general policy which McKenna followed in reconciling the exercise of State police power with congressional control of interstate commerce was fundamentally a willingness to allow play for the joints of the machine of government. Where there was no direct interference with interstate commerce or where the State law regulated only in a remote sense, he judged it to be a valid exercise of the police power. McKenna recognized that the prime purpose for employing police powers was to cope with the problems of daily social and economic life. Since those problems varied according to locality, the judiciary must tolerate legislative discretion if lawmaking was not to come to a standstill.

Police laws, enacted for the health and morals of the citizenry, were considered by McKenna to be matters of policy within the purview of the legislature to determine. Hence, he found no difficulty in sustaining regulations insuring the safety, health and morals of a community. He believed that saloons, hotels, restaurants, dance halls, theatres, amusement and recreation centers were subject to public supervision. Consequently in speaking for a unanimous court in *Miller v. Strahl,*[44] he upheld a State police law which obliged hotel owners to maintain watchmen as a precaution against fire.

Reminiscent, to some degree, of the attitude which he had adopted the year before in *German Alliance Insurance Company*

[43] 237 U. S. 220 (Apr. 1915). For the significance of this decision in the establishment of limitations on State police power, see Charles W. Gerstenberg, *American Constitutional Law* (New York: 1937), 273–274.

[44] 239 U. S. 426 (Dec. 20, 1915).

*v. Kansas,* he demonstrated that from the beginnings of common law inn-keeping was considered to be clothed with a public interest and hence subject to stricter supervision than other businesses. It was universally recognized that the State was vitally concerned in the proper conduct of hostelries and could make reasonable regulations for the safety of the guests therein. The act was reasonably calculated to promote the public safety; it had a real and substantial relation to that end; was not an arbitrary invasion of appellant's property rights; and if the legislature thought safety of guests would be better insured by employment of a special watchman, the court would not undertake to say that it was without a valid connection with the public interest and so unreasonable as to render the statute invalid.

Another facet of McKenna's conception of the police power was revealed in *Mutual Loan Company v. Martell* [45] when he sustained a State law which permitted the assignment of wages only after consent of wage earner's wife and employer. McKenna maintained that the validity of a police regulation depended upon the circumstances and it was within the power of the legislature to determine when those circumstances justified regulation. It was assumed that the legislature acted in the best interests of the community and dealt with conditions in order to bring out of them the greatest welfare of the people. In pursuance of its duty to promote the best interests of its constituents, a State might consitutionally provide that a wife and an employer approve an assignment of wages in order to avoid the results which almost inevitably followed extravagance or improvidence of the wage earner.

From the opinions of Justice McKenna on the nature and scope of the police power, there emerged a pattern of thought characterized by three or four prominent principles. He believed that the police power was one of the most extensive powers of government and in the absence of flagrant constitutional violation it must be sustained. The tests of common sense and reality must be applied to the exercise of the police power for it was not possible to

---

[45] 222 U. S. 225 (Dec. 11, 1911). "The Uniform Small Loan Law," *Harvard Law Review,* XLII (Mar. 1929), 691.

*Joseph McKenna*

enact legislation applicable to every condition with mathematical precision or classify subjects without inconvenience or cost. The personal rights of the individual in conflict with a proper exercise of police power must yield to the superior rights of society as protected by the police power. The indirect burden placed on interstate commerce by a police regulation was usually so remote as to be inconsequential and could be considered as an essential and unavoidable incident to the exercise of the police power.

# CHAPTER IX

## CONCLUSION

The interpretation of the thought of Justice McKenna, as expressed during twenty-seven years on the Supreme Court, should begin with some reference to his basic philosophic premises. The fundamental ideas in his conception of the origin and character of law should be considered if proper interpretation is to be given to his conclusions.

Justice McKenna's expressions on the nature and origin of law, government, society and man fell almost wholly within the school of the law of nature. The doctrine of natural law with its concomitant inalienable rights of life, liberty and property invested in the personality of man found ready acceptance and embodiment in the opinions of McKenna. Frequently he appealed to reason or the universal sense of mankind as to what was good or evil and justified a law because of its intrinsic reasonableness. The purpose of government was " to get all it can of good out of the activities of men and limit or forbid them when they become or tend to evil." The prime purpose of the State was the promotion of good and the inhibition of evil by preserving the peace and protecting the safety, health, morals and welfare of the citizenry.

In respect to the natural rights to life, liberty and property McKenna insisted that they could be reasonably regulated but not wholly taken away or substantially impaired by the State. He believed that private property was a necessary element in life and that everyone was entitled to the fruit of his labor. To him private ownership was far more conducive to human progress than any other form of ownership, for the individual tended to devote more attention and care to personal than communal goods. Human affairs would be more orderly if they were founded on the right of each citizen to manage something exclusively his own.[1]

---

[1] *Arizona Employers' Liability Cases,* 250 U. S. 437 (June 9, 1919); *Block v. Hirsh,* 256 U. S. 135 (Apr. 18, 1921).

In dissenting in the *Pipe Line Cases* [2] he claimed exclusiveness was one of the fundamental conceptions of property that is,

> the right of exclusive possession, enjoyment and disposition. Take away these rights and you take all that there is of property. Take away any of them and you take away property to that extent. The employment of one's wealth to construct or purchase facilities for one's business . . . constitutes no monopoly that does not appertain to all property. [3]

The deep respect which McKenna had for the historical foundation of the law induced him to attribute a sacrosanct character to precedent and previous legal pronouncements. However, there was some reason to believe that his lack of confidence in the early part of his career was equally responsible for the frequent citations and quotations which filled his early decisions. The present court librarian supported this observation when he recalled that McKenna was appalled at the magnitude of the task and responsibility which he had assumed. [4] In his early years on the bench he was frequently irritable, nervous and rather unhappy because he was not familiar with the law nor able to construct an opinion that would adequately express the convictions of his colleagues.

At the outset, McKenna cautiously felt his way and although his ideas were strong and forceful, yet he rarely struck out on an original line of thought. [5] He anchored his deductions on

---

[2] 234 U. S. 548 (Oct. 15, 16, 1913). Felix Frankfurter, "The Business of the Supreme Court of the United States," *Harvard Law Review*, XXXIX (Mar. 1926), 595; John B. Cheadle, "Government Control of Business," *Columbia Law Review*, XX (May, 1920), 571; Gustavus H. Robinson, "The Public Concept in American Law," *Harvard Law Review*, XLI (Jan. 1928), 297; Samuel C. Wiel, "Public Service Irrigation Companies," *Columbia Law Review*, XVI (Jan. 1916), 44–45.

[3] 234 U. S. 565.

[4] Oscar D. Clarke, Librarian, United States Supreme Court, personal interview, Jan. 12, 1944.

[5] For some illustrations of McKenna's thought at this time, see *United States v. Coe*, 170 U. S. 681 (May 23, 1898); *Orient Insurance Co. v. Daggs*, 172 U. S. 559 (Jan. 16, 1899); *Weyerhauser v. Minnesota*, 176 U. S. 550 (Feb. 26, 1900); *Fairbank v. United States*, 181 U. S. 283 (Apr. 15, 1901); *Cronin v. City of Denver*, 192 U. S. 108 (Jan. 4, 1904).

authority and filled the pages of his opinions with numerous references and a monotonous series of diffuse and uncritical quotations.[6] With passing years, he became more certain of his ability, and his expressions were characterized by greater breadth and independence of thought. He became increasingly assertive of his own views until his self-assuredness almost amounted to impatience with the conclusions of others.[7]

In *Norfolk & Western Railroad Company v. Holbrook* [8] the Court ruled that a jury had been unduly influenced by the appeal of emotion and prejudice. McKenna dissented and quite brutally asked his brethren if they thought a jury to be "without sense." McKenna's appeal for consideration of the widow and children involved was doubtlessly a manifestation of kindness for the helpless, but his was a tone of pugnacity and biting criticism when he instructed his confreres that:

> the court in the case was confronted with a serious difficulty to bring home to itself and to the jury the loss to wife and children. . . . The court in the present case ventured to say that these relations had something more in them and their destruction had something more of pecuniary injury than that injury to the mere next of kin and that there might be a loss to infant children greater than to adults. Would any one like to deny it? Would not its denial upset all that is best in sentiment and duty in life? [9]

Although McKenna was criticized for his adherence to *stare decisis* particularly in the initial part of his service, yet an overall survey manifested an endeavor to mould his thought to changing

---

[6] For examples of cases with frequent reference to past decisions, consult *Magoun v. Illinois Trust & Savings,* 170 U. S. 283 (Apr. 25, 1898) ; *Northern Pacific Ry. Co. v. Myers,* 172 U. S. 589 (Jan. 23, 1899) ; *Waters-Pierce Oil Co. v. Texas,* 177 U. S. 28 (Mar. 19, 1900) ; *Throckmorton v. Holt,* 180 U. S. 350 (Mar. 25, 1901).

[7] Somewhat sharp were his words, in *Arizona Employers Liability Cases,* 250 U. S. 400 (June 9, 1919) ; *Wilson v. United States,* 221 U. S. 341 (Apr. 15, 1911) ; *Weems v. United States,* 217 U. S. 349 (May 2, 1910) ; *National Prohibition Cases,* 253 U. S. 350 (June 7, 1920).

[8] 235 U. S. 625 (Jan. 5, 1915).

[9] *Ibid.,* 631.

conditions. This was especially noticeable in his interpretation of some of the more stable clauses in the constitution. Although he was not an advocate of change, for the sake of change, or for some transitory innovation in public opinion, yet, when he was convinced that modification was imperative, he did not hesitate to act. An instance of this adaptability was his attitude toward due process of law, which, he acknowledged, should be modified in its implications according to the thought of the time. When Justice McKenna took his place on the bench, it was already firmly established that due process of law was a flexible term endowed with sufficient elasticity to be enlarged or contracted as necessity dictated. Consequently McKenna set himself firmly against a precise limitation or definition of due process and even ventured to predict that nobody could mark out the precise and definite limits of its applicability. He noted that due process was the recognition of certain immutable principles inherent in democratic government and that as application was given to those basic elements in the past, so they could be adapted to circumstances in the future.

Perhaps the most striking instance of McKenna's willingness to see cause for modification was his expression in *Weems v. United States* where he insisted, in the face of Justice Holmes' dissent, that the essential elements of a "cruel and unusual punishment" had not been precisely defined, and that the phrase was liable to progressive interpretation. Hence the constitutional prohibition against cruel and unusual punishments not only interdicted punishments regarded as cruel and excessive in 1689 or 1787 but also those which were so classified by contemporary public opinion. He admitted that the judiciary might not oppose its power to that of the legislature in defining crimes and their punishment yet it was the obligation of the tribunal to determine

---

[10] 217 U. S. 349 (May 2, 1910). "Recent Decisions," *Columbia Law Review*, XI (Jan. 1911), 133, notes that McKenna considered not only the kind and degree of punishment and magnitude of the crime but also the conditions in a locality, in determining a cruel and unusual punishment. In addition McKenna noted "The clause of the constitution . . . may be therefore progressive, and is . . . not fastened to the obsolete and may acquire meaning as public opinion becomes enlightened by a humane justice."

whether the legislature had contravened a constitutional prohibition and " in that respect and for that purpose, the power
of the judiciary is superior to that of the legislature." These
illustrations demonstrated that McKenna was not irreconcilably
wedded to the past and that he brought to his explanation of the
constitution a proclivity for synchronizing the fundamental law
with contemporary conditions. He was favorable to rational
modification in constitutional construction whenever it was not
repugnant, in his opinion, to the purposes of the founding fathers.

In ferreting out the social theories of Justice McKenna, heed
must be paid to his reaction to the fundamental opposition which
lay at the bottom of most controversies involving social legislation. Intrinsically it was a conflict between individualism and
collectivism or in more concrete terms it was a question of construing " liberty of contract." In the United States, and in Great
Britain, the conflict began with Jeremy Bentham's extreme view
of individual liberty of contract and underwent a practical revolution as the police powers of the governments expanded at the
expense of liberty of action and free disposal of property.
Although constitutional limitations complicated the development
in the United States, the trend has been along parallel lines in
both countries.

The halo of liberalism could hardly be attached to either Justice
McKenna's social theories or pronouncements yet it would not
be correct to classify him as an incorrigible reactionary. Nor
did he concoct or champion innovations in social thought that
would later find their way as controlling factors into the mind of
the Court. Yet his isolated dissents for, and early acceptance
of, novel progressive legislation indicated his tendency to adopt
new modes of thought. There was some question however
whether this cautiousness was due to the sluggishness of his
thought processes or was the outcome of deliberate regard for
the force and protective value of precedent and progress, slow but
more certain.[11]

McKenna's contribution to the legal thought associated with

---

[11] For a criticism of Justice McKenna's opinions see, Richard J. Purcell,
" Justice Joseph McKenna," *Records,* The American Catholic Historical
Society, LVI (September 1945), 203–221.

social reform was his attempt to have the court recognize, in the absence of flagrant violation of constitutional prohibition, the unrestricted scope of police power. To him,

> Police power is but another name for the power of government; it is subject only to constitutional limitations which allow a comprehensive range of judgment, and it is the province of the state to adopt, by its legislature, such policy as it deems best.[12]

He would give to legislative judgment in social reform, a dignity and a weight that would have equal, if not superior, influence accorded to precedents. In this he partially jettisoned the extreme individualistic meaning given to " liberty of contract " by the courts. It was quite natural that McKenna with his deep understanding and esteem of the dignity of man should look with admiration on legislative efforts aimed at improving social conditions.

He was conscious that man had property rights to goods of body and of mind and that he was under obligation to self, his offspring and to his fellowmen. When individual workmen were deprived of their prerogatives, injustice was done, and hence McKenna concluded that organization of labor was lawful and necessary to protect natural rights. Labor unions were justified in striving to obtain for their members a proper share in the world's goods. To accomplish that aim there must exist true freedom in making of wage contracts. There was no true liberty when the worker had only the alternative of accepting conditions, wages, and hours of work as stipulated by the employer or of starving. In *Adair v. United States*,[13] he roundly condemned

---

[12] 222 U. S. 225 (Dec. 11, 1911) ; see also *Hadacheck v. Los Angeles*, 239 U. S. 394 (Dec. 20. 1915) ; *Bacon v. Walker*, 204 U. S. 311 (Feb. 4, 1907).

[13] 208 U. S. 161 (Jan. 27, 1908). Richard Olney, "Discrimination Against Union Labor—Legal ? " *American Law Review*, XLII (Apr. 1908), 884–890; Roscoe Pound, " Mechanical Jurisprudence," *Columbia Law Review*, VIII (Dec. 1908), 616; Maurice Finkelstein, " Judicial Self-Limitation," *Harvard Law Review*, XXXVII (Jan. 1924), 361; Henry Wolf Bikle, " Judicial Determination of Questions of Fact Affecting the Constitutional Validity of Legislative Action," *Harvard Law Review*, XXXVIII (Nov. 1924), 6.

" yellow-dog " contracts as an illegal interference with the independence of workingmen to select a bargaining agent.  Nevertheless labor unions must observe the proper limits of their privileges and hence McKenna censured their employment of unfair tactics, such as secondary boycotts, because

> a member of a labor union may refuse to work with non-union men, but this does not entitle him to threaten manufacturers for whom he is not working and with whom he has no concern, with loss of trade and a closing of the channels of interstate commerce against their products if they do not conduct their business in a manner satisfactory to him.[14]

It is in point to note that Justice McKenna did not wish to open the way to unimpeded action on the part of labor which would defy liability for unlawful acts.  He was persuaded that the deeds of unions were privileged only when performed to accomplish justifiable ends.  The record of Justice McKenna in behalf of legislation which promoted the welfare of working men and women could be typed as that of a moderate conservative.  In the first prominent State labor case in which he participated, *Lochner v. New York* [15] he shared the majority's interpretation of the Fourteenth Amendment.  The implication derived from this decision was that the judgment of a State legislature as to the necessity of an asserted health law was not without appeal, but that the need must be proved affirmatively to the Supreme Court.  Lacking such proof, the Court declared the State law unconstitutional, as beyond the police power of the State, and infringing the liberty of contract guaranteed by the Fourteenth Amendment.  The phrase " common understanding " as employed by the Court apparently meant the understanding of the tribunal rather than that of the legislature or of the general

---

[14] *Paine Lumber Co. v. Neal,* 244 U. S. 459 (June 11, 1917), 484.  Thomas R. Powell, " Commerce, Congress and the Supreme Court," *Columbia Law Review,* XXVI (May, 1926), 547; Albert M. Kales, " The Sherman Act," *Harvard Law Review,* XXXI (Jan. 1918), 445; Harris C. Lutkin, " The Sherman Anti-Trust Act, Injunction not Available to Private Party," *Illinois Law Review,* XII (Jan. 1918), 435–437.
[15] 198 U. S. 45 (1905).

public opinion of the State.  McKenna's support of this reasoning was a contradiction of his repeated expressions of confidence in the local law-making bodies to cope with provincial problems, and it contravened his theory of the extent of police power which he considered as "but another name for the power of government."

Through the gradual permeation of Justice Holmes' criterion that a State law could be accepted if it were deemed by a reasonable man to accomplish what the legislature intended, the attitude of the Court changed.  Holmes' theory was a repudiation of the unrestricted liberty of contract between employer and employee and during the ensuing twelve years McKenna realized the impossibility of sustaining the attitude to which he had adhered in *Lochner v. New York*.  In such classes of legislation as commerce, due process, personal rights and taxes, he imperceptibly approached the "reasonable man" standard.  In *Bunting v. Oregon* [16] he voiced the approval of his brethren for an hours-of-labor law which applied to adult males in non-hazardous occupations.

First then in *Adair v. United States,* McKenna sought to secure for the labor union wider rights in its encounters with the employer; later in *Bunting v. Oregon* he recognized as a proper exercise of the police power of the State the regulation of hours in the labor contract between master and servant.  Finally he supported a virtual combination of the two principles when the Federal and State governments endeavored to bestow positive protection on labor organizations and simultaneously to regulate the contracts of labor.  Thus Justice McKenna appreciated the intrinsic economic inequality between the positions of the capitalist and the artisan and was persuaded that the balance of power should be equalized by law for the general welfare of the community.

---

[16] 243 U. S. 426 (Apr. 9, 1917).  Felix Frankfurter, "Mr. Justice Holmes and the Constitution," *Harvard Law Review,* XLI (Dec. 1927), 143; Ray A. Brown, "Police Power Legislation for Health and Personal Safety," *Harvard Law Review,* XLII (May, 1929), 884; E. Merrick Dodd, "For Whom Are Corporate Managers Trustees?" *Harvard Law Review,* XLV (May, 1932), 1151.

Although he did not expressly criticize the prevalent industrial conditions, yet Justice McKenna believed that the workingman stood in need of the protection of the State in his dealings with his employer. To furnish this protection, the Federal Government found support in the commerce power while the States relied on their police power. A fairly adequate presentation of the need for governmental protection might be found in McKenna's dissent to *Adair v. United States* in which the majority concluded that the Erdman Law, forbidding discharge of an employee of an interstate carrier for union affiliation, was unconstitutional as an impairment of the liberty of contract. McKenna's line of reasoning was compatible with that expressed by Pope Leo XIII in his encyclical *"Rerum novarum"* in 1891 in which it was asserted

> inadequacy of his own strength, learning from experience, impels and urges a man to enlist the help of others . . . just as man is drawn by this natural propensity into civil union and association, so also he seeks with his fellow citizens to form other societies, admittedly small and not perfect but societies none the less.[17]

In opposition to the thought of the Court, McKenna argued that the labor unions were sufficiently connected with interstate commerce as to be subject to congressional regulation. Manifesting a breadth of view creditable to one enjoying wider reputation, McKenna insisted that the prohibition against discharge of workers for membership in a union be orientated to its proper status and relation to other parts of the bill. Assuredly it was

> an oversight in the proportion of things that Congress may not prevent the discharge of an employee in order to prevent the disastrous interruption of commerce, the derangement of business and even greater evils to the public welfare.[18]

Hence, McKenna's conclusions in the Bunting and in the Adair

---

[17] *Two Basic Social Encyclicals,* trans. Catholic University of America Press (New York: 1943), p. 65.
[18] 208 U. S. 161.

case might be viewed as his contributions to the movement opening up two new fields under the control of police power. For
the States, a general regulation of the hours of work; for the
national government, the unionizing of those railroad workers for
whom Congress was authorized to deal.

In the application of the Employers' Liability Act, McKenna
might be regarded as in one respect, a trail blazer. In a case involving the First Federal Employers' Liability Act, he maintained
that unless usurpation was patent, Congress must be presumed to
have acted within its constitutional powers.[19]  In applying the
" reasonable man " theory, which Holmes had applied as a gauge
for the constitutionality of a State hours-law, McKenna was instrumental in adopting the same criteria to the relations of a
master to his servants.

In *Northern Pacific v. Dixon,*[20] he opposed his colleagues'
assertion that the negligence of a train dispatcher was not that
of a vice-principal for which the railway was liable, but the
carelessness of a fellow servant. McKenna's dissent was at least
an indication of the breaking down of the atrocious fellow servant
doctrine of the common law. A few years later this principle
was applied in *Santa Fe Pacific Railroad v. Holmes*[21] in which
McKenna, as spokesman for the court, held that the omission
of an obligation by a train dispatcher was a violation of recognized responsibility of the master and for which the latter was
liable.

In recent years Justice McKenna's views have been vindicated
in at least one direction, his attitude in respect to the power of
the national government over the relations of employees in industries having direct relation with the movement of interstate
commerce. His dictum appears to have been accepted by the

19 207 U. S. 540.

20 194 U. S. 338.

21 202 U. S. 438 (May 21, 1906). J. A. Fowler, " Federal Power to
Own and Operate Railroads in Peace Time," *Harvard Law Review,*
XXXIII (Mar. 1920), 789; Frederick H. Cooke, " Nature and Scope of
the Power of Congress to Regulate Commerce," *Columbia Law Review,* XI
(Jan. 1911), 124; Alfred Hayes, " Partial Unconstitutionality with Special
Reference to the Corporation Tax," *Columbia Law Review,* XI (Jan. 1911),
129–130.

court, that labor disputes occurring in any part of an interstate railroad system were likely to burden and obstruct interstate commerce and that Congress may, therefore, take reasonable means to regulate the labor situation in the entire field.[22]

In view of this progressiveness, his dissent in the *Arizona Employers Liability Case*[23] was rather unexpected. However when the Arizona case was before the bar, McKenna was approaching his eightieth year and it could reasonably be presumed that he turned more readily to the past than to the future. It was only with reluctance that he disagreed with the majority for the motive and the purpose of the statute were good and " it required some resolution of duty to resist them."[24] The contested law made the employer, irrespective of negligence, liable for all injuries suffered by an employee in the course of employment. It abolished the employer's defense based on the fellow-servant rule, the employee's assumption of risk and his contributory negligence, and left the jury to determine the assessment of damages. The act was thus entirely for the benefit of the worker.

McKenna contended that the statute imposed liability without fault yet he hoped that it was " something more than timidity . . ." which prompted his opposition to his brethren. Chief Justice White and Justices Van Devanter and McReynolds joined McKenna in dissent. There was little likelihood to find such stalwarts of the *status quo* in the van of a social program which was a potential forerunner of socialistic legislation. McKenna's

---

[22] 313 U. S. 177 (Apr. 28, 1941). In overruling the Adair case and supporting McKenna's dissent, Justice Frankfurter ruled in *Adair Phelps Dodge Corporation v. National Labor Relations Board* that " so far as questions of constitutionality are concerned we need not enlarge on the statement . . . that there is 'no greater limitation in denying him (the employer) the power to discriminate in hiring than in discharging.' The course of decision in this court since *Adair v. United States,* and *Coppage v. Kansas* have completely sapped those cases of their authority."

[23] 250 U. S. 400 (June 9, 1919). John B. Cheadle, " Government Control of Business," *Columbia Law Review,* XX (May 1920), 573; E. Merrick Dodd, " The New Doctrine of the Supremacy of Admiralty over the Common Law," *Columbia Law Review,* XXI (Nov. 1921), 660; Ray A. Brown, " Police Power-Legislation for Health and Safety," *Harvard Law Review,* XLII (May, 1929), 866 ff.

[24] 250 U. S. 434.

words are those of a man who had himself toiled and labored
from youth and if he here forgot some truths of the present,
we must respect him for those which he recalled from the past.

The opinions concerning the power of Congress to regulate the
commerce and the prerogatives having their alleged source in
that power have been instrumental in opening up a new area for
the exercise of a so-called Federal police power,[25] a power deemed
to be imperative in the presence of new industrial conditions and
which came into being during McKenna's twenty-seven years on
the bench. The regulations of Congress and the interpretation
which the Court placed upon them had affected an increased centralization of authority in the national government. In the light
of McKenna's willingness to see in the legislature the ability and
the good sense to formulate adequate and reasonable remedies for
problems, it would be rather out of place to expect him to oppose
the right of the Congress to legislate under its commerce power
for the welfare of the common people.

When McKenna took his place upon the bench, the Sherman
Anti-Trust Act was coming to be of vital national importance.
In the *Northern Securities Case* [26] Justice Brewer expressed the
thought of McKenna that the acquisition of railroad stock by a

---

[25] For divergent views on the nature of the so-called Federal police power,
consult Ernst Freund, *The Police Power* (Chicago: 1904), pp. 62–83;
Freund states, "It is impossible to deny that the Federal Government exercises a considerable police power of its own. This police power rests chiefly
upon the constitutional power to regulate commerce among the states and
with foreign nations, but not exclusively so." Robert E. Cushman favors
Freund's position in "The National Police Power under the Commerce
Clause of the Constitution,'' *Minnesota Law Review,* III (May, 1919), 381–
412; (April, 1919), 289–319; (June, 1919), 452–483; Roy A. Brown holds
a similar view in "The Constitution, the Supreme Court and the N.I.R.A.,"
*Oregon Law Review,* XIII (Feb. 1934), 102–121; Arguments to the contrary are found in John J. Coughlin, "The N.I.R.A. Emergency Legislation
and the Federal Police Power," *Oregon Law Review,* XIII (June, 1934),
286–293; Paul Fuller, "Is there a Federal Police Power," *Columbia Law
Review,* IV (Dec. 1904), 562–588; William R. Howland, "Police Power
and Inter-State Commerce," *Harvard Law Review,* IV (Dec. 1890), 221;
Robert F. Cornell, "Police Legislation under Federal Powers," *Michigan
Law Review,* XXIV (May, 1926), 701–704.

[26] 193 U. S. 197 (1904).

holding company was an act restraining trade, preventing competition and instituting monopoly. Although no positive monopolistic or restrictive action could be attributed to the company, yet the possession of the power and the presumed threat to do so were sufficient justification to declare the combination illegal. Some years later, McKenna modified his view slightly in regard to combinations which could be held in violation of the Sherman Anti-Trust Act.

In *United States v. United States Steel Corporation*,[27] he ruled for the court that the mere ability to do wrong was in itself not illegal for

> Shall we declare the law to be that size is an offense, even though it minds its own business, because what it does is imitated? The Corporation is undoubtedly of impressive size and it takes an effort of resolution not to be affected by it or to exaggerate its influence. But we must adhere to the law, and the law does not make mere size an offense or the existence of unexerted power an offense. It, we repeat, requires overt acts, and trusts to its prohibition of them and its powers to repress or punish them.[28]

In 1918, McKenna again represented the Court and despite the disagreement of Justices Clarke and Day supported the contention that mere magnitude did not constitute a violation of the Sherman Anti-Trust Act.[29] In behalf of the United Shoe Machinery Company of New Jersey, he averred, " The company, indeed, has magnitude, but it is at once the result and cause of efficiency, and the charge that it has been oppressively used is not sustained." [30] However, McKenna believed that if intent to

---

[27] 251 U. S. 417 (Mar. 1, 1920). Mathew O. Tobriner, " Cooperative Marketing and the Restraint of Trade," *Columbia Law Review,* XXVII (Nov. 1927), 834; Myron W. Watkins, " The Change in Trust Policy," *Harvard Law Review,* XXXV (May 1922), 815; William W. Gager, " Efficiency or Restraint of Trade," *Yale Law Journal,* XXVII (June, 1918), 1060–1068.

[28] 251 U. S. 451.

[29] 247 U. S. 33 (May 20, 1918).

[30] U. S. Congress, Senate, Temporary National Economic Committee, *A Study of the Construction and Enforcement of the Federal Antitrust Laws, Monograph 38,* 76th Congress, 3rd Session (Washington: 1941), pp. 59–63.

restrain trade were proven, it was sufficient ground to enforce the provisions of the Anti-Trust Act and in this he agreed with Justice Holmes in *Swift v. United States.*[31]   The Beef Trust had performed acts which were in themselves not restraints of trade but were such as to "produce a dangerous probability" that commerce would be arrested.   McKenna had little trouble in differentiating it from the Northern Securities Case where the faculty was dormant and unexerted.   In the Danbury Hatters Case he agreed with Mr. Chief Justice Fuller's conclusion that it was incumbent upon labor unions to respect the prohibitions of the Sherman Act.[32]   The subscription of McKenna to this view proceeded from his desire to administer justice impartially to employer and employee alike.

For ten years following the Adair Case, which had brought McKenna into conflict with the rest of the Court, he was able to agree with them on the regulation of labor through the Commerce Clause.   In 1917, in *Hammer v. Dagenhart,*[33] he supported the dissent of Justice Holmes against the ruling that Congress had trespassed the bounds of its authority in attempting to control child labor through its supervision of interstate commerce.   The underlying principle of McKenna's action in this case was in line with his thought as expressed in *Riley v. Massachusetts* [34] and in harmony with the arguments of Chief Justice Hughes in *Miller v. Wilson.*[35]   In both instances he emphasized his confidence in the extension of the police power to cope properly and sensibly with the evils which were agitating society.   He was one

[31] 196 U. S. 375 (1905).

[32] *Loewe v. Lawlor,* 208 U. S. 274 (1908).

[33] 247 U. S. 251 (1918).   McKenna believed that Congress could exclude products produced by child labor from interstate commerce by exercise of its commerce powers but Congress could not do the same thing in virtue of its taxing powers hence his opposition to congressional legislation which sought to control child labor by taxation in *Bailey v. Drexel Furniture Company,* 259 U. S. 20 (1922).

[34] 232 U. S. 672 (Mar. 23, 1914).   Marion Cotter Cahill, *Shorter Hours* (New York: 1932), 74; John R. Commons and John B. Andrews, *Principles of Labor Legislation* (New York: 1920), pp. 248–262, summarizes the trend toward a standard eight-hour day.

[35] 236 U. S. 373 (1915).   The Court upheld an eight-hour labor law for women.

in mind with Holmes, who justified the exclusion of products produced by child labor from interstate commerce as an effective remedy for an abuse which was plaguing the nation for " It does not matter whether the supposed evil precedes or follows the transportation. It is enough that, in the opinion of the Congress, the transportation encourages the evil." McKenna believed that the power of Congress to regulate commerce could not be qualified because of interference with the domestic policy of a State for the national welfare might well require a different attitude than that of a self-seeking individual State. Justice McKenna's dissent in *Hammer v. Dagenhart* was probably the culmination of his labor opinions in which, for the most part, he had sought for the spirit or essential purpose of the law rather than for a literal rendering of its provisions. He endeavored to modify and mollify, without harshly or rashly revolutionizing, constitutional thought. In some respects his labors have not been in vain for he has left an impress upon the legal thought of the nation which has gradually been recognized by his successors.

In establishing a border line between national and State power over commerce, McKenna consistently favored the former. In *Southern Railway Company v. the People of the State of New York,*[36] he insisted " that the police power of a state could only exist from the silence of Congress upon the subject and ceased when Congress acted or manifested its purpose to call into play its exclusive power." [37] In spite of the firm determination of Justice McKenna to preserve the supreme right of the Congress in matters of interstate communication, he was not intolerant toward State regulations which incidentally affected that trade. While desiring to guarantee plenary powers to Congress and simultaneously give full recognition to State police powers, McKenna was more favorable to the latter than was the court. In frequently referring to *Western Union v. Massachusetts* [38] and in adhering to

---

[36] 222 U. S. 424 (Jan. 9, 1912).

[37] 233 U. S. 671 (May 25, 1914). Charles W. Needham, " Exclusive Power of Congress over Interstate Commerce," *Columbia Law Review*, XI (Mar. 1911), 251.

[38] *Western Union Telegraph Co. v. Massachusetts,* 125 U. S. 530 (Mar. 19, 1888).

Justice Holmes' dissent in *Western Union v. Kansas,*[39] McKenna
reiterated his belief that it was more valuable to continue inviolate
the fullness of the power of the States to supervise the entry of
foreign corporations within their confines than to extinguish the
mischievous practice of subjecting the agencies of interstate commerce to unnecessary burdens.   In the latter case Kansas had
based a tax on the total authorized capital stock of the company
and Justice Harlan in the name of the Court had declared such
a levy an unjustifiable burden upon interstate commerce.   To
McKenna this was a contradiction of his cherished theory that
the States had the prerogative to tax such business at will.
Presumably Justice Holmes enunciated McKenna's thought when
he remarked that Kansas did not attempt to tax Western Union
but had simply announced that before a corporation could engage
in business, it must pay a certain sum of money.

In somewhat a revealing manner McKenna outliberalized the
" great liberal " in *Louisville and Nashville R. R. Co. v. Central
Stock Yards Co.,*[40] in which Justice Holmes, as spokesman for
the Court, condemned a State statute obliging interstate carriers
to deliver their cars to connecting roads without being adequately
secured of their property.   Justice McKenna, supported by Justices Harlan and Day, attacked the conclusion of the Court in
that it weighed the effects of the statute only on interstate commerce but ignored its ramifications in the realm of domestic
intercourse.   For the Court to construct the supposition of unconstitutionality on the principle that a State tribunal had no authority
to compel a carrier to negotiate a contract with a competitor, was
confusing the issue.   Utilizing the very precedents Justice Holmes
had cited, McKenna insisted that the citations only proved the
judiciary was without authority, but the citations established no
limitation upon the powers of the legislature to prescribe a contract between two connecting transportation systems.   The com-

---

[39] 216 U. S. 1 (1910).

[40] 212 U. S. 132 (Jan. 25, 1909).   The principle of judicial tolerance of
legislative discretion lay at the basis of McKenna's declaration that "if the
State may so distribute its power of regulation it is certainly not within the
province of this court to say that it has not . . . against a contrary view, expressed or assumed, by the courts of the State."

petency of the State legislature, not that of the courts, to prescribe the conditions under which intrastate shipments were to be carried, was the issue involved and which was not decided by the majority.[41]

Justice McKenna was scrupulous in recognizing the province of the State's right to exercise its police power either before, or after, the current of interstate movement was in existence. He carefully stipulated its bounds and vigilantly saw that they were not infringed upon by the federal regulations. He endeavored to introduce a clearer definition of the time and the circumstances under which the federal power ended and the State competency began.

In *Texas and New Orleans R. R. v. Sabine Tram Company*[42] interstate commerce began when materials were committed to a common carrier for interstate transportation and ended· when the commodities arrived at the place where the shipper intended that they should finally halt.[43] This interpretation was subject to modification, but it was an attempt which created a sphere, however indefinite, within which the State could operate.

McKenna refused to entertain a specious defense of interstate business at the expense of the State police power in *Mutual Film Co. v. Industrial Commission of Ohio*.[44] The protection of interstate commerce did not suffice to inhibit the censorship of films which were to be exhibited in a State, even though they were sold in the original package. Justice McKenna readily supported the paramount position of the national government and at times unhesitatingly clarified his position, yet when circumstances or conditions warranted State action, even though it directly affected the current of business across State lines, he accepted such to be within the purview of the Constitution.

---

[41] 212 U. S. 147.

[42] 227 U. S. 111 (Jan. 27, 1913). Thomas R. Powell, "Supreme Court Decisions on the Commerce Clause and State Police Power," *Columbia Law Review*, XXI (Dec. 1921), 742; "Recent Cases," *Harvard Law Review*, XXVI (Apr. 1913), 554.

[43] *Diamond Match Company v. Ontonagon*, 188 U. S. 82 (Jan. 19, 1903).

[44] 236 U. S. 230 (Feb. 23, 1915). "Recent Cases," *Columbia Law Review*, XV (June, 1915), 546.

In estimating the power of the States to limit the rights of individuals, as guaranteed by the Fourteenth Amendment, Justice McKenna was inclined to reject rigid and predetermined definitions or a fixed procedure. He considered due process was satisfied if the fundamental ideals of democratic government were kept but their application was to vary with the distinctions peculiar to each problem.[45] Substantive rights were sheltered by the Fourteenth Amendment, but the extension of that protection was contingent upon the proportionate evaluation which the judiciary annexed to them in opposition to the police power. McKenna believed that if the legislature regulated a matter in which the rights of the individual were superior, the law should be outlawed as unconstitutional. Possibly Justice McKenna carried this principle further than his colleagues cared to go, and, rather significantly, the few times he denounced the State in due process cases was for the invasion of property rights.

In the Elevated Railway cases, he upbraided his brethren for deserting the cause of the individual whose rights were invaded by the State. Stressing the practical side of the violation of substantive rights, McKenna sharply criticized the conclusion of the Court, and implied it had lapsed into a rut of theoretical interpretation and had ignored the practical result of its adjudications.[46] "At times there seems to be a legal result which takes no account of the obviously practical result. At times there seems to come an antithesis between legal sense and common sense."[47] Although Justice McKenna jealously watched over the constitutional rights of individuals, he experienced little difficulty in reconciling this guardianship which consistently upheld the necessity of permitting the legislative judgment to determine the expediency and the facts of the situation. He believed that

---

[45] *Orient Insurance Co. v. Daggs,* 172 U. S. 559 (Jan. 16, 1899). On the same principles McKenna decided *New York Life Insurance Co. v. Cravens,* 178 U. S. 389 (May 28, 1900).

[46] *Sauer v. City of New York,* 206 U. S. 536 (May 27, 1907). In dissenting McKenna remarked that the abutting owners on the street "have an interest . . . for all time in the streets above their surface, and in having them kept open and unobstructed forever, of which they cannot be deprived without compensation."

[47] 206 U. S. 559.

the Court should not interfere or supplant the legislature in this sphere unless there was a flagrant and palpably unjust breach of the Constitution. Possibly the most outstanding trait of Justice McKenna was his strong desire to have this principle observed to the letter.

As has been noted previously, Justice McKenna was among those who would invest the State police power with the broadest possible extension. " The police power . . . is one of the most essential powers of government and one of the least limitable. In fact, the imperative necessity of its existence precludes any limitation upon it when not arbitrarily exercised." [48] Thus it might be reasonably accepted that McKenna's two cardinal maxims were first that the legislative judgment be accorded a liberal interpretation as to the justice and reasonableness of its measures and, secondly, that practical good sense, based on the fundamental elements of democratic government, be the criterion with which to estimate the antagonism to or harmony with, the prescriptions of due process.

McKenna might well be classified as an ardent advocate of State's rights, yet he did not permit that predilection to blind him to flagrant impingement of property under the guise of an exercise of the police power.[49] A municipality was not at liberty to oblige a service corporation to remove its poles and wires from its streets under the pretense that it was necessary for the public peace, health and safety. Yet McKenna upheld a municipality when it ordered the removal of poles and wires from its thoroughfares because the charter of the defendant telephone

---

[48] *Hadacheck v. Sebastian, Chief of Police, City of Los Angeles,* 239 U. S. 394 (Dec. 20, 1915), 410. George W. Wickersham, " Government Control of Corporations," *Columbia Law Review,* XVIII (Mar. 1918), 199; Alfred Bettman, " Constitutionality of Zoning," *Harvard Law Review,* XXXVII (May, 1924), 847; " Public Health Laws under the Police Power," *Columbia Law Review,* XVI (Mar. 1916), 239.

[49] *City of Los Angeles v. Los Angeles Gas and Electric Co.,* 251 U. S. 32 (Dec. 8, 1919). McKenna held as invalid a city ordinance requiring the utility company to remove and relocate poles and equipment without compensation, to afford space for installation for a municipally owned street lighting system.

company had been issued with the express reservation that the city had the authority to repeal the concession.[50]

Except through confiscation by eminent domain, the most obvious procedure to appropriate property was through the taxing power, and had litigants been allowed free reign, almost every levy could have been contested as seizure without due process of law. But Justice McKenna, uniformly discarding any but weighty reasons and arguments against the exercise of the taxing power, repulsed those who appealed for relief against any law that was inconvenient or unwise.[51] He applied the same standards of good sense and intelligence to the taxing as to the police power, rejecting any far-fetched or impossible requirement not ordinarily within the power of the legislature. When a delinquent taxpayer complained he had been given insufficient notice of the sale of his property, McKenna answered by referring to a practice among reasonable persons to familiarize themselves with whatever affected their possessions.

The hypothesis that property owners were cognizant of the laws was the basis upon which " the legislature was able to give efficiency to its operations." [52]   Justice McKenna likewise endeavored to bring home the point that the Fourteenth Amendment did not alter long-standing practices of the State which had become a part of the web and woof of the law. Furthermore he was convinced that the Fourteenth Amendment had not brought with it any additional requirements which the State was to fulfill in levying taxes. Thus in repudiating the charge of a discontented property owner, who alleged he had been stripped of his assets without a chance to contest, McKenna noted with evident satisfaction that the tax had been demanded in the same fashion by the city " for years " and there was no reason to

---

[50] *City of Ownesboro v. Cumberland Telephone and Telegraph Co.*, 230 U. S. 58 (June 16, 1913). The majority opinion, to which McKenna dissented, was written by Justice Lurton and held that an ordinance granting the right to place and maintain upon the streets poles and wires is the granting of a property right in perpetuity, unless limited in duration by the grant itself or as a consequence of some limitation imposed by the law of the state.

[51] 170 U. S. 293.

[52] *Ballard v. Hunter*, 204 U. S. 241 (Jan. 14, 1907).

believe that it had been abused in order to invade arbitrarily the property of the complainant.

Although the few dissents which Justice McKenna launched against State violation of the due process protection were concerned with street improvements, he opposed the doctrine that confiscation of property without compensation was an inevitable concomitant of the exercise of the tax and police powers. Without doubt, the policy of governments in improving roads, streets, bridges, and building conditions worked a hardship on property owners, but McKenna championed the view that unless the real estate was benefited, either directly or indirectly, there was no justification for assessment.[53]

In *Voigt v. Detroit City* [54] McKenna supported the assessment of the city, and he emphasized the fairness of the rule which had been followed when the municipality provided that

> the amount of the benefit thus ascertained shall be assessed upon the owners of . . . such taxable real estate, in proportions as nearly as may be, to the advantage which such lot, parcel, or subdivision is to acquire by the improvements.[55]

In the estimation of McKenna, it would be difficult to discover a more fair provision than this " which so essentially satisfied every requirement of due process of law." The Supreme Court of the State had ruled that if the aggrieved proprietor had been able to prove the assessment exceeded the advantages which accrued to his land he would " have relieved his land from tax." [56] McKenna was evidently convinced that some good should be

---

[53] 184 U. S. 122.

[54] *Voigt v. Detroit*, 184 U. S. 115 (Feb. 24, 1902).

[55] 184 U. S. 122.

[56] On the same principle McKenna decided *King v. Portland City*, 184 U. S. 61 (Jan. 27, 1902); *Bedford v. United States*, 192 U. S. 217 (Jan. 18, 1904); *Muhlker v. New York*, 197 U. S. 544 (Apr. 10, 1905); *Mead v. Portland*, 200 U. S. 148 (Jan. 2, 1906); *Chicago, Burlington & Quincy Railroad Co. v. Drainage Commissioners of Illinois*, 200 U. S. 562 (Mar. 5, 1906); *Cleveland, Cincinnati, Chicago and St. Louis Ry. Co. v. Porter*, 210 U. S. 177 (May 18, 1908); *District of Columbia v. Brooke*, 214 U. S. 138 (May 17, 1909).

derived from the payment of a tax and even went so far as to justify a State in levying upon non-abutting property owners.

In *Cleveland, Cincinnati, Chicago, and St. Louis Ry. Co. v. Porter* [57] he ruled that areas non-tangent upon the improved street yet within a distance of one hundred and fifty feet of the line of the improvement obtained sufficient advantage to warrant liability if the abutting land proved insufficient to sustain the cost of the improvement.

McKenna believed that States and municipalities could oblige citizens to pay for projects aimed at facilitating the health, welfare, or convenience of the community. However, when public works dispossessed an individual either of his easements or of his lands, the government was obliged to compensate for such loss. His most striking expression of this is a biting dissent in *Sauer v. City of New York* [58] when he accused his fellow justices of violating the principle they had enunciated in *Muhlker v. Harlem Railroad Company* [59] and *Burrell v. New York and Harlem Railroad Company,* [60] and *Kierns v. New York and Harlem Railroad Company.* [61] In each of these cases complainant was granted satisfaction for appropriation of the easement of light, air and access. The present case differed only in the fact that a municipality destroyed the easements rather than a private corporation. Somewhat impatiently McKenna queried, "Is it possible that the law can see no legal detriment in this, no impairment of the abutter's grant from the city, no right to compensation?" [62]

[57] 210 U. S. 177 (May 18, 1908).

[58] 206 U. S. 536 (May 27, 1907). In the case at bar the city deprived abutting property owners of easements of light and air by erection of a viaduct. McKenna claimed that a viaduct as well as an elevated railroad destroyed easements and the municipality should be compelled to pay compensation for the damage, as was done in *Muhlker v. Harlem R.R. Co.*

[59] 197 U. S. 544 (Apr. 10, 1905). This is one of the few cases in which McKenna condemned the action of the State in cases involving due process.

[60] 198 U. S. 390 (May 15, 1905).

[61] 198 U. S. 390 (May 15, 1905). In Kierns and Burrell cases Chief Justice Fuller and Justices White, Peckham and Holmes dissented but made no written comment.

[62] 536 U. S. 558.

The individual liberties protected by the first eight amendments to the Constitution were usually given an exact interpretation by the Court. However, McKenna was not an inveterate supporter of the school which insisted that an interpretation of a term by the fathers of the Constitution necessarily must be accepted by future generations. Through *Weems v. United States* [63] Justice McKenna initiated a wide departure from established precedent and gave to the courts a novel veto power over legislative discretion in the matter of criminal law. In his opinion, the Eighth Amendment, forbidding " cruel and unusual punishments," was not limited to its original meaning of body torture, but included unreasonable chastisement, excessive terms of imprisonment, or unnecessary deprivations.

The most important decisions of Justice McKenna, on the subject of personal rights, were those which affected indictment and the trial of accused individuals. Despite occasional lapses, Justice McKenna has recorded a number of well reasoned and commendatory defenses of personal liberties. One of his most vigorous dissents occurred when the court sustained the denial of the writ of *habeas corpus* to two union officials who had been kidnapped through the connivance of Idaho and Montana officials.[64] McKenna thought that to evaluate that act of the State authorities as one individual kidnapping another was not only disingenuous but naive for:

No individual or individuals could have accomplished what the power of two States accomplished; no individual or individuals could have commanded the means and success; no individual or individuals could have

[63] 217 U. S. 349 (May 2, 1910). In his dissent Justice Holmes maintained that the words of the Eighth Amendment prohibiting "cruel and unusual punishments," should be interpreted as they had been during the past three hundred years. The framers of the Constitution had the same meaning in mind as had the writers of the Bill of Rights in 1688 and no American court had ever given a different meaning. Therefore it was outside the province of the Court to read a new meaning into the Amendment.

[64] *Pettibone v. Nichols*, 203 U. S. 192 (Dec. 3, 1906); *Haywood v. Nichols*, 203 U. S. 221 (Dec. 3, 1906); W. J. Ghent, "William Dudley Haywood," *Dictionary of American Biography*, VIII (New York, 1932), 467–469.

made arrests of prominent citizens by invading their homes; could have commanded the resources of jails, armed guards and special trains; could have successfully timed all acts to prevent inquiry and judicial interference.

Justice McKenna disagreed with his colleagues again in *Trono v. United States*,[65] where the defendant had been tried and convicted for manslaughter in a Philippine court, and on appeal convicted of murder. Defendant assailed the second trial as double jeopardy and sought the intercession of the Supreme Court. The majority through Justice Peckham refused to see any violation of constitutional rights and sustained the conviction. Justice McKenna with Justice White condemned the procedure as twice jeopardizing the life and limb of complainant. He denounced the opinion of his colleagues as a contradiction of the principle which they had evolved in *Kepner v. United States*,[66] where they had classified as double jeopardy a second hearing after acquittal. The case at bar was an exact parallel, except it was an individual who challenged the constitutional integrity of the process rather than the government.

In *Hale v. Henkel*[67] he agreed with Justice Brown that a·corporation was not endowed with the same exemptions in the right of searches and seizures as an individual, and that an official of a company could not invoke his constitutional immunity against self-incrimination and thereby impede the government in its search for information on breaches of the Sherman Anti-Trust Law. However, when the books of a company were investigated solely

[65] 199 U. S. 521 (Dec. 4, 1905). "Notes," *Columbia Law Review*, VI (Apr. 1906), 261; "Recent Cases," *Harvard Law Review*, XIX (Feb. 1906), 300.

[66] 195 U. S. 100 (May 31, 1904). Ralph F. Colin, "The Evolution of the Doctrine of Territorial Incorporation," *Columbia Law Review*, XXVI (Nov. 1926), 843; "Current Legislation," *Columbia Law Review*, XXVI (June, 1926), 752; "Double Jeopardy," *Harvard Law Review*, XVIII (Jan. 1905), 216.

[67] 201 U. S. 45 (Mar. 16, 1906). Henry W. Taft, "The Tobacco Trust Decisions," *Columbia Law Review*, VI (June, 1906), 375–387; Osmond K. Fraenkel, "Concerning Searches and Seizures," *Harvard Law Review*, XXXIV (Feb. 1921), 374; Milton Handler, "The Constitutionality of Investigations by the Federal Trade Commission," *Columbia Law Review*, XXVIII (Nov. 1928), 917, 918.

in order to bring indictment against the person of the official, Justice McKenna considered that in such circumstances

> the constitution protected him from producing evidence against himself and he was certainly asked to produce such evidence. The books were in his possession in the transactions recorded, he was a participant and it may be the only doer. Let it be kept in mind that it was his own privilege that he claimed, not that of the corporation." [68]

Perhaps the most widely advertised, and in some circles the most popular, of McKenna's personal civil rights decisions was that in *Burdick v. the United States*,[69] in which the city editor of the *New York Tribune* was fined for refusing to reveal the source of his information for a number of articles which appeared in his paper. Despite the offer of a presidential pardon he persisted in silence and McKenna ruled that defendant legally exercised his right against self-discrimination.

Hence it was one of McKenna's greatest cares to fend off governmental encroachment on the immunities of citizens, in granting exemption from testifying, in his precedent-breaking adjudication of what constituted cruel and excessive punishments, in distinguishing between a lark and commercialized vice and in castigating law officers for illegally and forcibly preventing a man from invoking his constitutional right of *habeas corpus*. He championed the plight of the dispossessed and fulfilled what he believed was "the most serious duty of this court," that of protecting the liberties of those who looked to the Constitution for freedom from duress.

During his twenty-seven years on the bench Justice McKenna led a secluded and retired life. Although invited to numerous

---

[68] *Wilson v. United States,* 221 U. S. 361 (Apr. 15, 1911). Arthur M. Allen, "The Opinions of Mr. Justice Hughes," *Columbia Law Review,* XVI (Nov. 1916), 573–574, compares the language of Justice Hughes with that of McKenna and designates the latter's as "almost impassioned." Joseph M. Proskauer, "Corporate Privilege Against Self Incrimination," *Columbia Law Review,* XI (May, 1911), 541.

[69] 236 U. S. 79 (Jan. 25, 1915).

social functions he refused to accept lest he be deprived of the
time which he believed should be devoted to his heavy court
duties. He could invariably be found at his desk in his study
from eight o'clock in the morning and after dinner in the
evening, until in his later years, when poor eyesight compelled
him to forego night work. At his desk McKenna worked
arduously, " erect as a grenadier with a book in one hand, a
lead pencil in the other; and for one silent period upon another
there would not be the slightest movement of his features, not a
sound except the brushing of his pencil." [70]　Perhaps like his colleague, Justice Willis Van Devanter, the birth pangs of his opinions
were prolonged and torturous, but when completed they were
couched in precise terms. He bestowed the same care and industry on the insignificant as on controversies of pivotal import.
He was accustomed to study the facts in the briefs one by one,
ignoring none however trifling, and labored to fit each into the
composite picture, as he so well demonstrated in his dissent in
*Adair v. United States.*[71]　Because of his passion for exactness,
McKenna often deplored sloppiness and verbosity in the briefs
presented to him and therefore frequently advocated that lawyers
should have a ready facility in the use of Latin as a remedy for
ambiguous employment of language.

For recreation McKenna thoroughly enjoyed hunting at the
Carolina shooting box of Frank Thompson, the president of the
Pennsylvania Railroad.[72]　However innocent his motives in accepting the invitation of this magnate, such associations aroused
natural criticism among opponents of vested interests. McKenna's
detractors would have little trouble in utilizing this companionship as a basis for the charge that the industrialists influenced
the court. If not indiscreet, it was somewhat unfortunate that
a harmless pastime proved to be a ready tool for castigators of
entrenched wealth. The close affinity that Justice McKenna maintained with the executive of the Pennsylvania Railroad was a basic

[70] Statement by Davenport Brown to George D. Martin. Quoted in " A
Study of the Life of Joseph McKenna,". p. 39. A manuscript copy of which
is found in the *Brown Scrapbook.*

[71] 208 U. S. 161.

[72] Statement by Mrs. Pitts Duffield, personal interview.

reason why he was pilloried as a " tool of the railroads." In Washington his principal source of diversion was golf which he frequently played in the company of Justice Harlan at the aristocratic Chevy Chase Country Club.[73] McKenna was a close and scientific student of the game, and the story was told that he once detected a flaw in the swing of his professional who emphatically denied the fault but who admitted that McKenna's diagnosis was correct when slow-motion pictures supported McKenna's contention.

Although he possessed a good library, the Justice was not an omnivorous reader.[74] He did manage to keep abreast of political trends and he insisted that it was every judge's duty to keep posted on the development and progress taking place in the nation. When Felipe Espil, an Argentine diplomat, was a guest at the McKenna home, he commented on the discriminating taste with which the Justice had chosen his material. However, when he noticed the *Nation* and the liberal *New Republic* on the reading stand, the Argentinian became curious to know why a member of the Supreme Court indulged in such reading. McKenna explained that the type of existence in his position was fraught with the danger of losing a perspective on national problems and to avoid that hazard he read these liberal publications. Not only did McKenna remain well informed on economic progress but he continued to watch the ebb and flow of political fortunes and witnessed with lively interest the return to power of his own political party in 1920.[75]

Faithful in his religious observances, Justice McKenna regularly attended St. Matthew's Catholic Church each Sunday morning.[76] He followed the ceremonies and liturgy with intelligence and discrimination, and as he walked home he usually expressed a critical estimate of the sermon. He thoroughly approved prepared instruction, but he did not hesitate to make known his

---

[73] *Illustrated Sunday Magazine,* May 21, 1916.
[74] Statement by Robert F. Cogswell, law clerk to Justice McKenna (1921–1925), personal interview.
[75] Statement by Mrs. Pitts Duffield, personal interview.
[76] Statement by Robert Cogswell, personal interview.

dissatisfaction with a homily to which he had been an unwilling auditor.

Under the law Justice McKenna was eligible to retire at his seventieth birthday, but like his predecessor, Justice Stephen Johnson Field, it was difficult to impress McKenna with his limitations, physical and mental. Despite his age and a slight stroke of paralysis in 1915, he had no inclination to resign. While his hesitancy was reasonable during the Wilson regime, he might well have stepped down from office with the advent of the Harding Administration without breaking faith with the Republican Party. After McKenna, as the senior member of the Court, swore in William Howard Taft as Chief Justice of the United States (October 3, 1921), he soon placed that amiable individual in a dilemma as to the course to be pursued in order to convince Justice McKenna that he was no longer capable of performing his share of the work in a competent and intelligent manner. To his brother, Horace, the Chief Justice confided:

> I don't know what course to take with respect to him, or what cases to assign to him. I had to take back a case from him last Saturday because he would not write it in accordance with the vote of the court . . . and have taken it over myself.

A little later (June 11, 1923), Chief Justice Taft again referred to McKenna as "An Irishman, and he retains the old pugnacity . . . and he makes up his mind now on the impressionistic principle." And on another occasion he remarked:

> He is a Cubist on the bench, and Cubists are not safe on the bench. Holmes, though his senior by more than two years, has not lost his mental acumen so far as I can see, and his power of rapid work is still marvelous.

The Chief Justice was persuaded that both Justices Holmes and McKenna should retire but when the subject was broached to McKenna, he immediately assumed the position of self-righteousness by asserting that Holmes was "two years his senior"—a sort of rampart, it would seem, against retirement or possibly the hazard of death.[77]   McKenna was firmly convinced that with retirement would come oblivion in the world that he had been part and parcel of for forty years or as the Chief Justice phrased it, " He says that when a man retired, he disappears and nobody cares for him."   Taft sought again without success in the summer of 1924 to induce his declining confrere to retire.  Even Justice Holmes commented on McKenna's debility when he wrote to Judge Pollock:

> I have on the stocks two neat cases; one as to a trademark for a perfume, which awaits the oscillations of McKenna to determine whether it shall be the judgment of the Court.[78]

On the death of his wife, beloved companion for almost sixty years, McKenna was visibly affected.  It was with some effort that he continued to fulfill even the nominal duties of his office.[79] In November of the same year, the Chief Justice suggested to McKenna that he relinquish his post but McKenna defended himself this time with the assertion that he had fulfilled all of the tasks that had been allotted to him, " thus compelling the reply that only the simplest cases had been entrusted to him." Finally in January of 1925, McKenna consented to retire and the Chief Justice in adverting to this action noted:

> I want to say that while the attitude of the Justice was in some respects that of questioning the soundness of our judgment and the opinion that we had of his work, he was manly and just as knightly in his way of doing things as one might expect, and I told him so, and thanked him most cordially for making the conference as little painful as such a conference could be.[80]

On January 5, 1925, the resignation of Justice McKenna was received and accepted by President Coolidge who speedily nomi-

---

[77] Henry Pringle, *The Life and Times of William Howard Taft* (New York, 1939), 965, 971.

[78] M. de Wolfe Howe, ed., *Holmes-Pollock Letters* (Cambridge, Mass., 1941), II, 129.  March 7, 1924.  *Prestonettes, Inc. v. Coty,* 264 U. S. 359.

[79] Statement by Mrs. Pitts Duffield, personal interview.

[80] Pringle, *op. cit.*, p. 1059.

nated his old classmate at Amherst, Dean Harlan Fiske Stone of the Columbia Law School.  On the same day McKenna filed into the courtroom with his colleagues, read one of the twenty-one opinions and then Chief Justice Taft rose from his place and announced the proffered resignation.  In the midst of an impressively simple demonstration, the retiring justice was presented with a large bouquet of roses and a commendatory expression of his colleagues :

> Your pride in the Court, its high tradition and its courage has made deep impression on us who have enjoyed the benefit of your greater experience, example and esprit de corps.  Your fraternal nature, your loyalty toward each of us, your tenderness in times of strain and stress endear you to us and make us feel deeply sensible of our loss.[81]

He answered in a reply, touched with appreciation for the thoughtfulness of his associates and regret at the breaking of old ties, and while the members of the Court, lawyers, and visitors remained standing, the old man descended from the bench and with bowed head and firm step left the chambers by the same aisle he had entered twenty-seven years before.[82]

It might be presumed that he regretted his decision to retire, for he frequently visited the Capitol and wandered among the scenes of his more active days.  At one time he was seen lingering in his old haunts with tears in his eyes for evidently he missed his work and was lonely in his forced inactivity.  Almost to the very end, he was convinced that he should have remained on the bench for, on the occasion of his last illness, when Justice Holmes visited him, he remarked, " Don't you resign, you have a right to linger superfluous on the scene." [83]

During the last twenty-two months of his life he made it a daily practice to take a long motor drive for recreation.  On

---

[81] *Brown Scrapbook* contains a copy of the address delivered by Chief Justice Taft. There is also a copy of the letter of resignation sent by Justice McKenna to President Coolidge, Jan. 6, 1925.

[82] New York *Times,* Jan. 6, 1925.

[83] Statement by Mrs. Pitts Duffield, personal interview.

Labor Day, 1925, he had a premonition that it would be his last outing and desired to visit the Tomb of the Unknown Soldier and the graves of many of his friends in the Arlington National Cemetery. On his return home, he complained of a slight indisposition which gradually developed into a fatal illness. During the weeks that followed he repeated to his daughter, Mrs. Pitts Duffield, that he " could not wait for the time to be joined with your mother in oblivion." As the end approached, the pastor, Father Edward Buckey of Saint Matthew's Church, was called and administered the last rites of the Church. Early in the morning of November 21, 1926, he died in the presence ·of his son, Major Frank McKenna, and his three daughters, Mrs. Pitts Duffield, Mrs. Davenport Brown and Mrs. Edward Alsop.[84] Chief Justice Taft announced the news of McKenna's death to the court and recalled that " No one who was present will forget the affectionate scene of farewell in 1925, when the justice in this room took his leave of the Court and his colleagues." [85] Thereupon an unprecedented recess was declared in honor of the long service which Justice McKenna had rendered to his country.[86] A requiem Mass was held at St. Matthew's Church and a memorial service at his home in the afternoon presided over by Father Buckey and attended by President and Mrs. Calvin Coolidge, Chief Justice Taft, members of the Supreme Court and notables of political, diplomatic and social life. His remains were buried beside those of his wife in Mount Olivet Cemetery in Washington.

---

[84] Obituary notices: New York *Times,* Nov. 22, 23, 1926; San Francisco *Examiner,* Nov. 22, 1926; *Washington Evening Star,* Nov. 21, 1926 *Index to Register of Deaths,* Washington, D. C., states that Justice McKenna died at 1:50 A.M., Nov. 21, 1926. The attending physician, Dr. Sterling Ruffin, attributed death to "hyperae and urema, left side."

[85] 266 U. S. V; 275 U. S. V.

[86] Statement by Mrs. Pitts Duffield.

# BIBLIOGRAPHY

*Manuscript Letters.* In a scrapbook in the possession of Mrs. Davenport McKenna Brown there are the following letters in addition to a considerable number of news clippings: Joseph McKenna to J. G. Butler, Dec. 30, 1921; William Cardinal O'Connell to J. McKenna, Oct. 11, 1924; Secretary of Navy Curtis D. Wilbur to J. McKenna, Oct. 11, 1924; Mrs. Woodrow Wilson to J. McKenna, Oct. 11, 1924; Attorney General Harlan Stone to J. McKenna, Oct. 14, 1924; J. McKenna to President Calvin Coolidge, Jan. 2, 1925; Chief Justice William H. Taft to J. McKenna, Jan. 4, 1925; J. McKenna to Chief Justice and Brethren of the Supreme Court, Jan. 5, 1925; President Calvin Coolidge to J. McKenna, Jan. 6, 1925; John H. Clarke to J. McKenna, Jan. 6, 1925; Senator Hiram Johnson to J. McKenna, Jan. 8, 1925; James Hamilton Lewis to J. McKenna, Jan. 9, 1925; Frederic A. Delano, Jan. 9, 1925. The paucity of letters is explained by Robert F. Cogswell, secretary to McKenna (1921–1925), who said that McKenna ordered his personal papers destroyed.

William Howard Taft Papers, Library of Congress, used through the courtesy of Senator Robert A. Taft. Letters from Taft to J. McKenna, May 9, 1924; Taft to Pierce Stanford, May 13, 1924; Taft to Elihu Root, June 9, 1924; Taft to J. M. Dickinson, Oct. 20, 1924; Taft to Robert Taft, Dec. 14, 1924; Taft to Louis Brandeis, Jan. 4, 1925; and a memorandum of interview with McKenna pertinent to the latter's retirement from the bench, Nov. 10, 1924.

In the National Archives, Department of Justice, under Appointment Clerk file marked "Joseph McKenna," there are the following materials:

(1) Executive and Congressional Letter Books, Vol. XXX–XXXIII (Feb. 10, 1897–Feb. 1, 1898), contain over five hundred letters, orders, and directives written by McKenna.

(2) Letter-Press Copies of the Attorney General, Vol. XXVI (Sept. 2, 1897–Aug. 1, 1898).

(3) Letter-Press Copies of the Attorney General, Miscellaneous, Vols. LXXVIII–LXXXIII (Feb. 24, 1897–Mar. 30, 1898).

(4) Ninth Circuit Court of Appeals, files marked: 1889–1893; 1897–1901.

(5) Official Opinions of the Attorney General of the United States. The opinions are printed but the originals were consulted in the following files: 9187–1885; 6384–1886; 10709–1894; 14706–1894; 2856–1896; 8317–1896; 19365–1897; 8080–1897; 10862–1897; 11135–1897; 11247–1897; 11477–1897; 11659–1897; 11957–1897; 14477–1897. Files without a number and marked only with a date are: Apr. 28, 1897; May 19, 1897. Opinions issued by Solicitor General Holmes Conrad and countersigned by Attorney General

232

McKenna were consulted in files marked: 1066–1884; 1536–1893; 7635–1895; 7888–1896; 2039–1897; 2815–1897; 3409–1897; 3783–1897; 3435–1897; 5248–1897; 7546–1897; 8745–1897; 9414–1897; 11957–1897; 16430–1897. Files without a number and marked only with a date are: Apr. 28, 1897; July 23, 1897; Nov. 15, 1897.

(6) Southern Pacific-Central Pacific Indebtedness, 1890–1895, file 1203–87B.

(7) Union Pacific Indebtedness, file 1203–87A, Vols. V–IX.

In the following public and private archives and files, some valuable material was located. The Journal of the Assembly, 21st Session of the Legislature of the State of California, 1875–1876, Vol. I. Archives of the Secretary of the State of California, Sacramento, California. A List of Assemblymen in the Solano County Archives, Fairfield, California. Birth Certificate in the Church of St. Philip Neri, Philadelphia; school registers of St. Joseph's College, Philadelphia, and vital and religious information in the registers of Baptisms, Confirmations, and Burials of .St. Dominic's Church, Benicia, California. Death certificate in Bureau of Vital Statistics, Washington, D. C.

Printed sources included the *Annual Report of the Superintendent of Public Instruction of the State of California,* Sacramento, 1855–1858, *The Journal of the Senate,* 19th Session of the Legislature of the State of California, 1871–1872, Sacramento, 1872, *United States Statutes,* Vols. XXIV–XXVIII, Washington, 1888–1894, *Report of Cases Determined in the Supreme Court of the State of California, Oct. 1870–Jan. 1871,* Sacramento, 1872; the *Federal Reporter,* Vols. XLIX–LXXVII, St. Paul, 1893–1898, *United States Supreme Court Reports,* Vols. 170–266, Washington, 1898–1924, *Congressional Record,* 49th–52nd Congress, Washington, 1885–1892, *Congressional Directory,* 49th Congress, Washington, 1886, *Senate Executive Document 52,* 54th Congress, 2nd Session.

A great deal of secondary material has been used in the way of articles, essays, dissertations, biographies, histories and the like which are herein listed.

## 1. PUBLISHED VOLUMES

*American Law Reports, Annotated,* Rochester, 1907.

Bancroft, Hubert H., *History of California,* San Francisco, 1890, II, VI, VII; *History of Central America,* San Francisco, 1890, III.

Bates, E. S., *The Story of the Supreme Court,* Indianapolis, 1936.

Biddle, E. C. and John, *McElroy's Philadelphia Directory,* 1842–1855, Philadelphia, 1842–1855.

*Biographical Directory of the American Congress,* Washington, 1928.

Burns, J. A., *The Catholic School System in the United States,* New York, 1908.

Butler, C. H., *A Century at the Bar of the Supreme Court of the United States,* New York, 1942.

234        *Joseph McKenna*

Cahill, Marion C., *Shorter Hours,* New York, 1932.
Carson, Hampton L., *History of the Supreme Court,* Philadelphia, 1902, II.
Chafee, Zechariah, *Freedom of Speech,* New York, 1920; *Free Speech in the United States,* Cambridge, Mass., 1942; *The Inquiring Mind,* New York, 1928.
Clark, G. A., *Leland Stanford,* New York, 1931.
Cleland, Robert C., *History of California, the American Period,* New York, 1922.
Cowan, R. G. and R. E., *A Bibliography of the History of California (1510–1930),* San Francisco, 1933, I, II, III.
Commons, J. R., and Andrews, J. B., *Principles of Labor Legislation,* New York, 1920.
Croly, Herbert D., *Marcus Alonzo Hanna,* New York, 1912.
Cummings, Homer, and McFarland, Carl, *The Department of Justice of the United States,* Baltimore, 1927.
Daggett, Stuart, *Chapters on the History of the Southern Pacific,* New York, 1922.
Davis, Winfield, *History of Political Conventions in California, 1849–1892,* Sacramento, 1893.
Dille, Elbert R., *Rome's Assault on Our Public Schools,* San Francisco, 1889.
Dodge, Arthur J., *Origin and Development of the Office of Attorney General,* Washington, 1930.
Dobie, Edith, *Political Career of Stephen Mallory White,* Stanford University, 1927.
Duffield, Isabel McKenna, *Washington in the 90's,* San Francisco, 1929.
Ellison, Joseph, *California and the Nation, 1846–1869,* Berkeley, 1927.
Engelhart, Zephyrin, *The Missions and Missionaries of California,* San Francisco, 1915, II, IV.
Ewing, C. A. M., *The Judges of the Supreme Court, 1789–1937,* Minneapolis, 1938.
Farrand, Max, *Framing of the Constitution of the United States,* New Haven, 1913; (ed.) *Records of the Federal Convention of 1787,* New Haven, 1923, 3 Vols.
Fessenden, Otis N., *Illustrated History of the Panama Railroad,* New York, 1861.
Finch, James A., *Digest of Official Opinions of the Attorney Generals of the United States, 1881–1906,* Washington, 1908.
Gerstenberg, Charles W., *American Constitutional Law,* New York, 1937.
Gleeson, William, *History of the Catholic Church in California,* San Francisco, 1872, II.
Gregory, Thomas, *History of Solano and Napa Counties,* Los Angeles, 1912.
Haines, Charles G., *American Doctrine of Judicial Supremacy,* New York, 1914.

Hasse, Adelaide, *Index of Economic Material in Documents of the States of the United States, California, 1849–1904,* Washington, 1907.

Hinsdale, Mary, *History of the President's Cabinet,* Ann Harbor, 1911.

*Historical Sketches of the Catholic Churches and Institutions of Philadelphia,* Philadelphia, 1895.

Hittell, Theodore, *History of California,* San Francisco, 1897, I–IV; *The General Laws of the State of California from 1850–1864,* San Francisco, 1865, I.

Hornblower, William, *Modern Legislation as Exemplified by the Sherman Anti-Trust Act,* New York, 1909.

Hunt, Marguerite, *History of Solano County,* Chicago, 1926.

Keep, Rosalind A., *Fourscore Years—A History of Mills College,* Oakland, 1921.

Kimble, John H., *The Panama Route to the Pacific Coast,* Seattle, 1937.

Kirlin, Joseph L., *Catholicity in Philadelphia,* Philadelphia, 1909.

Klinkhamer, Sister Marie Carolyn, *Edward Douglas White, Chief Justice of the United States,* Washington, 1943.

Kohlsaat, H. H., *From McKinley to Harding,* New York, 1923.

Lamar, Clarinda P., *The Life of Joseph Rucker Lamar,* New York, 1926.

Leach, Frank A., *Recollections of a Newspaper Man,* San Francisco, 1917.

Lerner, Max, *The Mind and Faith of Justice Holmes,* Boston, 1943.

Lewis, Oscar, *The Story of the Big Four,* New York, 1938.

Lynch, Jeremiah, *Buckleyism: The Government of a State,* San Francisco, 1888.

Maguire, John F., *The Irish in America,* New York, 1873.

Mott, Rodney, *Due Process of Law,* Indianapolis, 1926.

Moulder, Andrew, *Commentaries on the School Law of California,* Sacramento, 1858.

Myers, Gustavus, *History of the Supreme Court of the United States,* Chicago, 1918.

Olcott, Charles, *Life of William McKinley,* New York, 1916.

Palmer, Benjamin W., *Marshall and Taney: Statesmen of the Law,* Minneapolis, 1939.

Pell, E. L., Buel, J. W., and Boyd, J. P., *McKinley and Men of Our Times,* Washington, 1901.

Phillips, Catherine C., *Cornelius Cole–California Pioneer and United States Senator,* San Francisco, 1929.

Prendergast, Thomas F., *Forgotten Pioneers,* San Francisco, 1942.

Pringle, H. F., *The Life and Times of William Howard Taft,* New York, 1939; *Theodore Roosevelt,* New York, 1931.

Quigley, Hugh, *The Irish Race in California and on the Pacific Coast,* San Francisco, 1878.

Rhodes, James Ford, *The McKinley and Roosevelt Administrations,* New York, 1922.

Ribble, F. D., *State and National Power over Commerce,* New York, 1937.

Richardson, James D. (ed.), *Compilation of the Messages and Papers of the Presidents, 1789–1897,* Washington, 1896–1899, 10 Vols.

Rooney, Miriam, *Lawlessness, Law and Sanction,* Washington, 1937.

Royce, Josiah, *California from the Conquest in 1846 to the Second Vigilance Committee in San Francisco,* Boston, 1886.

*Sadlier's Metropolitan Catholic Directory,* 1851–1855, New York.

Scharf, J. Thomas, and Thompson, Wescott, *History of Philadelphia,* Philadelphia, 1884, II.

Shuck, Oscar T., *Bench and Bar in California,* San Francisco, 1889; *History of the Bench and Bar in California,* Los Angeles, 1901; *Representative and Leading Men on the Pacific,* San Francisco, 1870.

Sullivan, Mark, *Our Times,* New York, 1926, 5 Vols.

Swett, John, *History of the Public School System of California,* San Francisco, 1876; *Public Education in California,* New York, 1911.

Swisher, Carl B., *Motivation and Political Technique in the California Constitutional Convention, 1878–1879,* Claremont, California, 1930; *Stephen J. Field, Craftsman of the Law,* Washington, 1930.

Talbot, Francis X., *St. Joseph's College, Philadelphia, 1851–1926,* Philadelphia, 1927.

Thayer, W. R., *Theodore Roosevelt,* New York, 1919.

Thompson, Robert A., *Historical and Descriptive Sketch of Sonoma,* Philadelphia, 1877.

Thompson, William, *Reminiscences of a Pioneer,* San Francisco, 1912.

Thorpe, Francis N. (ed.), *Federal and State Constitutions,* Washington, 1909, I.

United States Senate, *Memorial Addresses of Life and Character of Leland Stanford,* Washington, 1894.

United States Supreme Court Bar, *Proceedings . . . in Memory of Joseph McKenna,* Washington, 1926.

Warren, Charles, *Congress, the Constitution and the Supreme Court,* Boston, 1925; *History of the American Bar,* Boston, 1911; *Supreme Court in United States History,* Boston, 1926, II.

Weed, Joseph A., *A View of California as It Is,* San Francisco, 1874.

Wicher, Edward, *The Presbyterian Church in California, 1849–1927,* New York, 1927.

## 2. SPECIAL STUDIES AND CRITICAL LEGAL REVIEWS

Abbot, Edwin H., "Patents and the Sherman Act," 12 *Columbia Law Review* 709–723.

"The Acquisition of Patents as a Restraint of Trade," 24 *Columbia Law Review* 654–660.

Adler, Edward A., "Labor, Capital and Business at Common Law," 29 *Harvard Law Review* 241–276.

Albertsworth, E. F., "Judicial Review of Administrative Action by the Federal Supreme Court," 35 *Harvard Law Review* 565–584.

Allen, Arthur M., "The Opinions of Mr. Justice Hughes," 16 *Columbia Law Review* 565–584.

Armstrong, Robert D., "The Municipality as a Unit in Rate Making Cases," 32 *Michigan Law Review* 289–324.

Arterburn, Norman F., "The Origin and First Test of Public Callings," 75 *Pennsylvania Law Review* 411–428.

Ballantine, Arthur, "A Compensation Plan for Railroad Accident Claims," 29 *Harvard Law Review* 705–723; "Railway Strikes and the Constitution," 17 *Columbia Law Review* 502–522.

Beale, Joseph H., "The Carrier's Liability," 11 *Harvard Law Review* 158–168.

Bettman, Alfred, "Constitutionality of Zoning," 37 *Harvard Law Review* 834–859.

Bikle, Henry Wolf, "Judicial Determination of Questions of Fact," 38 *Harvard Law Review* 6–27; "Mr. Justice Brandeis and the Regulation of Railroads," 45 *Harvard Law Review* 4–32; "The Silence of Congress," 41 *Harvard Law Review* 200–224.

Bird, Francis, "The Evolution of Due Process of Law in the United States Supreme Court," 15 *Columbia Law Review* 37–50.

Bohlen, Francis H., "Duty of Master to Supply Safe Appliances," 20 *Harvard Law Review* 14–34.

Bordwell, Percy, "The Function of the Judiciary," 7 *Columbia Law Review* 520–528.

Bornstein, Samuel, "Statutes as the Source of Title in Descent and Distribution in Wills," 15 *Boston Law Review* 205–211.

Brown, Ray A., "Due Process, Police Power and the Supreme Court," 40 *Harvard Law Review* 943–968; "Police Power-Legislation for Health and Personal Safety," 42 *Harvard Law Review* 866–898.

Buchanan, John G., "The Ohio Valley Water Case and the Valuation of Railroads," 40 *Harvard Law Review* 1033–1069.

Buford, Edward P., "Assumption of Risk under the Federal Employers Liability Act," 28 *Harvard Law Review* 163–185.

Burdick, Charles K., "The Adamson Law Decision," 11 *Cornell Law Review* 320–324.

Canfield, George F., "Corporate Responsibility," 14 *Columbia Law Review* 469–481.

Carey, Homer F., and Oliphant, Herman, "The Present Status of the Hitchman Case," 29 *Columbia Law Review* 440–460.

Carpenter, Charles, "Court Decisions and the Common Law," 17 *Columbia Law Review* 593–637.

Carroll, Thomas F., "Freedom of Speech," 17 *Michigan Law Review* 621–665.

Carver, T. N., "The Theory of the Shortened Working Week," *American Economic Review* (Sept. 1936) 451–462.

Chafee, Zechariah, "Freedom of Speech and States' Rights," 25 *New Republic.*

Cheadle, John, "Government Control of Business," 20 *Columbia Law Review* 550–585.

Cobb, Frank M., "Maximum Rates and Rate Regulation," 21 *Harvard Law Review* 175–194.

Colby, Elbridge, "Occupation under the Laws of War," 26 *Columbia Law Review* 146–170.

Colman, William, "Constitutional Limitations upon State Taxation of Foreign Corporations," 11 *Columbia Law Review* 393–427.

Colin, Ralph F., "The Evolution of the Doctrine of Territorial Incorporation," 26 *Columbia Law Review* 823–850.

Collins, Charles W., "Stare Decisis and the Fourteenth Amendment," 12 *Columbia Law Review* 603–612.

Conner, James T., "The Nature of Succession," 8 *Fordham Law Review* 151–165.

Conway, James, "Rights and Duties of Family and State in Regard to Education," 9 *American Catholic Quarterly Review* 105–127.

Cooke, Frederick H., "Nature and Scope of the Power of Congress to Regulate Commerce," 11 *Columbia Law Review* 35–40.

Corwin, Edward S., "The 'Higher Law' Background of American Constitutional Law," 42 *Harvard Law Review* 149–185, 365–409.

Coudert, Frederic R., "The Evolution of the Doctrine of Territorial Incorporation," 26 *Columbia Law Review* 823–850.

Cushman, Robert E., "Social and Economic Interpretation of the Fourteenth Amendment," 20 *Michigan Law Review* 737–764.

Denis, William C., "Notes on Some Recent Supreme Court Cases Relating to the Situs of Intangible Personal Property," 15 *Columbia Law Review* 377–398.

"Deportation of Aliens," 20 *Columbia Law Review* 680–684.

Dodd, E. Merrick, "For Whom are Corporate Managers Trustees?" 45 *Harvard Law Review* 1145–1163; "The Problem of State Constitutional Construction," 20 *Columbia Law Review* 635–651.

Earle, John J., "Sentiment of the People of California with Respect to the Civil War," *Annual Report of the American Historical Association, 1907,* 123–135.

Edgerton, Henry W., "The Relation of Mental States to Negligence," 39 *Harvard Law Review* 849–870.

"Eight Hour Law," 17 *Columbia Law Review* 422–426.

Fairleigh, David W., "An Inquiry into the Power of Congress to regulate the Intra-State Business of Interstate Railroads," 9 *Columbia Law Review* 38–50; "Federal Regulation of Intrastate Railroad Rates," 21 *Columbia Law Review* 352–358.

Finkelstein, Maurice, "From Munn v. Illinois to Tyson v. Banton," 27 *Columbia Law Review* 769–783; "Judicial Self-Limitation," 37 *Harvard Law Review* 338–364.

Foik, Paul, "Anti-Catholic Parties in American Politics, 1776–1860," 36 *Records,* The American Catholic Historical Society, Philadelphia, 41–69.

Fowler, J. A., "Federal Power to Own and Operate Railroads in Peace Time," 33 *Harvard Law Review* 775–793.

Fraenkel, Osmond K., "Concerning Searches and Seizures," 34 *Harvard Law Review* 361–387; "Recent Statutes Affecting Labor Injunctions and Yellow Dog Contracts," 30 *Illinois Law Review* 854–883.

Frankfurter, Felix, "The Business of the Supreme Court of the United States," 39 *Harvard Law Review* 587–627; "Mr. Justice Holmes and the Constitution," 41 *Harvard Law Review* 121–164; "Hours of Labor and Realism in Constitutional Law," 29 *Harvard Law Review* 353–373; "Mr. Justice Brandeis and the Constitution," 45 *Harvard Law Review* 33–105.

Frankfurter, Felix, and Landis, James, "A Study in the Federal Judicial System," 40 *Harvard Law Review* 1110–1129; "Business of the Supreme Court at the October Term, 1931" 46 *Harvard Law Review* 226–260.

Freeman, Robert H., "Retroactive Operation of Decisions," 18 *Columbia Law Review* 230–251.

Fuller, Paul, "Expansion of Constitutional Powers by Interpretation," 5 *Columbia Law Review* 192–214.

Gager, William W., "Efficiency or Restraint of Trade," 27 *Yale Law Journal* 1060–1085.

Green, Leon, "The Duty Problem in Negligence Cases," 28 *Columbia Law Review* 1014–1045.

Grosvenor, Edwin P., "The 'Rule of Reason' as applied by the United States Supreme Court to Commerce in Patented Articles," 17 *Columbia Law Review* 208–229.

Hackett, Frank W., "Federal Employers Liability Act," 22 *Harvard Law Review* 38–47.

Haines, Charles, "The Law of Nature in State and Federal Decisions," 25 *Yale Law Journal* 617–657.

Hayes, Alfred, "Partial Unconstitutionality with special reference to the Corporation," 11 *Columbia Law Review* 120–146.

Hohfield, Wesley N., "The Individual Liability of Stockholders and the Conflict of Laws," 10 *Columbia Law Review* 520–549.

Howland, Charles P., "Monopolies: the Cause and the Remedy," 10 *Columbia Law Review* 91–117.

Hubbard, Harry, "The Fourteenth Amendment and Special Assessments on Real Estate," 14 *Harvard Law Review* 1–19, 98–115.

Hull, Henry, "Jurisdiction and Causes of Action Arising under the Act to Regulate Commerce," 17 *Columbia Law Review* 309–319; "Some Legal Aspects of Federal Control of Railroads," 31 *Harvard Law Review* 860–874.

Hunting, Warren B., "The Constitutionality of Race Distinctions," 11 *Columbia Law Review* 24–35.

Hurt, Peyton, "The Rise and Fall of the Know Nothings in California," 9 *California Historical Society Quarterly*.

Isaacs, Elcanon, "The Federal Protection of Foreign Corporations," 26 *Columbia Law Review* 263–292.

Jaffe, Louis L., and Tobriner, Mathew, "The Legality of Price Fixing Agreements," 45 *Harvard Law Review* 1164–1195.

"Juristic Theory and Constitutional Law—Liability without Fault," 33 *Harvard Law Review* 86–88.

Kales, Albert M., "The Sherman Act," 31 *Harvard Law Review* 412–446.

Kirchway, Karl W., "The Interstate Commerce Commission and the Judicial Enforcement of the Act to Regulate Commerce," 14 *Columbia Law Review* 210–228.

Larremore, William, "Stare Decisis and Contractual Rights," 22 *Harvard Law Review* 182–189.

Laylin, Clarence D., "The 'Ohio Blue Sky' Cases," 15 *Michigan Law Review* 369–385.

Lilienthal, David, "Regulation of Public Utilities during Depression," 17 *Columbia Law Review* 745–775.

Littlefield, Charles E., "The Insular Tariff Cases in the Supreme Court," 15 *Harvard Law Review* 164–190.

Lowry, Philip, "Strikes and the Law," 21 *Columbia Law Review* 782–800.

Lutkin, Harris C., "The Sherman Anti-Trust Act," 12 *Illinois Law Review* 435–437.

McAllister, Breck P., "Lord Hale and Business Affected with a Public Interest," 43 *Harvard Law Review* 759–791.

McCarthy, Frank L., "White Slave Traffic Act," 26 *Yale Law Journal* 509–510.

McClain, Emlin, "The Hawaiian Case," 17 *Harvard Law Review* 386–399.

McGovney, Dudley, "American Citizenship," 11 *Columbia Law Review* 526–529.

Magruder, Calvert, "A Half Century of Legal Influence upon the Development of Collective Bargaining," 50 *Harvard Law Review* 1071–1117.

Marshall, W. M., "Secular Education in England and the United States," 11 *American Catholic Quarterly Review* 278–312.

Meeker, J. Edward, "Preventive Punitive Security Laws," 26 *Columbia Law Review* 318–328.

Montague, Gilbert, "Anti-Trust Laws and the Federal Trade Commission," 27 *Columbia Law Review* 650–678.

"Nature and Validity of License Restrictions Imposed by a Patentee," 12 *Columbia Law Review* 445–447.

Needham, Charles W., "Exclusive Power of Congress over Interstate Commerce," 11 *Columbia Law Review* 251–261.

Olney, Richard, "Discrimination Against Union Labor—Legal?" 42 *American Law Review* 884–890.

Oliphant, Herman, "Trade Associations and the Law," 26 *Columbia Law Review* 381–395.

Parkinson, Thomas I., "Congressional Prohibitions of Interstate Commerce," 16 *Columbia Law Review* 367–385.

Patterson, Edwin W., "The Transfer of Insured Property in German and American Law," 29 *Columbia Law Review* 691–714.

Peaslee, Amos J., "The Effect of the Federal Anti-Trust Law," 38 *Harvard Law Review* 394–406.

Philbrick, Francis, "Joseph McKenna," 12 *D.A.B.* 87–88.

Pope, Herbert, "Municipal Contracts and the Regulation of Rates," 16 *Harvard Law Review* 1–21.

Pound, Roscoe, "Mechanical Jurisprudence," 8 *Columbia Law Review* 605–623.

Powell, Thomas R., "Commerce, Pensions and Codes," 49 *Harvard Law Review* 1–43; "Due Process and the Adamson Law," 17 *Columbia Law Review* 114–127; "The Constitutional Issue in Minimum Wage Legislation," 2 *Minnesota Law Review* 1–21; "Indirect Encroachment on Federal Authority by the Taxing Powers of the States," 31 *Harvard Law Review* 572–618; "The Judiciality of Minimum Wage Legislation," 37 *Harvard Law Review* 545–573; "The Nature of a Patent Right," 17 *Columbia Law Review* 663–686; "The Supreme Court and the Adamson Law," 65 *Pennsylvania Law Review* 607–631.

"The President's (Grant) Speech at Des Moines," 22 *The Catholic World* 707–711.

Proskauer, Joseph M., "Corporate Privilege against Self-Incrimination," 11 *Columbia Law Review* 445–452.

Purcell, Richard J., "Civil Service versus the Spoils System in the Federal Government," 30 *Catholic Educational Review* 549–560; "Fists Across the Sea," *Columbia*, April, 1926; "Irish Educational Contribution to Pennsylvania," 37 *Catholic Educational Review* 425–439; "John C. Heenan," 8 *D.A.B.* 499–500; "John Ireland," 9 *D.A.B.* 494–497; "Michael C. Corrigan," 4 *D.A.B.* 450–452; "Senator David Broderick of California," 28 *Studies* (Dublin) 415–430; "William Henry Aspinwall," 1 *D.A.B.* 396–397; "Chief Justice Roger B. Taney," 40 *Catholic Educational Review* 3–18; "Chief Justice Edward D. White," 40 *Catholic Educational Review* 321–333; "Justice Pierce Butler," 42 *Catholic Educational Review* 193–215; "Justice Joseph McKenna," *Records,* American Catholic Historical Society 56 (Philadelphia), September, 1945, 177–223.

Radin, Max, "Statutory Interpretation," 43 *Harvard Law Review* 863–885.

Randolph, Carmen F., "The Insular Cases," 1 *Columbia Law Review* 436–470.

Reynolds, Jackson E., "Railway Valuation—Is It a Panacea?" 8 *Columbia Law Review* 264–280.

Richter, Erwin, "The Application of State Safety Statutes to Actions under the Federal Employers Liability Act," 15 *Columbia Law Review* 649–661.

Robinson, Gustavus, "Public Utility Concept in American Law," 41 *Harvard Law Review* 277–308.

Rooney, Francis, "The Legality of Combinations in Foreign Trade," 17 *Columbia Law Review* 404–416.

Saylor, Harold D., "Blue Sky Laws," 65 *Pennsylvania Law Review* 785–787. "The Scope of the White Slave Traffic Act," 4 *Virginia Law Review* 653–660.

Seavey, Warren A., "Negligence—Subjective or Objective," 41 *Harvard Law Review* 1–28.

Sharp, Malcolm P., "Movement in Supreme Court Adjudication," 46 *Harvard Law Review* 361–403.

Shea, John G., "Catholic Free Schools in the United States," 9 *American Catholic Quarterly Review* 713–725.

Shoene, Lester P., and Watson, Frank, "Workmen's Compensation on Interstate Railways," 47 *Harvard Law Review* 389–424.

Simpson, Sidney Post, "Constitutional Limitations on Compulsory Industrial Arbitration," 38 *Harvard Law Review* 753–792.

Stern, Robert L., "That Commerce which Concerns More States than One," 47 *Harvard Law Review* 1335–1366.

Tobriner, Mathew O., "Cooperative Marketing and the Restraint of Trade," 27 *Columbia Law Review* 827–836.

Taft, Henry W., "The Tobacco Trust Decisions," 6 *Columbia Law Review* 375–387.

Trickett, William, "The Original Package Ineptitude," 6 *Columbia Law Review* 161–174.

Wallace, M. G., "Constitutionality of the Sedition Laws," 6 *Virginia Law Review* 385–399.

Wambaugh, Eugene, "Workmen's Compensation Acts," 25 *Harvard Law Review* 129–139.

Warren, Charles, "A Bulwark to the State Police Power—The United States Supreme Court," 13 *Columbia Law Review* 667–695; "The New 'Liberty' under the Fourteenth Amendment," 39 *Harvard Law Review* 431–465; "The Progressiveness of the United States Supreme Court," 13 *Columbia Law Review* 294–313.

Warren, Frank, "The Federal Employers Liability Act of 1908," 22 *Harvard Law Review* 38–47.

Watkins, Myron W., "The Change in Trust Policy," 35 *Harvard Law Review* 815–837.

Whitney, Edward B., "The Insular Decisions," 2 *Columbia Law Review* 78–91.

Wickersham, Cornelius, "The N.I.R.A. from the Employers' Viewpoint," 48 *Harvard Law Review* 187–207.

Wigmore, John H., "Freedom of Speech and Freedom of Thuggery in Wartime and Peacetime," 14 *Illinois Law Review* 539–561.

Wiel, Samuel C., "Public Service Irrigation Companies," 16 *Columbia Law Review* 37–47.

Wyman, Bruce, "Jurisdictional Limitations upon Commission Action," 27 *Harvard Law Review* 544–569.

## 3. NEWSPAPERS

The newspapers used included:

Alameda *Argus*, February 12, 1892; January 21, 1897.

Alameda *Encinal*, July 16, 23, 26, 1884; September 1, 1886.

Arcata *Leader*, August 9, 1879.

Bakersfield *Echo*, January 14, 1897.

Baltimore *Sun*, November 22, 1926.

Benicia *New Era*, August 23, 1879; August 4, 11, 18, September 1, 1886.

Berkeley *Advocate*, July 12, 19, 1884; August 15, 1888.

Berkeley *Gazette*, February 5, 1897.

Brooklyn *Daily Eagle*, October 18, 1897.

Butte *County Register*, July 11, 1897.

Butte *Weekly Record*, September 16, 23, 1876; August 2, 16, 1879.

Chicago *Legal News*, May 7, 1898.

Chico *Enterprise*, September 8, 22, November 3, 1876; August 1, September 12, 1879.

Colusa *Independent*, October 22, 28, November 4, 1876.

Colusa *Weekly Sun*, October 18, 28, 1876; September 6, 1879.

Contra Costa *Gazette*, May 17, 24, July 12, 19, 26, August 2, September 6, October 4, 8, November 1, 1884; October 23, 30, 1886; August 1, September 15, October 31, 1888; August 30, September 24, October 11, 1890.

Dixon *Tribune*, September 5, 13, 1879.

Downieville *Weekly Peoples Cause*, August 2, September 20, 1879.

Healdsburg *Enterprise*, October 18, 1876.

Inyo *Index*, February 17, 1892.

Lake *Democrat*, November 4, 1876.

Lassen *Advocate*, September 27, 1876; July 19, 1879; February 9, 1897.

Los Angeles *Herald*, February 9, 1897.

Marin *County Journal*, July 17, October 16, 1884; September 30, 1886.

Marysville *Daily Appeal*, October 22, 1876; September 2, 1879; January 19, 1897.

Marysville *Democrat*, August 30, 1886.

Mendocino *Democrat*, October 14, 1876.

Modesto *Herald*, February 4, 1897.

Mountain *Messenger*, September 16, 20, 1876; July 19, 26, 1879.

New York *Herald,* September 11, December 10, 11, 1854; March 14, April 6, July 2, 1855.

New York *Journal,* October 15, 1897.

New York *Times,* January 6, 1925.

Napa *Register,* September 5, 1876.

Oakland *Daily Evening Tribune,* February 13, July 15, 16, October 15, 1884; September 8, 1890; February 12, 13, 1892; January 20, 21, 1897.

Oakland *Daily Times,* July 15, 16, 17, 26, October 15, November 5, 1884.

Oakland *Enquirer,* August 1, 18, October 19, 25, 1888; February 5, 1897; January 21, 1898.

Oakland *Morning Times,* August 27, 1886; August 18, October 25, 1888.

Oroville *Weekly Mercury,* August 29, 1879.

Philadelphia *Enquirer,* November 22, 1926.

Philadelphia *North American,* May 7, 10, July 8, 9, 10, 1844.

Philadelphia *Pennsylvanian,* May 7, 10, July 8, 9, 10, 1844.

Sacramento *Daily Union,* August 12, 1876; June 20, 1879; August 26, 30, October 6, 1886; February 12, 1892.

St. Helena *Star,* October 2, 1876.

San Diego *Tribune,* January 20, 1897.

San Francisco *Alta California,* June 27, 1850; November 30, 1852; August 10, 11, 1876; June 28, September 7, 1879.

San Francisco *Argonaut,* July 24, 26, 1884; September 18, 1886; July 23, 1888.

San Francisco *Bulletin,* June 10, 11, 22, 30, September 9, 12, 13, 15, 1875; January 9, February 14, 17, 18, March 15, August 8, 9, September 2, 12, 15, 16, 18, 20, 22, 25, October 2, 10, 17, 19, 25, 28, November 1, 4, 9, 15, 1876; June 18, July 2, 9, September 17, 1879; February 5, 21, 1897.

San Francisco *Call,* March 1, 1876; February 5, 6, 21, 27, 1897.

San Francisco *Chronicle,* February 12, 1892; February 6, 27, March 8, 1897.

San Francisco *Daily Report,* February 16, 18, 1892.

San Francisco *Examiner,* February 12, 1892.

San Francisco *Post,* July 20, 1893; February 5, September 7, 1897.

San Francisco *Reporter,* March 31, 1897.

San Francisco *Wave,* January 27, 1897.

San Francisco *Monitor,* March 13, May 29, June 5, 12, September 11, 1897; April 23, 1898.

San Leandro *Reporter,* August 1, 1884; August 14, 1886.

San Rafael *Journal,* January 21, 1897.

Santa Rosa *Daily Democrat,* October 17, 1876.

Scott Valley *News,* July 30, August 7, 9, 1879.

The *Sentinel,* July 29, August 9, 1879.

Solano *Weekly Republican,* August 27, September 16, 1875; January 20, February 24, July 27, August 26, 1876; August 26, 30, September 4, October 28, 1879; July 11, 1884; August 27, September 17, 24, October 15, November 5, 1886.

Sonoma *Democrat*, August 23, 1879.
Stockton *Record*, January 20, 1897.
Suisun *Republican*, January 20, 22, February 23, 1897.
Tacoma *Daily Ledger*, February 24, 1892.
Tehama *Tocsin*, September 24, 1876.
Tulare *Register*, January 19, 1897.
Ukiah *City Press*, August 8, 15, 1879.
Vallejo *Evening Chronicle*, October 20, 22, 1876; August 30, 1879.
Vallejo *News*, January 19, 1897.
Visalia *Equal Rights Expositor*, October 18, 1862.
Weaverville *Journal*, January 23, 1897.
Wheatland *Free Press*, November 4, 1876.
Woodland *Democrat*, February 18, 1897.
Yolo *Democrat*, August 21, 28, 1878.
Yolo *Mail*, October 8, 1886.
Yreka *Journal*, February 9, April 19, May 10, August 23, November 15, 1876; February 9, 1897.
Yreka *Union*, January 15, April 1, 1876; August 9, 16, 1879.

# INDEX

Adams, Alvin, 8
Adamson Act, 135, 141 n., 142
Agreement, 114
Agriculture, 26, 27
Alameda, 49, 69
Alaska, 69
Alcohol, 55
Alemany, Archbishop Joseph S., 13, 48
Aliens, 84, 85, 89
Allen, William V., 105
Amendment, 29, 72
American Party, 58, 59, 61, 64, 65, 68, 72
American Protective Association, 78, 104
Anti-Catholicism, 1, 4, 50, 54, 60, 65, 66, 68, 72, 78, 90
Anti-Chinese Party, 58
Anti-Monopoly Party, 52
Aspinwall, William H., 7 n.
Attorney General, United States, appointed to, 90–92
Austin, John, 111 n.

Bagging, 62
Banks, Jerome C., 42
Bargaining Power, 134, 137, 140
Barrundia Affair, 71
Bayne, Thomas, 68
Benicia, Calif., 9, 10, 11, 12, 14, 49, 50, 53, 56, 57, 61, 71, 74
Benicia Collegiate Institute, 15
Bentham, Jeremy, 137, 205
Berry, Campbell, 43–48
Bigotry, 1–4, 6
Bland-Allison Silver Purchase Act, 57, 59, 60
Blaine, James G., 52, 54
Boggs, Lilburn, 9 n.
Bonus, 72
Bornemann, Amanda (Mrs. Joseph McKenna), 20, 21, 229
Bounties, 70
Boycott, 165, 207
Brandeis, Louis Dembitz, 129 n., 143, 159, 162, 181
Breckenridge, William, 68, 69
Brewer, David J., 110, 115, 128, 138

Brown, Mrs. Davenport (Marie McKenna), 21, 231
Buckley, Christopher, 11 n.
Burlingame Treaty, 45, 66
Burns, A. B., 52
Business, 118, 123, 136, 176
Bynum, William, 63

Cable cars, 86, 87
California, 6, 16, 44, 56, 62
California, Assembly of, 18, 23, 27, 28, 31, 33, 34, 67, 82, 93
California, Senate of, 18
California-Oregon Railroad, 56
Camron, W. W., 49–51
Campaigns for Congress, in 1876, 33–42; in 1879, 42–49; in 1884, 49–54; in 1886, 56–61; in 1888, 64–68; in 1890, 72–73
Canadian Pacific Railroad, 57
Cannon, Joseph, 75
Carpenter, Gideon J., 28
Carrier, public, 127–128, 133, 148, 168, 175, 196
Casey, Col. Silas, 10 n.
Catholicism, 2–4, 6, 12, 29, 30, 41, 60, 65, 66, 90, 97
Catholic Indian Mission Schools, 90, 91
Central Pacific Railroad, 23, 24, 26, 47 n., 70, 99
Chamberlain, Charles, 61
Charters, 113, 114, 123
Child Labor Law, 52, 159 n., 214 n., 215
Chinese, 24, 25, 42, 43, 45, 52, 58, 63, 66, 69, 70, 72, 83–86
Chinese Exclusion Bill, 63, 84
Civil Rights, 178–190
Civil service, 52, 53
Clarke, John H., 129 n., 147, 158, 159, 161, 162, 169
Classification, 118, 125, 129, 184, 193, 194
Cleveland, Grover, 52, 53, 55, 56, 60, 61, 93
Cobden Club, 66
Cogswell, Robert F., 227 n.
Colton, David, 40 n.

246